The terrifying choice, someone once warned me, is between a comfortable life or an abundant one. [...] voted with her heart. She tells the tru[...] writing with unnerving grace.

STEVE DUIN, columnist, *The Oregonian*

In a world of hot takes and sound bites, Jillana Goble has written a rich, complicated memoir of what happens when we open up our lives to radical hospitality—both as receivers and givers. Heartbreaking and eye-opening, it is a call for mutual aid in our communities and neighborhoods. There is love written into every line; there are grief and joy too, just like how life is. We will be stretched if we allow ourselves to pay attention to the stories in this book.

D. L. MAYFIELD, author and activist

Sometimes a memoir is written to highlight a special grace given to a person in power or with fame. Jillana's story, found in *A Love-Stretched Life*, is filled with a special grace of a different sort. Her story is powerful because it highlights the beauty and danger of what happens when we live a self-sacrificing, others-centered life. This is what the world needs now. Jillana lives in a way that will challenge the reader to ask the question *Can I live this way too?* The answer is *yes*!

BEN SAND, CEO, The Contingent and author of *A Kids Book about White Privilege*

From the moment I first met Jillana and heard her story, I was struck by her authentic and relentless commitment to ensuring that children and families impacted by the child welfare system are seen and feel loved. In *A Love-Stretched Life* she challenges decades of practice and presumption that for children and families facing the greatest challenges of trauma and adversity, short-term, transactional interventions just don't work. Jillana is someone who not only talks about the power of love and unconditional relationship, she lives it.

For anyone desiring to change the world for children and families encountering significant obstacles, this book will inspire you to love more deeply.

ERINN KELLEY-SIEL, chief officer of Expansion and Policy for Friends of the Children and former director of the Oregon Department of Human Services

In a culture where unrelenting voices of fear, judgment, and even hatred seem to be louder than any others, Jillana's gentle voice in *A Love-Stretched Life* is a salve of humility, compassion, and love that our battered spirits so desperately need. Her story is a beautiful illustration of consistently offering what one can in the oft-paralyzing battle against injustice. Readers will close these pages with opened eyes, challenged minds, and love-stretched hearts of their own.

KIMBERLEE COOPER, founder and executive director of The Family Room, Portland, Oregon

It's easy to buy into the idea of a perfectly curated life, one that is neatly tied up in a bow. With raw authenticity and genuine warmth, Jillana Goble instead gives readers of *A Love-Stretched Life* permission to enter into the complications of a real, messy life—a life that accepts pain, clings to hope, and believes in a faith, hope, and love bigger than anything else.

CARA MEREDITH, author of *The Color of Life*

The stories Jillana shares in *A Love-Stretched Life* are raw and real. You won't want to put this book down as you read time after time of heartbreak and struggle. But the stories are not only hard, they are beautiful too. They are about choosing to "love against the grain." For anyone who has considered stepping into the story of a vulnerable child, this book is for you.

RYAN AND KAYLA NORTH, cofounders of One Big Happy Home

In *A Love-Stretched Life*, Jillana shows us how to walk in an "all in" kind of faith that is authentic and real. Jillana puts flesh on what it means to walk by faith for the sake of others; and the result is a holy, messy, beautiful picture of heaven breaking into earth and souls being transformed. You will find a friend in Jillana as you walk this uncommon path; we believe that these pages will show you the grace of knowing you are not alone.

RICK AND JEANNE McKINLEY, founders of Imago Dei Community in Portland, Oregon; parents and full-time caregivers of a child impacted by disability

What an outpouring of heart and soul! With humility and grace, Jillana Goble invites you into the intimacy of her family for an eye-opening glimpse into the rigors of foster care and adoption. Despite the ever-present shadows of grief and loss, not once does she falter in her ability to shine light where it's most needed. You will not want to say goodbye to this labor of love.

KENDRA MORRIS-JACOBSON, director of Oregon Post Adoption Resource Center

A Love-Stretched Life is Jillana's story of faith and hope alongside the reality of the heartache and struggles that come with choosing to love vulnerable children (and their families) with your whole heart. From our very first conversation with Jillana when we heard her desire to uplift the children, families, and staff impacted by the foster care system, we knew we wanted to be part of it. It's been amazing to watch as Every Child has become a statewide movement, born out of Jillana's heart to come alongside, embrace, and be part of the solution.

MARC AND SUSAN ESTES, pastors of Mannahouse and adoptive parents of two children with disabilities from the foster care system

In this book, Jillana shares an honest portrayal of a life stretched by love. Her story is one of struggle, faith, hope, and connection—but most of all, love. As an adoptive and special needs mom, I felt like I was reading a letter from a dear friend. Her wisdom and insight will be an encouragement to the reader.

AMY J BROWN, writer and cohost of *Take Heart* podcast for special needs moms

In *A Love-Stretched Life*, Jillana and Jennifer, "two imperfect moms [who] walk toward one another for the sake of loving the same child" draw you in to rescript the assumption of family and create room for those who need a home. If we all lived like this, the world would truly be a very different place.

DIANN R. TAKENS, founder and executive director of Peace of the City, Buffalo, New York

This raw and gritty story depicts a life that hasn't chosen the easy road. *A Love-Stretched Life* cuts to the heart of getting to know others' stories before jumping to judgment. It's made me pause and reflect on the relationships in my own life. This evolving story doesn't have a neat and tidy ending but in the stretching, there is love.

ALLIE ROTH, president and founder of With Love

If parenting is in your heart, this memoir will captivate you. Jillana's journey of childhood to adulthood, becoming a teacher, parent, neighbor, and friend, gave me a broader, more beautiful definition of family. She reminded me of the wild capacity I have been given to love. You will be inspired.

JOY EGGERICHS REED, author of *Get to the Publishing Punchline: A Fun (and Slightly Aggressive) 30 Day Guide to Get Your Book Ready for the World*

A LOVE-STRETCHED LIFE

Stories on Wrangling Hope, Embracing the
Unexpected, and Discovering the Meaning of Family

JILLANA GOBLE

TYNDALE
MOMENTUM®

A Tyndale nonfiction imprint

Visit Tyndale online at tyndale.com.

Visit Tyndale Momentum online at tyndalemomentum.com.

Tyndale, Tyndale's quill logo, *Tyndale Momentum*, and the Tyndale Momentum logo are registered trademarks of Tyndale House Ministries. Tyndale Momentum is a nonfiction imprint of Tyndale House Publishers, Carol Stream, Illinois.

A Love-Stretched Life: Stories on Wrangling Hope, Embracing the Unexpected, and Discovering the Meaning of Family

Designed by Lindsey Bergsma

Edited by Bonne Steffen

Published in association with Creative Trust Literary Group, 2006 Acklen Ave., P.O. Box 121705, Nashville, TN 37212-9998. www.creativetrust.com

All the stories in this book are true, but some names and identifying information have been changed to protect the privacy of the individuals. As the author, I take seriously the sharing of any story that intersects with my own. I weighed heavily the decision to write about my youngest son and share his diagnosis. With his permission, I have done so, with the hope that it will increase awareness, understanding, and compassion for individuals with invisible, brain-based differences and for the families who love them.

For information about special discounts for bulk purchases, please contact Tyndale House Publishers at csresponse@tyndale.com, or call 1-855-277-9400.

Library of Congress Cataloging-in-Publication Data

A catalog record for this book is available from the Library of Congress.

ISBN 978-1-4964-5340-2

Printed in the United States of America

28	27	26	25	24	23	22
7	6	5	4	3	2	1

To Luke
whose steadfast and supportive partnership
has kept equilibrium in our love-stretched life

CONTENTS

THERE, WHERE THE FOREST FELL

DARK AND DEEP

THERE WAS NO PATH.

SO I TROD ONE.

~ Edwina Gateley ~

LEANING IN

HAVE YOU EVER COME TO THE realization that a normal day for you may be the very definition of what someone else would squarely label "overwhelming"?

In my household, we are acutely familiar with how a lighthearted moment can suddenly tip into a nerve-racking one, but on this *nothing special* afternoon in our home, there's a vibrant fullness—a delightful chaos.

My two teenage daughters, Sophia and Eleni, are in the kitchen, the room in our house that is continually filled with hustle and bustle and crumbs on the countertop. Fifteen-year-old Eleni is doing homework at the breakfast bar. I'm suspicious of the homework part because even though she's holding a pencil, she also holds up her phone every five minutes and asks, "Do you think this would look good on me?" while showing me photos of models with their hair dyed burgundy. Sophia, who is admittedly a better cook at seventeen than I am at forty-five, is stirring something on the stove. Sophia turns on some music to accompany the stirs, and before I know it, she starts tap dancing barefoot. It's taken years of practice to get to the place where all those fast, skilled taps look effortless, and Eleni, who also has taken dance classes for years, joins in. Our black Labradoodle, Theo, and our kids-are-lonely-during-the-pandemic-decision cat, QT, look on. I would love to tell you my daughters got those cool moves from me, re-creating my glory days, but that would be a lie. I had exactly zero dance glory days. They got them from their father.

In the midst of this, my husband, Luke, walks in the door, ending his workday. Charlie, my ten-year-old, squeals, "DADDY!" and throws his arms straight behind his back, fabricating his own invisible superhero cape as he sprints down the hallway toward him. Charlie entered our family via a phone call asking us, "Can you foster a baby for the weekend?" He's our weekend baby turned lifelong family member. As Luke hugs Charlie and hangs up his coat and work bag, he passes by the gray sign with white letters hanging in our front entry hallway that declares *Goble Family Established 2000.* He gives me a quick kiss.

Charlie immediately starts peppering Luke with questions about heading out the door to go gold mining right *now.* (Charlie's backpack is full of gold-mining supplies that he keeps on his person at *all* times because one never knows when they might stumble upon gold.) If he can't mine gold before dinner, he wants to drive to Target right *now* to buy the LEGO set he saw the last time he was there, because what if another customer picks it up to look at it and then puts it back in the wrong place and then he goes back to the store and can never find it again? Or what if LEGO suddenly stops making that set? There's a daily urgency involving all sorts of things Charlie *has* to do before it's too late!

When Charlie was four years old, he was diagnosed with an invisible, brain-based disability. Charlie is smart and interesting, clever and unique, and the way he experiences brain differences affects every single aspect of his life—and ours—at every moment. Corey, a trusted family friend who helps Charlie navigate the world, serves as Charlie's developmental disability aide. When school is out, Corey's full-time job is to be in our home with us or in the community with Charlie, helping him stay safe and regulated. Now that Luke is home, Corey grabs his keys and heads out the door saying, "See you tomorrow, Goble family," giving friendly waves or fist bumps on his way out.

As soon as Corey disappears out the front door, my thirteen-year-old son, Micah, comes into the kitchen through the back door. He is sweaty from bouncing on the trampoline in our backyard with his friends from across the street. Our home is a revolving door for his friends, who are always in and out, and Micah is just as welcome at their houses. Micah stands shoulder to shoulder with me at five foot eight and will be taller than me any minute. Behind him I spy a cherished photo of our family from years ago when he was only up to my knees—an oldie but goodie photo that will always have a place of prominence in our home. In the frame, three adults and lots of kids are crowded together, smiling, on our front porch: Luke and me, Sophia, Eleni, Micah, and Charlie, alongside Micah's first mom, Jennifer—a cherished part of our family—and Micah's three biological siblings. The happy photo of all of us leaning together was taken a few years after we adopted him.

My phone starts vibrating on the counter. I make a

concerted effort to limit phone time when my kids are home in the afternoons, but I spy the name on the screen. It's Royal, the son of my heart. I pick up and hear, "Hi, Mom," in the deep voice of a twenty-four-year-old young man in whom I delight. Royal was six years old when we met, and he walked through my front door with his possessions in a garbage bag. He was the first child Luke and I ever welcomed in foster care. Through an improbable series of events, Royal and I reconnected after thirteen years apart and today claim one another as family. In the broad, miscellaneous category of life and parenthood labeled *Things I wasn't grateful for at the time, but now I am*, this phone call qualifies. I appreciate the gift of being able to talk with Royal now on a normal phone call from his home to mine, and not one where I pick up the phone and hear an audio recording from a correctional facility where his name is inserted into the script, asking if I'll accept the call, like in the past.

• • •

I wonder if your days have ever felt like mine: real and complicated, messy, colorful, exhausting, and exhilarating—often simultaneously. Starting in 2003, my parenting journey as a foster, biological, and adoptive mom (in that order) has certainly given me a unique path, but a universal fact remains: Intentionally caring for and cultivating a family is hard. Yet just like in the classic children's story *The Velveteen Rabbit*, I would not trade my worn-down, real life for something shiny and new, as tempting as it may feel some days. Stretching to love and love well, even when it's hard—*especially* when it's hard—is what has given me the life that is mine.

If you saw the Family Rules that we put together sitting around the dinner table (written in crayon on green construction paper and taped to one of our kitchen cupboards), you'd read such things as

Be safe with your body and words
Respect one another
Celebrate each other's unique qualities
Promote one another's well-being

Some of you might be tempted to think we've got things dialed in and figured out, but don't be fooled. We have had to work, reconcile, ask for forgiveness, take deep breaths, and keep plugging along. I don't have all the answers. Honestly? I don't know if I have *any* answers. But here is what I'm learning: We're divinely created to engage this world, be connected to others, and prop one another up.

• • •

This compilation of stories is my way of inviting you to my (proverbial) table. If I were to host you at my house someday, I'd want you to know this in advance: You might get the white linen tablecloth with fresh flowers, or you might get a smudged table with leftover crumbs from the Take 'N' Bake Pizza shop down the street. I've always aspired to have the skills to put together a dazzling charcuterie board like I see on Pinterest, but it's highly likely my grapes will be clumped in an ordinary bowl sitting on the table. Though expertly snapped Instagram photographs surround us, perfectionism never breeds authentic connection. Bringing our *real* selves to the table and sitting shoulder to shoulder, eating those grapes from a plain old bowl, is what allows us to come as we are. Whatever I may lack in inspirational food presentation, however, I hope I would make up for in this: my genuine interest to sit with you, to listen and lean forward as you share the stories of what has shaped you and what makes you come alive in this world.

Like you, I wear many hats. My roles as a daughter, a sister, a wife, an employer, a neighbor, a leader, and a friend all indelibly shape me. It is specifically through my role as a mom, however, that I have been invited on many of life's detours and the ever-expanding lessons that accompany them. When life and family and relationships proceed less like a nice, neat line and more like something that closely resembles a scribble, I am shored up by this truth: *Difficult* and *worthy* are not mutually exclusive—they are often intertwined.

The details of our lives may look similar or completely different, but as you hold this book, I hope you find truth in these pages. I'm delighted you're here. You belong here. Your story matters to me. As we lean in together, know this: I am unequivocally *for* you. May these stories of walking across a suspension bridge between reality and hope anchor you, gently giving you what you need to navigate your own love-stretched life.

1

PRESENCE THAT SHAPES YOU

Influence

SOMETIMES IN ORDER TO BETTER understand the "What led me here?" of the present, we must go back to the past. The reality is that an ordinary, nothing-special afternoon in my home—the place that shelters the people and photographs of those I hold dear—would have looked entirely different if I had skipped this part of my story. Many people would not have been present. Sometimes when we embark on a journey, we are aware that a person or a place will forever change us and give direction to our lives. I had none of that awareness when my plane landed in Central America in 1999.

I stood alone at the curb outside La Aurora International Airport in Guatemala, excited about the adventure ahead but missing my fiancé, Luke. I had only had two weeks to wear my engagement ring before I put it in a safe-deposit box as

I left for Central America. Luke's proposal was memorably romantic. We were on a rugged Northern California beach at sunset. Luke strummed his guitar and sang an original love song to me, finishing just before high tide had a chance to soak our blanket. I tackled my husband-to-be with my eager yes and momentarily admired the sparkly diamond on my finger, and then we sprinted to the car hand in hand. We were both twenty-two and fresh out of college.

Since Luke was heading off to Kazakhstan for a year and I had committed to teach at an orphanage in Guatemala for six months, we had barely a week together to plan our wedding for the following summer. We sampled cake, chose our invitations, and found a beautiful vineyard for an outdoor wedding ceremony. The first dress I tried on is the one I chose for our wedding. All the main details were taken care of, which enabled us to wholeheartedly concentrate on our separate adventures ahead.

I looked at my watch. *Did the director of the school receive my flight information? How long should I wait before I call someone?* Just then, a rickety maroon minivan rounded the corner, music blaring. The friendly driver who worked at the orphanage introduced himself to me as Juan Carlos. He said, *"Mucho gusto,"* and took my suitcase and my bag of teaching materials as I slid into the passenger seat. In English he asked me, "Have you been to Guatemala before? Are you nervous to be here? Have you worked with kids before?"

The answers were all no, but I added, "I'm excited to be here and use my Spanish. I know I'll learn so much being here." As we drove out of the city and got on the highway, we passed numerous humble roadside markets, houses, and tin-roofed shacks. The glass birdie dangling from the van's rearview mirror almost went flying when Juan Carlos suddenly turned sharply onto an unmarked road. As the gravel crunched under the tires, we approached a compound of buildings that I recognized from the photos on the website. I saw a two-story building in the middle of a large compound. I recalled from what I'd read that the school classrooms, a kitchen, and an open concrete area for assemblies and church gatherings were all located there. On the second floor of the same building was a three-bedroom apartment with a large living space that served as the infant and toddler live-in nursery.

When I got out of the van, I was given a quick tour. The main building was surrounded by a covered pigpen enclosure, a flock of free-range chickens, and six numbered trailers that housed kids divided by age and gender. There was at least one adult assigned to each trailer as a house parent, all of them native Guatemalans. Over sixty kids called this orphanage home. Some were truly orphans, while others were there temporarily.

I knew from the emails I had received that I would be living in trailer number three, only a stone's throw from the school. I put my one suitcase in my small, laminate wood–paneled room, while the six school-age girls who lived there watched me from the doorway. I introduced myself and they all eagerly told me their names. A moment later, Teresa, the house parent for trailer three and a fellow teacher, appeared. Before I had a chance to open up my suitcase, the American director of the school came by to offer a heartfelt welcome and then delivered some unexpected news.

"The teacher for the second- and third-grade combination class just up and quit! Jillana, would you be willing to finish out the school year as their teacher so the children can end on a positive note?" He knew I was prepared to teach ESL (English as a second language) daily to all the grades, but now the most urgent need was for a regular classroom teacher.

"I know Spanish was your major in college and was hoping you could show up tomorrow morning at 8:00 a.m. and fill in the gap." This was not what I had signed up for, but I found myself nodding my head and saying I'd try my best. It was good I hadn't known this last-minute change ahead of time. I would have been so overwhelmed with my self-professed inadequacy that I might not have come.

Twenty-four hours after setting foot in Guatemala, I took a deep breath to calm my nerves as I smiled at the sixteen kids in the classroom and was introduced as "Maestra Jillana." Since I had looked over the curriculum beforehand and paged through all the books I was given, I was mildly confident about teaching all the subjects—with the exception of Guatemalan history. That subject would keep me on my toes the most. Thanks to the students, I learned about the *quetzal*, the country's national bird and also the name of the country's currency, through a song and presentation the class had already prepared for the school assembly that week.

During our first science class, we planted seeds in a garden patch behind the main building. Weeks later, as I crouched down, excitedly examining a student's budding plant, a group of boys clustered together erupted in laughter. Francisco, a little boy with a huge scar across his head, visible under his buzz cut, was peeing on the sprouts. *Oh, Francisco.*

Francisco sat in the back of my classroom with a ready, amiable smile on his face at all times, but he had no volume control. After he missed every spelling word for a few days, I told him I'd love for him to sit closer to me in the front of the class. He responded with an eager "Of course, Maestra Jillana," in what I would soon discover was his happy-go-lucky attitude toward everything.

As the days went by, I increasingly noticed the kids didn't play or interact much with Francisco. He was loud, and he was always dirty. The sink for washing hands was located in an open common area, and I often winked at Francisco, whispering for him to go back and wash his hands during recess. More times than not, however, he would wriggle his second-grade hand into mine before washing and ask me, "How are you doing today, teacher?" As I washed my hands later, I thought of this endearing boy.

When the house parents in Francisco's trailer had to leave for a few hours one evening, I volunteered to supervise the boys. I sat in the trailer with seven mid-elementary-age boys as we slurped our dinner of broth with sliced carrots and bits of chicken. *I never expected to do this as an ESL teacher!* I somehow managed to oversee the post-dinner cleanup, made sure they got their jammies on and brushed their teeth, then read them a story. The boys were on triple-stacked bunk beds on both sides of the room. Except for Francisco.

He slept outside the room on the living room couch. When the house parents returned late that evening, I asked them why Francisco slept there. They motioned for me to follow them outside.

Standing on the steps of the trailer in the dark, the woman told me in a hushed tone with absolutely no emotion, "Francisco was sold to a pimp when he was young. When he returned one day with no money, the pimp tied him up, strung him upside down from a tree, beat him, and let a dog attack him. That's where the scar on his head came from. He was about five years old. Francisco was found that way and was brought here. He is separated from the boys because he tries to act out with them, you know, what was done to him."

Because I was one of only a handful of non-native Spanish speakers living on the compound, I wanted to be sure I understood what they had said. My mind recognized the words, the sentence structure, the syntax, but I couldn't comprehend what I was hearing. So I repeated it back to them with a lingering question mark in my voice.

"*Sí*," they nodded, and they bid me goodnight.

There was one buzzing fluorescent light hanging above the short concrete path between our two trailers that flickered like a faint strobe light. I was grateful for the strict lights-out policy on the compound, so I didn't have to talk or interact with anyone as I crept past the sleeping girls into my small bedroom in the trailer. I stayed up half the night, feeling like the dark wood-paneled walls in my tiny room were closing in on me. Sleep wouldn't come. In just a few hours, I'd be standing at my classroom door greeting the kids by name. I pictured Francisco in the front row, missing almost everything, yet raising his hand, speaking too loudly, and flashing a full-toothed smile. I stared at the moon outside my little window with my mind bouncing around like a pinball machine, wondering how a compassionate God could allow such heinous things to happen to an innocent child.

I must have dozed off at some point during the night because I was awakened the next morning by a squealing pig being butchered. I sat on the edge of my bed, head in my hands, and suddenly felt overwhelmed. I wanted to pack up and head to the airport.

The dial-up internet at the one communal computer didn't work consistently, so I found myself scribbling things down in a little journal, both as self-therapy and so I wouldn't forget details.

At an afternoon staff meeting two months into my stint at the orphanage, we were told that a pregnant sixteen-year-old named María would be coming to live at the orphanage.

I first met María when I was returning our trailer's dinner trays to the kitchen where she was washing dishes. She looked much younger than her age with a flawless complexion, a few gold-capped teeth, and long black hair pulled back into a braid. She was dressed in a mid-eighties secretarial outfit, wearing a mid-calf length, yellow polka-dotted dress with buttons down the front and a tie in the back. She was also wearing slightly oversized heels that clicked loudly on the cement floor. It was clear her outfit was from a donation clothing barrel.

María and I would greet each other in the kitchen each night and wave to each other when I'd see her wandering around the compound throughout the day. I started inviting her to my class to help me with a few tasks, more to include her than for any specific purpose. She could easily pass for a middle-school student if she didn't have a protruding belly. María sat at my desk since I was always up and moving around. When Francisco loudly announced in the middle of class that he was hungry, María broke off a piece of her granola bar and gave it to him.

One night as I dropped off the trays, she asked if I wanted to see her room when she was done with dish duty. I said I'd like to, and she smiled ear to ear. I helped her finish cleaning up the kitchen, we turned the lights out, and I walked with her to the trailer.

She shared a small room with another teenage girl. Her bedspread was beautiful with deep indigo-colored embroidery, and there were three stuffed animals on her pillow. She invited me to sit down on the bed and then, one by one, she silently handed me each of her stuffed animals to hold. She smiled again and said, "I like you. You talk to me."

I've learned and experienced over the years how people respond to trauma. One response can look like being significantly overwhelmed by a dire sense that one can never do enough. While I was falling in love with Guatemala, the people, their culture, and the kids who called this orphanage home, I also was aware there was never enough time, never enough money, never enough resources, never enough adults to help. Despite the good intentions of those present, scarcity abounded.

One night as María and I were finishing up with dish

duty, she smiled her soft, shy smile and asked, "Ms. Jillana, can I talk with you?"

"Of course. Let's go somewhere quiet."

We put away everything in the kitchen and headed toward the auditorium. María's heels clicked on the concrete floor as we walked together. She wore the same yellow dress that tied in the back, and her black hair was gathered in a loose bun. We pulled up two green plastic chairs close to each other in the empty auditorium. Sitting across from her, I asked her how she was feeling about the baby coming soon. With her unassuming smile, she told me she wanted me to name her baby.

I was flabbergasted. "Wow. What an honor, María. Are you sure?"

She nodded and informed me that immediately after the baby was born, she planned to leave the hospital without the baby and return home. "I need to be there to protect my little sister," she said, "so my father doesn't do this (pointing to her belly) to her too. But you will make sure the baby is okay, right, Ms. Jillana?"

Her brown eyes looked into mine, and her smile was as pure as the moon shining through the skylight, creating a circle of light where we sat.

"I will do my best," I told her. I walked her back to her trailer, and we hugged.

I spent that night staring out my little window, thinking about how unqualified I was at twenty-two to be engaging in such a conversation with María. Shouldn't I have a PhD in counseling or something? Everywhere I turned, there were high-needs situations. Every single one of the sixty children had experienced some twist of the life-altering common denominators of abuse, neglect, and trauma. Despite my inability to change this situation, I could offer her the one thing that was within my own capacity—the ability to see her and talk with her. Presence. Human presence.

After I finished my classes the next day, I told a few adult leaders that María would continue to be around her abuser. I knew the kind lawyer at the orphanage was a dedicated advocate in the courts for the children, and admittedly, it wasn't my place to know what was going on behind the scenes. Those with whom I shared seemed already aware. They nodded compassionately but could only offer a resigned "There's not much we can do" shrug.

• • •

Two weeks later, María went into labor and delivered a baby girl. When I visited her at the hospital, she was her shy self, yet I saw a resolute strength in her.

It wouldn't be until five years later when I was lying in a hospital bed after pushing out my own baby girl that I would be able to fully recognize the emotional weight of what was missing from that hospital scene with María—a baby being placed in her arms, a body depleted and a heart full.

You might blame it on the *telenovelas* (Spanish soap operas) I watched with my Dominican host mother the semester I studied abroad, but I gave this six-pound peanut a whopping eight-syllable first and middle name—a name that rolled off the tongue with flair and meaning. Esperanza (hope) was her middle name.

Two days later, María was gone. I never saw her again.

Esperanza was taken to the second-floor nursery above the school, where every day after school, after high-fiving my students and releasing them to go back to their trailers, I'd walk up the stairs to rock and sing to her. The nursery had full-time staff who lived and worked there, so Esperanza was lovingly held and bathed and fed by them, but I had a unique connection to this girl.

I had known her mother.

A single American woman named Kayla came to the orphanage and volunteered in the baby room. She quickly fell in love with Esperanza and was determined not to leave her. This assuaged the feeling that I was abandoning Esperanza when I had to return home.

Six months later, as I rode in that same rickety van back to the airport, the school director thrust a letter of recommendation into my hands, citing my contribution to the orphanage as I waited to board my plane. I didn't know it then, but I'd be back. Guatemala would shape the trajectory of the rest of my life.

• • •

Luke and I started our married life in a tiny apartment in San Francisco, decorated with an array of framed wedding photos: me in my bridal gown getting out of a horse-pulled carriage; my arm intertwined with my dad's; Luke dipping me back in his arms, my veil touching the ground, as we gazed into one another's eyes with giddy smiles plastered on our faces.

I would take the N Judah train into downtown San

Francisco to teach English, while Luke commuted over the Golden Gate Bridge every day to his job at an after-school tutoring center. We rented an apartment that didn't have an oven, so we used a convection oven/microwave placed on a TV tray in the living room. We also lacked kitchen counter space so a card table in the corner of the living room became our food prep station and dining table. It would shake every time we cut up our food.

We made friends, attended a small church in the heart of the city, and spent some of our wedding gift money on the quintessential sporting goods item of 2000: Rollerblades. We bladed around Golden Gate Park, with Luke looking cool as he weaved around confidently, with me, not quite as cool but more safety conscious, fully decked out with kneepads and wrist guards. We lived two blocks from the ocean and would saunter down to the beach any ole time. In fact, on our one-year anniversary, we pulled out a piece of frozen wedding cake to celebrate the occasion. The cake was crumbly and flavorless, but the seagulls liked it. Life was unbelievably good.

Strolling down the beach, I jokingly told Luke, "You're my dream guy in every way but I always kind of thought I'd marry someone who spoke Spanish." When I playfully suggested we move to Guatemala for a little while, he smiled and said, "Let's go!" I looked to see if he was joking, but he wasn't. His added "Carpe diem!" made it official.

Six months later, we packed up and headed to Antigua, Guatemala, with barely enough money to pay for six months' rent and Spanish language school for Luke. I now had my master's degree in teaching ESL and was hired to teach English at a private high school during the week. On most weekends, we went to the same orphanage where I had lived and taught two years before. We offered respite to the house parents, giving them a break from their 24/7 parenting duties. It was the perfect way for Luke to dip his toes into what life had been like for me at the orphanage when we were separated during our engagement. Many of the same kids were still there two years later. I immediately looked for Francisco but couldn't find him.

When I asked a staff member where Francisco was, the staff person said he had been sent to the juvenile detention facility "for the safety of others." I knew immediately what Luke and I needed to do. We boarded a bus crowded with people and their animals. There were chickens in small cages and others fluttering around on the bus. We shooed away a goat that was attempting to eat our clothing.

The juvenile detention facility was in the middle of nowhere. As soon as I walked in, I knew that the "therapeutic" in the title of the facility was meaningless. We waited in a large visitation room for Francisco. He was escorted by a staff member, and I immediately recognized his smile. The scar on his head was fully visible and dirt smudged his face. When he stretched out his hand for me to grab, I couldn't help but notice the dirt clumped underneath his fingernails. I grasped his hand tightly, as I had two years earlier on recess breaks when he was in my classroom.

"¡Hola, Maestra Jillana! ¿Como estás?" he eagerly asked me.

"I am so happy to see you! How about you, Francisco? How are you?"

"Great!"

Luke and I had been allowed to leave the premises for an

hour with Francisco. We took him out for ice cream. The time passed way too quickly, and we returned to the facility. As we were escorted back to his room, Francisco asked if we could visit him again.

I wanted to say we would make our best effort, but I knew in my heart this would be our one and only visit, and I didn't want to set him up for disappointment. Instead, I looked deep into Francisco's eyes and told him I would always remember him.

He smiled and made a grand gesture as if taking a bow and said, "Thank you for always remembering me, Ms. Jillana."

I squeezed his hand one more time as a staff member arrived. Francisco turned and waved goodbye. I waved back and then I walked out, biting my lower lip to keep my quivering chin from cuing a bucket full of tears. Luke, emotionally steady as a rock, put his arm around me.

In that moment, one of Jesus' beatitudes came to mind: "Blessed are the pure in heart, for they shall see God." It is Francisco's blessing to claim forever.

• • •

Luke and I lived in a two-bedroom furnished apartment in Antigua, in an alleyway off a main street. Every morning, like clockwork, a shepherd would herd his flock of bleating sheep right by our front door. There was a market nearby selling all sorts of meats, spices, produce, and—my favorite—fresh flowers. Much to my delight, carnations are actually the most expensive flower in Guatemala and roses are among the cheapest, so our apartment always had a vase of fresh roses on the table.

At Spanish language school, Luke met a couple in their forties with four young children who were preparing to work for a non-profit in the Dominican Republic. Since I had lived in the DR as part of my college Spanish studies and had lived in the same city where they were headed, we had a natural connection. Luke and I went to Pete and Lola's house for dinner a few times, then planned to hike together on Acatenango, the two-peaked volcanic mountain that towered over the city as an impressive backdrop.

We packed a small picnic and set off on a trail that wound around the mountain with a gentle incline. There weren't many other people on the wide main trail this particular afternoon. Nevertheless, we had been advised to stick together. As we climbed a little higher, Lola handed me their camera and asked me to take a photo of her and her family. The scene behind them was postcard-perfect: blue skies, fluffy clouds, green pastures in the valley below the mountain. I snapped several shots of them as two men walking their donkeys came around the bend.

We continued on until we decided it was time to turn around and head back down the mountain. Luke and Pete started engaging in a playfully obvious game of hide-and-seek with the children, zigzagging across the trail. Lola, carrying their toddler in a hiking backpack, and I were engrossed in conversation and kept a steady pace in front of them as we kept heading back to the base of the mountain. Soon, without realizing it, we had left them behind. We looked back and could no longer see Luke, Pete, or the kids.

Suddenly two men, wearing black ski masks and brandishing machetes, jumped out of the bushes in front of us. The one closest to me held two blades high in the air and spoke rapidly in Spanish.

"Don't move. Don't scream. Give us the camera and your money. Now!"

How do they know we have a camera? These must be the men with the donkeys, I thought. The camera was in Lola's cargo shorts pocket, and I didn't want them to get it.

I locked eyes with the black slits peering at me through the opening in his mask and said with an eerie calmness, "Lola, don't move or scream." I knew how deadly a machete was since Luke had been using one to help clear land around the orphanage. A few whacks from a machete could take down a tree with a trunk as wide as a pineapple. Lola couldn't control herself—she primally screamed her husband's name and took off, sprinting up the trail with her toddler wobbling back and forth in the backpack.

The man I was still staring at commanded his sidekick to follow Lola. I was now alone with this man menacingly wielding two machetes. My initial calm boiled over into red-hot rage. I jerked the straw bag off my shoulder and turned it upside down. A DVD, a few half-eaten sandwiches, and some coins fell on the ground. In a Spanglish rant I screamed, "Leave me ALONE! What do you WANT from me? I don't have ANYTHING!"

"Shut up! Shut up!" he hissed.

I slowly turned my head to look up the mountain, and I saw Pete handing the other thief his wallet. The courteous robber took the money out and handed back the billfold as if to say, "Nice doing business with you," and then half-jogged back down the hill toward me, machete in hand.

Then, seemingly out of nowhere, Luke, my now Spanish-speaking dream-guy-in-every-way, sprinted toward me so fast he left a red dust cloud in his wake. When he arrived on the scene, he assured me, "Honey, I can totally take these guys!"

Yes, no exaggeration. Hand over my heart, those were his *exact* first words to me in my moment of peril with two men and three machetes between them. My confident husband was going to "take" them.

If you ask Luke for his version of the story, he'll tell you that he thought they were amateurs because they stood with their backs to the small ravine. They were also at least six inches shorter than either of us. They demanded Luke's watch, which he reluctantly handed to them, and they immediately slinked into the brush. Pete, Lola, Luke, and I scooped up the children and ran down the hill.

At the police station, I reported the incident. As I explained what had happened, the officer kept yawning as if I were reciting long sections out of an encyclopedia.

We then got on a crowded bus for home, squeezed in between people and animals. All of us adults looked out the window with blank expressions on our faces, but the older kids, sheltered from a lot of the up-close drama, peppered us with questions. "Why were those men mean? What did they want?"

We adults were acutely aware that this was a case of Robin Hood taking from the rich for the sake of the poor. Our appearance and language tipped them off that we had resources. The camera had sealed the deal. At that particular moment, those men who likely had few material resources had an opportunity to get something. It's not an excuse, but it was reality.

One of the children who saw the man holding up the machetes said with childlike innocence, "Let's just pray for those bad guys, so they can be good guys, and when they're good, we can have them over for dinner."

We were grateful that no one had been physically hurt, but Pete and Lola admitted they could never feel safe in Guatemala again. To make matters worse, while we were being robbed on the mountain, their washing machine and dryer were stolen, hoisted up and over the six-foot stucco wall that surrounded their house.

• • •

A decade after Kayla adopted Esperanza, she contacted me. We were both living in the States now. Esperanza was a teenager, and she was asking questions about her biological mother, María.

"You're the person who knew her," Kayla said. "Would you be willing to talk to Esperanza?"

"It would be a privilege. Put her on the phone."

I told Esperanza everything I could remember, from María's sweet demeanor to the way she walked and talked. "I liked having her sit in my classroom. We enjoyed washing dishes and talking together." When Kayla adopted Esperanza, I'd given her a copy of every picture I had of María. My favorite was the one I'd snapped of María on her embroidered bedspread, holding her stuffed animals over her large belly. As I talked to Esperanza now, it was clear she had studied those pictures well by the way she referenced them, the yellow polka-dotted dress, the high heels, the shy smile, the braided, jet-black hair.

Even in the midst of hideous abuse, there can still be life, brimming with love and meaning. It's something Emily Dickinson captures beautifully in a line from one of her poems, one I framed and have sitting on my bedroom dresser:

"'Hope' is the thing with feathers that perches in the soul."

Hope is not a fluffy word to sugarcoat the real pain and lifelong effects of abuse and trauma. Hope is not a cover-up side story. Hope still acknowledges that all adoption, even under the best of circumstances, starts with a story of loss— loss that may be felt in the marrow of the bones, even if it can't be articulated. Even in the midst of loss, hope was braided into the fiber of cords of grace, tethering our lives together.

• • •

Before Luke and I had left for Guatemala in 2002, he had submitted several applications for grad school. An acceptance letter arrived while we were in Guatemala for a doctoral program in American Studies at the University of Buffalo in New York, the place where he grew up. We celebrated as bleating sheep scurried past our front door. Our six months were coming to an end, and it was time to return to the States.

On our last day in Guatemala, we bought a painting of the colorful city streets of Antigua with a large purple mountain (*the* mountain) as the backdrop. We've lived in six homes since we purchased that painting, and it's always been displayed in a prominent place in each one. It reminds me that Guatemala is where I was first exposed to the jagged reality that I will see and hold suffering that seems beyond comprehension. Guatemala showed me the pain of swaddling a newborn baby girl in the hospital with a cloth of suffering and hope and bringing her to an orphanage without her beautiful mama. It also allowed me to see a tenderhearted woman step into that role.

In Guatemala, I experienced fear as I never had before, giving me a sliver of understanding of the body's "fight, flight, freeze" instinctive response to trauma, preparing me for what I would later witness with many children in my home. Guatemala gave me the privilege of feeling fingers wrapped around mine both in a classroom and in a lockdown facility. A humble offering of undivided presence, though it feels inadequate when there's an ocean of pressing needs, is still *something*.

This place showed me that vivid color and quiet beauty can still exist amidst traumatic, injustice-filled stories that brought children to live at an orphanage in the first place. Our time in Guatemala is what ultimately led Luke and me to ask, "Where are the vulnerable children here?" as we stepped off the plane to make our home in New York.

It was that very simple and straightforward question that led us straight to the doors of foster care.

2

A ROYAL STORM

A New Understanding of Faith

I WAS IN MY LATE TEENS. I had just finished my workout at the Airport Health Club and was walking out of the gym locker room with a towel slung over my shoulder, when a poster on the bulletin board caught my eye. "Who can help a child in foster care? You can! Learn all the ways you can help." A childlike drawing of stick figures depicted a family with varying shades of skin color. I stopped and read it. With the exception of that one poster, I can't remember ever hearing about foster care. There was zero mention of it in the suburban cul-de-sac I grew up in. I never heard anyone anywhere *talk* about foster care, let alone personally engage it. The question "Where do vulnerable children go when they don't have a safe family who can adequately care for them?" had never really crossed my mind. It was so far outside the realm of my personal experience of having a loving, caring family and of those in my bubble of friends.

Our family attended church every Sunday where a few hundred people came together in a building located off a main road in our suburb. I remember singing, "Jesus loves the little children." I remember participating in impactful "mission trips" helping to build and paint medical clinics just over the border in Mexico. (For a split second I was fired up to become a doctor so I could help even more, but the fact that I was squeamish dashed that idea.) I knew Scripture about the vulnerable being close to God's heart. Yet I can't recall a single sermon that nudged people off the high-speed freeway of well-constructed lives, generous intentions, and manicured lawns and directed them to explore the disruptive exit ramp marked "Foster Care."

Thankfully, more and more faith communities today, with varying degrees of commitment, attempt to hang a spotlight over this exit ramp. But despite being immersed in multiple Christian contexts at that point in our lives, Luke and I hadn't seen or experienced them. We attended our first foster parent training with Child and Family Services in 2002, bringing only our experience working with orphaned children in Guatemala, our good intentions sprinkled in faith and the hazy concept of foster care gained from a safe distance.

If I had put together a mixtape of sound bites (clearly, I became a teenager in the late eighties) of what I *thought* foster care was before living it, you'd have heard, "Foster care is kids needing to be rescued from awful situations and people."

"Foster care is all about helping a child." "Foster care is when you get to love a child who's never been shown the love of family." After all, I *had* watched the movie *Annie*. My favorite part is when Annie and Daddy Warbucks find each other, wiggle their way into each other's heart, and arm in arm belt out songs about togetherness and not needing anyone but each other.

When Luke and I finished our ten-week training in Buffalo, New York, we were asked to invite our "support people" to a gathering to hear about the impact of foster care. Luke's family who lived nearby came, along with a few close friends. Our intention was to ease into foster care by doing weekend respite care. We were both twenty-five, had no kids, and lived in a two-bedroom apartment. Little did we know that there's no such thing as "easing in." It would be a helicopter drop in the middle of the ocean.

Because Luke and I each had a pulse and no criminal records, we were immediately granted status as *caregivers* to meet the urgent need in our community at the end of our ten-week training. We were tapped on the shoulder and asked to consider "therapeutic" foster care, the highest level of care. While a case could be made that any child brought into state custody needs a high level of attention and care from a team of foster parents and professionals, "therapeutic" is the label reserved for cases when trauma manifests in high behavioral needs. This requires extra skillful parenting. We were a bit flattered at this invitation, and curiosity piqued our interest. Luke and I were not overly confident—we knew this wouldn't be a breeze—but we were willing to say yes in our youthful optimism and energy, motivated by our understanding of what it meant to put our faith into action.

With the ink still drying on our foster certificate, I said yes to the phone call asking us to take nine-year-old Dion and his six-year-old brother, Royal, who were in the therapeutic foster care program. They were the twelfth and fifteenth children born to their mother. The state vehicle pulled into our long driveway with two mocha-skinned boys buckled in the back seat. I hospitably held their garbage bags as I swung wide our front door to the boys and helped them inside. I knew they were coming from a relative's home. I don't recall thinking how frightening this must have been for them to leave their aunt's house and to be driven to a stranger's.

As my heart pounded behind my welcoming smile, I showed them their room with new comforters on the beds and a brightly colored rug. I watched as they took it all in, their eyes darting around the room. I gave them a tour of the kitchen, stopping at the fully stocked snack cupboard. Not more than an hour after the caseworker dropped them off, I snapped a picture of Royal licking gooey brownie batter off spoons. That afternoon included a game, dinner around the table, a TV show, and several bedtime stories.

"How does it feel to be a mom?" a friend asked me on the phone after I said good night to the boys.

"So far so good" was my happy, confident reply, seven hours in.

At 3:00 a.m., the wall between our bedroom and the boys' reverberated with gleeful shouting. I put on my robe and opened their door. The floor, pillowcases, and bedspreads were completely covered in a sea of white, waxy paper strips. Both boys were jumping on their beds, throwing Fruit-by-the-Foot snack wrappers in the air like confetti. Just a few hours after I had prayed for the boys to feel love and safety in our home and had drifted off to sleep, they silently tiptoed into the kitchen, and joyfully devoured a month's worth of individually wrapped treats.

I took a deep breath. We had learned about the prevalence of food hoarding in our training class, a response to chronic food scarcity that so many children have faced. This would be the first of countless times I'd be exposed to the difference between neatly taking notes in a journal during a training class and staring at the lived reality. I gently told the boys, their mouths full of snacks, "Let's get you back in bed. We'll clean up the wrappers in the morning." It was 3:15.

The next day, without a hint of shame, I took the boys to the grocery store, and they each picked out boxes of their favorite snacks as well as food they liked. We let them sleep with a box of individually wrapped snacks under their pillow, with the deal it would stay wrapped, unless they asked to open it. It was a symbol of reassurance that food would be there whenever it was needed. Walking into a wrapper-littered room soon stopped.

Royal had lots of energy that kept us on our toes, but he also had a tenderness to him. Despite our best efforts to engage Dion, he overtly indicated to us that he was not pleased to be with us. He figuratively spit venom and literally spit on both his brother and us. One afternoon while Royal was doing his homework at the kitchen table, I walked into the boys' bedroom and discovered the trash can outside underneath an open window.

Dion was gone.

I ran outside and called his name, my adrenaline racing. I couldn't see him anywhere. With my heart thumping, I dialed the agency to inform them he was missing. They called the police. An hour later, which felt like an eternity while I paced inside the house, Dion arrived in the back of a police car. The supervisor of therapeutic foster care was waiting for him in our driveway. "Foster homes do not get any better than this, young man," she warned, her mirrored sunglasses on the bridge of her nose. Dion's chest was still heaving, a scowl pasted on his face. Royal stood close to me. My stomach was in my throat. I didn't need to say out loud what I already knew.

I'm a total failure.

Why didn't Dion want to stay? I knew it had very little to do with me and everything to do with the grossly unfair, trauma-filled cards that life had dealt him before he'd ever walked through my front door. I was trying to create a peaceful home environment with adequate structure and plenty of fun, just like our training had recommended. We had a positive-reward system. We engaged in lots of physical exercise together. When someone suggested we buy a punching bag for the boys to get out their aggression, we set it up in the basement and let them play loud music while they hit it again and again.

Nothing was working. Two days after the police were in our driveway, an argument between the brothers erupted in the living room after school. Dion cleared our bookshelf, throwing books at his brother and at our windows. We tried every technique we knew but couldn't calm him down. Dion clawed at Luke like a frightened animal fighting for his life. We immediately called our social worker. She asked if we could please hold on for a few more days until another foster home could be found.

The next day, Dion knocked Royal off a kitchen chair and was mercilessly kicking him while Royal screamed "Stop!" and cowered in fear. I pried Dion off him, fervently wishing Luke was home. I carried Royal into our bedroom and shut the door; I needed to check how badly he was hurt. Dion continued to rage like a tornado, throwing items around the kitchen.

Suddenly Dion was pounding on our bedroom door with his fists, demanding to be let in. I took a deep breath and calmly said, "I'll be out in a minute." I slid the hook latch on the top of my bedroom door so he couldn't barge in. While checking out Royal's shiner, I heard a faint scratching sound by the door. I paused to listen, then stiffened when I saw the sound was caused by the blade of a steak knife slowly sliding between the door and the frame, lifting up the lock. Instinctively, I flung open the door and grabbed the handle of the knife from Dion, who was standing on a kitchen chair pulled up against the door. He was gone from our home the next day.

If Royal was unhappy to be separated from his brother, he didn't show it, but sadness enveloped me. Luke and I curled up in bed, feeling like we had come to the end of ourselves. As a relatively comfortable, educated, well-adjusted couple with a "can do" attitude, in barely no time at all, foster care had disavowed us of our faulty belief that we were self-reliant.

Staring at the ceiling, we wondered, *How do people do this?* I expected many things in my life to shift naturally now that our focus was on parenting, but my life as I'd known it had been thrown off a cliff.

• • •

Growing up in church, I'd always had a predisposition toward being impacted by vulnerable people living on the margins, but I wasn't actually close to anyone who fit this description. Church seemed to be a place made up of people whose lives looked more or less like mine, living in the same neighborhood with a heavy emphasis on having a respectable family and a good job. There's nothing wrong with that, but it didn't occur to me until decades later to ask the salient question, "Who's not present, and why don't they feel welcome here?" In the absence of proximity to people whose burdens are often more than they can bear, I oversimplified their struggles to fit within my narrow paradigm. Though I can't recall having this exact thought, it wouldn't have been too far off for me to believe at that point in my life that if parents who have kids in foster care could "just get it together, stop choosing drugs over their kids, get into church, and surround themselves with community," they'd be on the right track! To be clear, I believe in the utmost power of belonging and true community as primary ways that Love shows up! I must confess, however, that my head-shaking, judgy "just get it together" sentiment did exist. I too easily made a linear connection between the redemption of people's souls and the prosperity of their lives.

Upward mobility and Luke's and my own ability to "make life work for us" was like a buffet of privilege spread out before us, where faith could very well be a side dish, not the main course. The two of us already had a helping of "looks like you're on the right track in life" piling up high on our plates with ease—with our graduate degrees, our burgeoning ability to provide financially for ourselves, and our sense of connectedness in multiple settings. Sure, we had God, but also, up until that point, we were also able to dine until we were full on our own self-reliance.

This parenting road, however, toppled that plate off the table, and it cracked on the floor. I didn't have a single friend who was fostering. While we had supportive friends and family, I felt lonely and in way over my head. Sipping a latte from the coffee bar at church began to feel isolating.

If someone had said to me, "Just get it together," or worse yet, "You got yourself into this situation so you can get yourself out of it," I would have been furiously disillusioned by the over-simplification of the struggle.

Diving into parenting kids from hard places was disrupting life as I knew it. But even in the wreckage, as I curled up in a ball on my bed, I knew God hadn't abandoned us. "God, help me to trust you as if my very life depended on it and not as a feel-good aside," I prayed. In the past I had prayed for help on a test or for writing my master's thesis. Now, "Help me!" was a cry that reflected a deep need born out of the inability to make things right on my own.

Before I could pull out my holey parachute of self-reliance, I was swept out into the sky and free-falling, grasping only a cord of faith that promises strength amidst weakness, a faith that can hold the tension of injustice with no easy answers, and a faith that clings to humility when navigating the mountain of things I have not experienced. Foster care was my first personal, handwritten invitation to meet people, places, and situations I'd never encountered, wrecking my life as I knew it while saving me from unexamined privilege.

Luke and I had learned in our foster care training classes that it was "best practice" for siblings to be placed together. This haunted me. The brothers were now separated. "You can't sacrifice one to save another, Jillana," the social worker tried to reassure me with a heavy sigh during her next home visit.

I was never under the illusion that I was "saving" anybody.

• • •

Royal's given middle name was Storm. Royal Storm—fitting. Now that Dion was gone, Royal was free to be his own hurricane. When he started first grade at the nearby charter school, Luke and I learned to see and define progress in new ways, such as only hearing from the teacher or principal about exasperating behaviors every *other* day. We praised Royal, gave him high fives, and celebrated what many people might consider little things. We picked one thing to work on at a time so Royal wouldn't become overwhelmed, and we tracked it on a colorful chart hanging on the fridge. When Royal met his goal, we rewarded him with trips to the toy store and to the (dreaded on my part) Chuck E. Cheese with our neighbor his same age.

While there were plenty of Kodak moments, there were still occasions I would rather have gone without. For example, the time he locked himself in his room and peed all over his bed and pillowcase, and in his brand-new boots when I told him "not right now" in response to a request. He innocently asked me afterward, "Ms. Jillana, are you dis-a-boob-ed in me?" I assured him I wasn't disappointed in *him*, just the behavior. We stripped the sheets together, stuffed them into the washer in our basement, hosed out the boots, and then went on with the rest of our day.

Most of our friends hadn't started a family yet, so the fact that we had a six-year-old was unusual. As a result, Royal Storm was a little celebrity wherever he went. Many of our friends and family members interacted with him and intentionally poured time and energy into his life. I could sense him standing up straighter. A photo in our home shows his winsome smile, and his missing two top teeth, as he glided around on his new scooter. Every day, Royal was gaining confidence that he was, indeed, the really good kid we told him he was and believed him to be.

Luke and I let Royal in on our pregnancy news before anybody else on the day it was announced. He smiled shyly, with one hand covering his mouth and his brown eyes twinkling. The plan was to have Luke casually drop the announcement into the dinner conversation at Thanksgiving. My parents had flown out from the West Coast to join us around the table with Luke's family, but Luke couldn't contain it. Immediately after the blessing, Luke clanged his glass and happily blurted out the news. There were shouts of joy around the table, hugging and hearty congratulations from everyone.

I immediately looked at Royal, playing in the living room not too far away. He walked over to me, and I drew him close. I couldn't help but wonder how the news of him, baby number fifteen, had been received in his family. Throughout my pregnancy, Luke and I were intentional to make Royal feel included and not threatened. He sincerely asked us to name the baby "Kewpie." We compromised and said that could be the baby's name while *inside* the womb.

Royal had been part of our family for ten months when his social worker told us he would not be reunited with his parents. Royal now needed a permanent adoptive home. There were no strings attached to the announcement, pressuring us to fill that need. She knew our baby was coming in the summer and that we had stepped into foster care desiring to be a bridge, not a permanent destination. Still, we didn't want to give Royal the impression he was being kicked out to make room for the baby. So we agreed to care for him until a good situation arose for him, regardless of the timing. It simply never occurred to me, being young and new to foster care, that someone might not go the extra mile, find him to be a total delight, and be fully committed to him. I mean, that's why people engage in foster care in the first place, right?

I was painfully naive.

Royal and I made a scrapbook together of his year with us. Pictures of Royal on his first flight, his eyes wide in amazement as he looked out the window, and our time at Disneyland were pasted on colorful pages. There were photos of Royal holding hands with Luke as they ice-skated together, Royal participating in the school choir concert (in which he looked noticeably less than thrilled), and Royal standing in the middle of my family as we smiled by the Golden Gate Bridge. We captured the special and the ordinary. We rewatched family home videos, the favorite one being Luke running behind Royal on his shiny new Christmas bicycle before Royal skidded in the snow and smacked into a parked car. Despite crashing, that charming smile still shone for the camera.

The agency told us they were moving forward with transferring Royal to a potential adoptive placement, an older woman all three of us had been spending time with and getting to know in preparation for this transition. A few days before Royal left, Luke gave me a ring to honor my first mothering experience. Though Royal only ever called me Ms. Jillana, he was the first child I'd ever had the privilege of caring for, and my heart was connected to his. Royal asked to hold the ring and accidentally dropped it, chipping the aquamarine stone and revealing a noticeably jagged edge if turned toward the light. This gem signifying my parenting journey wasn't perfect, but I didn't want to replace it. That rough edge was fitting.

• • •

"Hello?"

I picked up the phone to hysterics. Royal's pre-adoptive mom, who had weekly contact with me, shared with me a preventable yet alarming situation. She no longer wanted to proceed with adoption. We asked the agency to have Royal placed back with us, but due to the nature of what had transpired, we were told no.

For the next eighteen months, we maintained a relationship with Royal while he, at just eight years old, lived in a group home. He spent time with us on Fridays, and we had many photos of him proudly holding baby Sophia under a watchful eye. He threw the football with Luke. We went out for ice cream. We were the one constant presence in his life for two and a half years.

One day, I called to make arrangements for our family to pick him up for a visit and was dryly informed, "He's been transferred."

"What does that even mean?" I asked. Due to confidentiality protocols, I couldn't be told where, only that it was to another agency. I pushed back to no avail. I even showed up in person at the other agency to inquire if I could leave my contact information for his new foster mom to contact me.

"Trust that things will work out as they are meant to be," I was told. They were shallow words with nothing of substance to stand on. Without the dignity of an official goodbye, I suddenly lost contact with our good-hearted Royal Storm.

I circled his July birthday on my calendar. I wore the mother's ring with that chipped gem. On many ordinary days, I would be walking from the kitchen to the bedroom and stop and look at framed photos of him on the hallway wall. I missed him. I worried about him. I wondered about him. And still, the fullness of life, swirling the ordinary and the sacred, carried on.

The supervisor at the foster care agency who had stood in our driveway waiting for the police to return with Dion became a personal friend. Through backyard dinner conversations, she told me she needed to get out of the world of abandoned and abused children before she became "too callous to care." After two decades, she wanted to pursue a career as a doula, to see babies born into families where immediate interventions to keep babies safe were not needed. She soon left the world of foster care for good. But we'd see each other again: She was in the room when our second daughter was born!

3

BONDS OF
BROTHERHOOD

Ties That Bind

TWO AND A HALF YEARS AFTER we lost touch with Royal, we moved from New York to Portland, Oregon, to be closer to my family. After the birth of our second daughter, Eleni, Luke and I made an intentional decision to take a break from foster care. We decided to give it at least a year in our new city and state before jumping back in. In late January 2009 I called the local Department of Human Services (DHS) office to inquire about the process of becoming foster parents in Oregon. I am pretty sure the call was on a to-do list sandwiched between rescheduling a dental appointment and calling a landscaper.

I answered some simple questions and told a warm and kind woman named Anna that we were still certified foster parents in New York. She asked me a few more clarifying questions about what type of child or children we'd be willing to welcome in our home. I told her that when we were ready to foster—sometime in the future as this call was simply to do my homework for a later date—we'd like to welcome a child younger than our youngest child, yet we wanted to remain open.

Four days later Anna called back. "Jillana, it's Anna from Child Welfare. We spoke a few days ago. A case came across my desk, and I couldn't stop thinking of you. I was wondering if you and your husband might be interested since you're still currently certified foster parents."

I stood in a patch of rare January sunlight shining on the tan carpet in my bedroom and listened to Anna with rapt attention. She told me that the biological mom struggled with methamphetamine addiction and nobody currently knew her whereabouts. During her pregnancy, she had been living in a clean-and-sober apartment and was working as a drug and alcohol counselor. The biological father was currently incarcerated. The baby was six months old, and his name was Micah.

Luke, now a university professor, was in his office, surrounded by overflowing bookshelves, answering email, and eating his bagged lunch when I called him.

"Hey, babe, how's your day going?" I was casual at first, but after he responded, I slowly said, "So . . ." and then rapidly blurted out all the information. "What do you think?"

The last question he expected from me was if he was interested in coming home to a six-month-old baby. Luke is a deep thinker and always asks thoughtful questions without getting overly worked up. "I'll think about it, and we'll talk later tonight." That kind of one-step-at-a-time approach keeps my head grounded and my heart from racing when I'm tempted to start prematurely sprinting.

I don't remember much from that evening conversation, but a few days later, on a dreary, cold afternoon in early February, I unbuckled Micah from his car seat in the back of the government vehicle sitting in our driveway. I was handed two Post-it notes, a plastic tote, and a garbage bag full of possessions by his social worker, Karina, a stylish woman wearing a leopard-spotted trench coat. She explained more of Micah's backstory. "His great-aunt was a wreck about this decision, but she just couldn't handle his needs amidst her home-based business. This great-aunt who fostered Micah had also fostered Micah's mom decades earlier." Before I could take in the full circle of the same relative caring for this boy and his mother in foster care, Karina kindly said to call if I needed her. "I'll be back in a month." And then she drove away.

Micah had large brown eyes and an unruly mop of fuzzy-dandelion-meets-shaggy-surfer-boy hair.

Our girls, four-and-a-half-year-old Sophia and two-year-old Eleni, instantly oohed and aahed over him. They emptied their entire toy box in two minutes flat to encircle him with all his options. We took lots of "capture the moment" candid pictures. My parents made the thirty-minute drive over, and we just so happened to be hosting my grandma for a weeklong visit. When Luke walked in the door from work that day, he was greeted by a household of people buzzing with excitement.

"How's my little man?" he said as he reached out to greet Micah. "Whoa! He's only six months old?" We quickly realized the six-month-size diapers we'd just purchased would have to be returned since he was filling out twelve-month overalls.

A few minutes later, Micah was asleep on Luke's shoulder, his shaggy mop of hair pasted to his face with sweat. The two of them were in a rocking chair, center stage in the welcoming chaos.

The next week, I took Micah to our pediatrician for a basic examination. Although Micah sometimes flashed quick, shallow smiles, there was a hollowness to both his smile and his eyes. He did not make direct eye contact with people and usually gazed downward. At six months old, he could not sit up on his own and his head had a tendency to flop to one side. The back of his head was as flat as a board, presumably from being left lying down for long periods of time, the pediatrician surmised. Most noticeably, he sweat profusely. Watery beads would regularly roll down his temples, despite the rest of his body being at a reasonable temperature. His hair was often soaked, as if he'd just been dunked in the bath. The pediatrician wondered aloud if Micah had cried incessantly while being left on his back and nobody responded. He also suggested this could be a physiological reaction to internal stress Micah had endured in his first six months of life.

For the first few days, I scanned the Post-it notes on the fridge several times, wanting to be sure there was no pertinent information I was missing. I was frustrated at how little there was. Still, I knew from experience that even two scribbled notes is much more information than many foster parents receive about the neglected and abused kids they embrace.

One Post-it had Micah's tentative sleep schedule scribbled

on it: bedtime by midnight (*midnight?*) and one short nap at midday. The other note had scribbled, "Favorite show— Kipper and Pingu." I had no idea what that was or why a six-month-old had a favorite TV show. I later learned it is a cartoon about a talking dog and a Claymation penguin.

Luke and I tried to be extra intentional with this baby regarding healthy attachment. We wanted to make up for lost time, if such a notion is even possible. We carried Micah in a baby carrier or sling nearly all the time. He was so heavy my shoulders sagged, but we wanted him to feel our skin and get to know our voices. We swaddled him to sleep, rocked him, and made eye contact while we fed him his bottle. We sang him lullabies, and within a few weeks, I put words to a little tune and sang a personal lullaby over him every night, just as I'd created for my girls.

Micah responded well to being snuggled, held close, and put down for naps on a quasi-consistent schedule. We thought he was a good sleeper, but quickly realized that Micah never cried and hardly even stirred when he woke up. We would walk into his nursery and find him staring at the wall or ceiling. Presumably, he had grown accustomed to no one coming when he cried, so he had just stopped, even though he would be restless and covered in sweat. He was quiet for all the wrong reasons.

We moved him to my bedside so I could respond to his every whimper when he woke up. It was important for him to trust that he would get his needs met, and so it meant retraining him to know that someone would be there for him day or night.

Four weeks after his initial placement with us, Karina,

the social worker, dropped by on her first home visit and exclaimed, "This is not the same little boy who was dropped off last month." When Luke scooped him up and swung him high and low, saying in a singsongy voice, "Micah, you're my little man," he would genuinely belly laugh. Everything we were pouring into him was changing his countenance. His eyes were beginning to have a spark of wonder and his mouth was more willing to curl up and show off a gummy smile.

As a mom, I did not put up a wall in my heart toward this little one, but I certainly did not plan to bond with this baby so fast. I couldn't help it. *Boom.* All the extra intentional eye contact into those big brown eyes, rocking him, and watching him sleep in the bassinet next to our bed put my heart on a fast track. My motherly protective heart swelled, and Micah was fully inside it, just like that. It wasn't a decision. It simply was.

Foster care is temporary; the goal is to reunite children with their parents when at all possible. I knew that. I was on board with that goal. I was not fully prepared, however, to hear the message from Karina on my phone two months later.

"Jillana, we have located Micah's mom, Jennifer. She'll be at court next week. She's ready to do whatever it takes to get him back."

• • •

Keys in hand on my way out the door, I was already running late. I needed to get across the city for a court date at the juvenile courthouse. As I gathered my things, my eyes fell on the beautiful 8 × 10 photograph of baby Micah that was framed and sitting on my piano. I swiped it, frame and all, and locked the door behind me.

It had been four months since Micah had been removed from the custody of his mother, Jennifer, in a scene that involved a SWAT team. A staff member at the state's child welfare office had described it as "dramatic." In Micah's short six months of life, for a variety of reasons, we were his third foster home, and his fourth home if you counted the first two months he lived with Jennifer. I didn't know much more than that. "She is his mom, and the photo of her child is the one framed in my home," I reassured myself as I drove to court, the large photo frame sticking out of my purse. I'd never been to court or had the opportunity to meet a parent of a child I was fostering before.

Outside the courtroom in a carpeted hallway, I saw a disheveled-looking woman, her hair pulled up into a messy bun, huddled up with her attorney. When they stopped whispering, our eyes met and I took a few steps closer to her and quietly asked, "Are you Micah's mom?" When she nodded and responded that she was, I introduced myself, "I'm Jillana, Micah's foster mom. I brought this for you." I held out the framed photograph for her to take. She took it, and tears overwhelmed her. I instinctively reached out and told her, "I'm rooting for you."

We embraced as she wiped her eyes. This was certainly not planned. I was surprised to hear myself give such encouragement, but in that moment, from one mom's heart to another, it was honest and true.

The caseworker stood up in court and shared with the judge that we were an "excellent foster family," but I was struck with how empty this adjective seemed. Jennifer and baby Micah were court-ordered to have time together for one hour each week. The child welfare office where visits occurred was located close to my house, so I decided to pass on the offer to have a staff person pick Micah up and instead do my own transportation. It was an intentional move to be able to look Jennifer in the eyes at drop-off, say hello, give her a personable update about her son, and then say goodbye as I brought him back to my home.

On this particular morning, a few months into this weekly visitation rhythm, I pulled into the Department of Human Services parking lot for their scheduled one-hour visit. For once, we were actually a few minutes early, so I unbuckled my two girls, ages two and four, and we went into the lobby.

"Are we gonna see Jennifer?" Eleni wanted to know. They were used to seeing Jennifer when we'd take Micah to visit her every Wednesday. When I told her we would, Eleni clasped her pudgy toddler hands together and exclaimed, "Goody!"

When Jennifer appeared, Eleni ran up and said enthusiastically, "Hi!" Jennifer said hello back, then scooped Micah up and held him close.

As Jennifer headed to the long corridor of visitation rooms, Eleni pointed her pudgy finger and sternly called out to her, "Hey! Where are you going with my brudder?"

Jennifer turned around. "Don't worry, honey. I'll have him back in an hour."

"But where *is* my brudder?" Eleni worried a minute later when I buckled her up in the car seat in the parking lot. Luke and I did not use the term *brother* for Micah. We had been intentional about framing foster care accurately to our girls. Micah was entering our home because his parents needed some time to learn to be "safe and healthy" parents and make "safe and healthy" choices for Micah. It was our job to love Micah and keep him safe and healthy until he could be reunited with them. And yet, instinctively, the girls had deemed Micah their brother.

Pulling out of the DHS parking lot, I stopped at a red light and picked at my nails. As Micah visited with Jennifer and I pulled into my driveway with my girls, Eleni's forcefully emphatic "Hey! Where are you going with my brudder?" rattled inside me.

I remembered asking that question myself as a child. It was the early eighties, and I was a six-year-old who seemingly had it all—a yellow Lab named Buffy, a huge backyard swing set, a sandbox, a garden, and plenty of neighborhood friends. But the one thing I desired more than anything was a sibling.

I remember praying in my bed at night with my parents sitting near the footboard, asking God to *please* give me a brother or a sister. I asked my mom why she didn't have a round tummy with a baby in it like so many of my friends' mommies. As an adult, I've had several friends who have walked the grief of infertility. I have a fresh understanding of how my straight and pointed questions as a child must have pierced my mom's heart. And yet, she calmly and lovingly explained that families can be formed in many ways. When I was an adult, my mom shared how many nights her pillowcase was soaked in quiet, salty tears from the many miscarriages and failed adoption attempts she and my dad had endured in that season. I lived blissfully unaware of just how traumatic this was for them, and then, in the winter of 1982, my parents got the long-awaited call—our family had been chosen at last.

Finally, I had the baby brother I'd been waiting for! My parents named him Ethan Joseph. My bedtime prayers instantly changed from pleading tones to jubilant ones, and I often begged to sleep in Ethan's beautifully decorated room. I hovered over him, running to retrieve anything for the baby, ceaselessly asking to hold him on the couch, and covering the walls of his room with crayon drawings professing my love for him.

Life is finally perfect, I thought. And then, with another phone call, my perfect life was upended.

I was at the piano, plunking away at the latest Suzuki piece my teacher had given me to memorize. Ethan was beside the piano in a dark, woven bassinet cooing with contentment when the phone rang. My mom picked up the clunky rotary wall phone with the long extension cord attached. I looked at her and she winked as she answered it. I started plunking down on the keys again, entertaining my baby brother, when I heard her shriek "No, no, no!" My dad zoomed home from work early. Later, my parents sat with me on the brown striped couch in the living room. With bloodshot eyes, they shared the news that Ethan's birth mom had changed her mind. She wanted him back. It was within the legal window when she could do that. There was nothing my parents could do.

When Ethan's birth mom and her family came to claim him, I stood by the curb in front of our house. My mom handed him over, along with everything from his baby shower that was in his nursery. My mom wanted her to have it all. "I plan to change his name," she said, "but I will keep his middle name Ethan to honor the time he spent with your family."

I gave him one last kiss and ran into the house as fast as my feet would take me.

I collapsed, sobbing uncontrollably on the same brown striped couch. The upholstery was scratchy as I pressed my face into the cushions. I wanted that ugly couch to swallow me up. My kindergartner mind couldn't comprehend what had just happened. The devastation that "I had a baby brother and now suddenly I don't"; the emotional complexities of a mother carrying a child for nine months, then placing him into another mother's arms before ultimately reversing that choice; the ripple effects of heartache impossible to quantify on both sides.

A year later, my family was chosen again, this time by an expectant sixteen-year-old. I was swimming in my grandparents' backyard pool, and my parents walked onto the back patio with my two-day-old brother. "Jillana, we want to introduce you to your baby brother." I distinctly remember getting out of the pool, drying off, and admiring him for the first time. A few photos were snapped of the once-again proud big sister with wet braids plastered to the side of my face. I walked around our neighborhood pulling my Radio Flyer red wagon and going door-to-door passing out zucchini from our garden and giving all our neighbors See's candy suckers with blue wrappers announcing, "It's a BOY!" Less than two years later, I was passing out pink "It's a GIRL!" suckers after my mom gave birth to my sister, a pleasant surprise to us all. Life was good, and yet, from time to time, I would think about Ethan.

Fast-forward sixteen years: A local news story reported that two eighteen-year-old young men had burglarized a home, presumably in search of drugs. When the police arrived, one of the young men fatally shot himself. That young man? It was Ethan, my first baby brother. Apparently, he had grown up his whole life in a town twenty minutes away from me.

I wondered if our paths had ever crossed without our even knowing it, perhaps as we were standing in line at the grocery store or walking past each other at a community event. The wondering and the hypotheticals can feel downright haunting, set against the backdrop of love and longing. If he had been raised in our family, would he have been in that house on that day with a gun? Would he have been a totally different kid? Was the pain of being separated from him at the beginning sparing us this anguishing fate down the road?

This first painful memory morphed into my very first funeral experience. When my mother, father, and I arrived, I signed the guest book with my maiden name and perused the many photos on the cardboard posters. In a few of the baby photos, my mom recognized baby items she had given to Ethan's mother.

A little bookmark with a Scripture and his picture was given to us as we entered the church. I put it in the middle of a small Bible, where it remains to this day, a reminder of love, loss, and a different life—both his and mine—that might have been.

My mind flipped back to the present, my girls itching to get out of the car and into the house. What happens when the time comes when Micah doesn't return in an hour . . . or ever? I was on board with the goal of foster care being reunification with family when safely possible—I signed up with my eyes wide open—but what in the world was I doing to my girls? Was I signing them up for heartbreak?

• • •

When we first started fostering Micah, I received a post-card from my friend Diann. She runs an inner-city after-school program that provides a respite of hope for children in generational poverty and trauma so deep that resilience and despair play a daily tug-of-war in their lives. I placed the postcard on my windowsill where I could see it every day. Against a black background, a burning candle illuminated a quote by Eleanor Roosevelt.

It is better to light a candle than to curse the darkness.

I needed this daily reminder. Our love and care for Micah was our way of offering something sacred, something sacrificial into the world. Our family was toppling head over heels in love with this baby, and the weight of Micah leaving some-day would certainly devastate us all. Yet from the darkness of neglect, we had the jaw-dropping privilege of lighting a candle for this child. And Micah, receptive to the goodness being poured into him, was already reflecting light back to us.

Someone earnestly asked me the other day, "How do you protect your heart in all of this?" This is my least favorite question, even if it may be well-intentioned. Avoiding pain is not the ultimate prize of a life well lived.

C. S. Lewis reminds us,

To love at all is to be vulnerable. Love anything, and your heart will be wrung and possibly be broken. If you want to make sure of keeping it intact, you must give your heart to no one, not even an animal. Wrap it carefully round with hobbies and little luxuries; avoid all entanglements; lock it up safe in the casket or coffin of your selfishness. But in that casket— safe, dark, motionless, airless—it will change. It will not be broken; it will become unbreakable, impenetrable, irredeemable.

Sometimes we arrive at this vulnerable path of love by choice. Other times, we find ourselves in the middle of it, and there's no getting around it other than to keep putting one foot in front of the other. The truthful answer to that well-intentioned question is this: Micah deserves healthy attachment more than I need to keep my heart protected from shattering. Love is a risk, a vulnerable heart move. There is no risk-free path in parenting, no matter how our children come to us. We know that at any moment, our hearts could be scraped by tragedy, trauma, or rebellion. This doesn't stop us, however, from loving our children and continually being shaped by them.

There is a painting my mom created that hangs on our living room wall. The scene features a weathered barn set against a background of a thick forest of yellow-leaved trees. A winding, uphill path starts at the edge of the woods, before it's swallowed up by fog. Our parenting journey resembles that path in the painting—a path that begins clearly but becomes overwhelmed in a fog of unknowns. And yet, love compels us to keep walking.

And so we continued to love Micah—and his mother—for whatever time we had.

One day after Jennifer and Micah finished a visit, she held Micah on her hip as she walked with him out to my car in the DHS parking lot.

"Did you know I grew up visiting my mom in this same office—even in the same room—where I now visit with *my* baby?"

I shook my head; I wasn't aware.

"I hate it here," she said straightforwardly. "Would you ever be open to supervising visits for me outside of the office, Jillana?"

Though I'd never heard of a foster mom doing this, I replied that I'd check in with the caseworker.

With an email requesting that I inform her if Jennifer appeared "under the influence of drugs or alcohol," the caseworker granted me permission to supervise visits between Jennifer and her baby. Week after week at 10 a.m., I would pull my green Volvo to the corner of 122nd and Division Street in the Payless Shoes parking lot, and Jennifer would hop in the front passenger seat. We'd zoom off to the park, the zoo, the community center. Her presence was the best gift she could give to Micah, which was more than what she had often received as a child.

Every week, I unbuckled Micah from his car seat in the back, handed him to Jennifer, and literally walked and sat beside them, often photographing them together. I fully loved and adored my son in foster care whom I was raising for a season. But Micah was Jennifer's son, and I did want her to succeed. I had begun to care for her with a determined sisterly love. The risk of heartache on all sides for both her and me felt palpable—there was no way under or over it— and yet I was extended a quiet yet radical invitation. Love was inviting me to walk squarely down the middle of the road and root for the flourishing of Micah's mother.

Months later, I received another letter from Diann.

"Jillana," she wrote, "it's all eternal, your love—unable to be destroyed, no matter which way this story goes. It is better to light a candle than to curse the darkness, yes, but here's another Eleanor Roosevelt quote as you care for Micah and his mother."

> *What is to give light
> must endure the burning.*

As I cradled Micah in my rocking chair that night, his intense brown eyes locked on mine, I knew that if I were hyper-focused on the ending of this story, I'd miss the every-day gift of being shaped by these tender-heart circumstances. If my girls grew up with their own story of a baby brother who they were wildly attached to for only a season, I would know what they're feeling and would be present to their pain. I would point to their grandmother's painting of an uphill, foggy path headed toward a forest and assure them that in our moments of living out stories riddled with question marks, love is present with us on the path.

4

WE ALL MISS
THE MARK

Empathy

MICAH'S ONE-YEAR BIRTHDAY WAS APPROACHING. When I handed Jennifer party invitations for her and her family members, she was thrilled that they were illustrated with frogs. She rolled up her pant leg to reveal a frog tattoo on her calf. It was another sign that Micah was "meant to be" living with our family, she said.

Micah's party was held at our local city park with a playground, picnic tables, and an abundance of food, balloons, and games. About twenty-five people were there, and it was a gathering of two worlds—our friends and family and Jennifer's. Was it awkward and stilted? A bit. If we had polled random strangers walking down the street about the two different camps of "family" and asked who belongs in which group, could they have divided us up? Probably. But none of that mattered. We were all there to love one sweet boy.

When it was time to open presents, I said quietly to Jennifer amidst the birthday party buzz, "Why don't you let him open yours first?"

"I didn't bring him one," she replied softly, looking uncomfortable.

I immediately felt sheepish at my insensitive blunder. My intent was to honor her, and I blew it. Jennifer didn't know how she would pay rent at her halfway house in two weeks and whether she'd be homeless as a result. *Why in the world did I assume she would have a present for Micah?* Her gift was her presence—clean and sober—a present worth infinitely more than anything she could have bought. But it was invisible, even to her.

Later, away from everyone and in a quiet moment, I put my hand on her back and apologized. "Jennifer, I didn't know. I'm so sorry." Instead of a snarky response out of shame or sadness, she quietly replied, "That's all right."

There was a gentle earnestness to those three words that made me believe that she wasn't merely being polite. She was gracious to me. Other than my cringe-worthy comment, the party was a success. Micah mowed down his cupcake and gave everyone the coveted frosting-on-the-face first birthday photo.

After the party ended, I nuzzled Micah's nose and gave him his bottle. He was freshly bathed with hair smelling of honey shampoo, swaddled in his favorite blankie. He stared at me for the longest time and then reached up and cupped my cheek. I took his little fingers and kissed them twice.

"This kiss is from me because I love you so much. And this kiss is from your mama because she loves you so much too."

• • •

Jennifer and I are relatively close in age, and yet our lifetime experiences are worlds apart. When I was seven, I enjoyed riding my bike with its glittery streamers on the handlebars in my suburban cul-de-sac. When Jennifer was seven, she was molested by her stepdad in a city trailer park. When my parents were tucking me in at night, Jennifer was bouncing from foster home to foster home and began to run away. At age ten, when my mom was teaching me how to curl my bangs with a curling iron, Jennifer's mom was giving her a bottle of hard liquor. When I was thirteen, I had a big sleepover party with friends that my parents helped me to plan. When Jennifer was thirteen, her mom offered her meth. When I was fifteen and was out with my friends, I honored a strict curfew so my parents wouldn't panic. When Jennifer was fifteen, she landed in a lockdown facility for running away from countless foster homes. She can only recall one foster family in her entire childhood who expressed kindness to her.

I went to one high school and graduated with many of the same peers with whom I'd attended elementary school. Jennifer went to five different high schools, and with every transition, she lost both academic potential and a place to belong. When I was seventeen, my parents took me on several college tours. When Jennifer was seventeen, she dropped out of high school and ran away for the final time. At nineteen, I was a sophomore in college, experiencing travel and buckling down on my college majors. At nineteen, Jennifer had two babies, both involved with Child Welfare. Her third child, Micah, would be in foster care with me six years later.

As Micah's plight dragged on for the next eight months, the story we were living became more of an ongoing saga and less of a catchy, heartwarming sound bite, depending on the week. For the first time in her twenty-six years of life, Jennifer started attending a church for something other than an AA or NA meeting. She asked if I might join her one Sunday, so I made arrangements to skip my church service and to show up at hers. Micah was in a huge attachment stage and often buried his head on my shoulder when others reached out for him. Jennifer was no exception.

I walked into the church a few moments after the music had started and found where Jennifer was seated. She reached out for him, but he hid his face and clung to me. The song "Blessed Be Your Name" was being played by the worship band. After a few minutes of holding and snuggling Micah, his arms were no longer glued around my neck. I turned him around and held him with his back against my chest and swayed with him. He loved music, and I could feel him relax. Slowly, I quietly passed him over into Jennifer's arms. Micah let Jennifer hold him for a few minutes as the lyrics sank into my being: "You give and take away . . . blessed be your name . . ."

At our third court date, Jennifer looked like a different person than she did when I first met her. She was dressed in clean clothes, her hair was combed, and she was sporting a fresh haircut. The judge praised the "tremendous progress" Jennifer had made. She was completing the services the court had required, and she was on track to reunite with Micah. But even though Jennifer was doing well in some respects, she was now living out of her van and sleeping in the living room of a friend in recovery.

A few weeks after that court appearance, Jennifer and I, along with two of my friends, met at a park. A court-appointed parenting coach for Jennifer watched her push Micah in the swing for ten minutes, handed her a piece of paper saying her parenting class was now complete, and then drove away. It was another hoop successfully jumped through for reunification.

A few minutes later, Jennifer casually told me, "Last night I decided to drive to my dealer's house. Everything just feels like too much right now. But on the way I realized I didn't have my debit card. It was lost somewhere in my room, so I turned around and went home. So I'm still clean. God works in mysterious ways," she said with a shrug.

I was not prepared to hear this. I couldn't process it all. Wait, *what* did she just share with me? Still stunned, I clarified the most important question first.

"Your dealer takes debit cards?"

She chuckled and explained a few background details. We went back to the car and she buckled Micah in his car seat as she often did and kissed him goodbye. When I was alone in the car later that day, I did a lot of steering-wheel slapping as I processed the conversation. I was incredulous and angry. *Mysterious ways? Your son whom I love and am pouring my life into every second of the day to make sure he's healthy so he can be reunited with YOU is being left to the chance that you didn't have your debit card? That's why you're still clean?*

Even though I found her tone offensively casual, I still could not shake the nugget of truth that God *does* work in mysterious ways. I was worn out and ready for the mystery to be solved.

Our next visit was great. I picked Jennifer up for a trip to the park. She was hands-on, loving, and thoroughly engaged with Micah. They played in the fountains together. She fed him. She tickled him, and he laughed heartily. We exchanged small talk about weekend plans.

And then Jennifer fell off the face of the planet for the next month. No showing up for weekly visits. No phone calls. No texts. It didn't take much intuition to know something was off.

Right about that time, Karina, Micah's social worker, came for a routine monthly visit. She implied something was going on but wasn't at liberty to discuss it with me. She asked me how I'd feel about an open adoption. My heart was leaping out of my chest. *Did she really just ask me that?* After I told her we'd like to discuss that, she reminded me, "Anything can happen, so don't get your hopes up."

As a foster parent, I am mandated to pass along questionable or unsafe comments to the social worker, so I mentioned to Karina what Jennifer had told me at the park, though my heart dropped. I know some foster parents have a "gotcha" attitude with birth parents, and my heart was heavy as I passed it along. She told me the comment would be repeated in court, so she suggested I talk with Jennifer before she heard it in front of the judge.

But where *was* Jennifer? I woke up at night worried about

her. I placed two engraved rocks on my windowsill. One said "Peace" and the other "Hope." I found myself staring at those rocks while doing the dishes, and they became my breath prayers.

Then Jennifer left me a voicemail. She wanted to know if she could schedule a visit for the *next* day. My pulse quickened listening to that message. Over the previous six months, we had spent more than 150 hours together. I did not regret the time invested in our community visits one bit, but I made the confident decision that for my own emotional well-being, I needed to back off. After a flurry of phone calls with the caseworker, it was decided that Jennifer would now be meeting with Micah weekly at the agency instead of with me out in the community.

Even though I felt like I needed some space with supervising visits, I had a sudden prompting to call and talk with Jennifer. She actually picked up and told me she was at a tire store having her tires changed. Baby Micah was sleeping, and the girls were reading books quietly on the couch. I heard myself purposefully speaking slowly and gently because I didn't want her to feel threatened in any way. I told her I cared about her and wondered where she'd been. I told her she was under no obligation to tell me anything, but that I needed her to know that I knew something was going on.

"What am I supposed to think here, Jennifer, given the comment you made at the park followed by you disappearing for a month?"

There was a long hesitation and then an admission that she wanted to give up.

It was my turn for a long pause.

I took a deep breath, and I told her I'd like to sing her the song I sang to Micah every night. Now, I am not a singer. I have never sung anything serious to anyone before in my life unless you count my reflection in the mirror when I was a child singing into my hairbrush. Deep down, I know the reason God did not bestow on me the gift of a good voice was because I likely would have been vain about it, and who knows how that would have derailed me in life? Well before adulthood, I'd reached a peace about my lack of singing prowess, which is why I was just as surprised as Jennifer probably was when I told her I wanted to serenade her at the tire store.

I assure you this was not a typical move from my repertoire, but sometimes life invites you to pivot and swerve in and out of all kinds of uncomfortable moments. Pacing back and forth on my front porch with one hand lifted high, I sang the words only baby Micah had heard up to that point. The song mentions all the people in his life who love him, Jennifer included. I finished and could hear that her voice was teary and emotional.

I also shared with her about passing along the comment from the park. "My first priority is Micah and his safety. I hope you understand." She said she did, and we agreed to follow up on Monday morning when I dropped Micah off at the agency for his first visit with her in five weeks. Though I felt a tremendous weight was lifted with that conversation, I knew there was no predicting what our Monday morning check-in conversation would hold.

I tried to stay present in the moment, and not four steps ahead. Easier said than done.

On Monday morning, I drove to the government office to pick up Micah from an hour of spending time with Jennifer. Micah reached out when he saw me, and Jennifer handed him over to me. Jennifer quietly shared news with me. "I'm pregnant again." I shifted Micah from one hip to another in my arms.

Quietly and with a slower cadence I said, "You don't have to answer this if you don't feel comfortable, but is this baby's father the same as Micah's?"

"Yes, it's Simon's again." Then she started crying.

I took a deep breath. "How did you find out?"

"I went to the hospital last month for my chipped elbow. Before the nurse gave me some anti-inflammatory meds, she did a pregnancy test. It came back positive. When I burst into tears, the nurse asked me if they were tears of joy.

"I said, 'I don't have custody of any of my kids. I'm homeless. I just got back together with this guy, and I'm a drug addict, so you tell me.'"

"I bet you scared that nurse," I said, gently teasing her.

"I bet I did," she said, chuckling as she wiped away the tears streaming down her face.

• • •

Jennifer tearfully announced her pregnancy at a big meeting the next day. Its purpose was to collectively check in outside of court, assessing how things were progressing in the case. Simon was seated across from her. Twelve of us, including their attorney's assistants and their parenting coaches, were sitting at the long rectangular table in a sterile room at the foster care agency under humming fluorescent lights. Jennifer lamented how long she and her kids had been in the system and how tired she was, but there was no mention of giving up as she had told me. "I would like to start drug and alcohol treatment again at a new facility." You could have heard a pin drop. I flashed Jennifer a weary half-smile. She just looked down and away.

I willed my emotions to remain calm as I told everyone there how baby Micah was doing, my relationship with Jennifer, how much we care about her and care for baby Micah, and our family's openness to whatever the future may look like.

But in the end, the caseworker announced we were moving from plan A (reunification) to plan B (adoption). Both Simon and Jennifer buried their heads in their hands. "If you guys do really great from here on out, it can still be changed," the caseworker offered.

The assistant for Jennifer's attorney joined in, "Look how far you've come! You still have a lot of positives going for you, despite some setbacks."

"Yes! Yes!" Many people in various roles around the table affirmed that the plan could be changed back to reunification.

I willed myself to not squirm in my seat though I was feeling antsy on the inside. It felt to me like the story of the emperor's new clothes where the townspeople were praising something that didn't actually exist—in this case "success" meant completing necessary treatment programs and services in a timely manner, and that was obviously not happening. I did understand it, however, to be a motivating rallying cry. This wasn't something to be taken lightly. Losing custody of a child would impact their lives and Micah's life forever.

Later, Luke walked up to Simon. With quiet confidence, he said, "Simon, as a father myself, I just want to tell you that when I look at you, I see a man who desires to be with his son. We want you to know we see you as a person."

Simon shook Luke's hand and gave him a "bro hug," pulling him close and patting him on the back for a second. "Thanks for everything you're doing for Micah. I know you guys are a great family and everything. But I want the chance to be a father. I never had one."

As I pulled out of the parking lot and considered the future on the short drive home, I finally allowed tears to come. Tears of love for Micah. Tears of deep care for Jennifer. Tears of seeing Micah's parents' lifelong unhealthy habits result in a meeting with Child Welfare. Tears from having a front-row seat to the suffering of others. Weary tears of surrender. Tears at the privilege it was to be Micah's foster parents for *today*.

I woke up the next morning to a text message from Jennifer. This is what it said:

God is going to fix two big things today in your favor.

My heart was beating fast. What in the world did she mean? Was this her way of telling me she'd reached an important decision about Micah's future?

I scrolled down further.

If you believe in God, send to 10 people. Do it now and put Him first!

I felt on edge from the whiplash and let out an exhausted sigh. It was a forwarded chain message, sent to everyone in her phone.

In the months that followed, Jennifer and I continued to talk but it was more polite and stilted than before. As long as Jennifer was engaged in her parenting classes and required services, I was not a threat to her. But now I clearly was. She made it explicit through her lawyer and with the caseworker that she wanted Micah back, and she had several more months to prove herself.

The way the system is set up, if Jennifer and Simon didn't show progress in the next few months and yet refused to relinquish their parental rights, there would be a trial in an attempt to terminate their parental rights to Micah. A few weeks later, I received a letter in the mail as the state began their trial preparation. The letter stated I would be called as a "witness for the state." *All the intentional relationship building would be jeopardized.* I would be called to testify against Jennifer. I had done all I could to prioritize loving her in this relationship and now that connection would potentially be used as evidence that her ties to her son should be legally severed forever? I wanted to throw up as I held that letter. I envisioned how betrayed I would feel if I were in Jennifer's shoes.

"Breathe, just breathe," a well-meaning woman reminded me. "It's a long process, and I don't envy you one bit. The hypotheticals will drive you crazy and rob your life. Just trust the process and see where the cards fall."

The cards were about a little boy I loved with my whole heart and whom I stood to lose.

And those same exact cards were falling for Jennifer.

．　．　．

A month after our meeting around the table, Jennifer called to cancel her visit with Micah. I was standing in the frozen food section of the grocery store with my girls holding on to the grocery cart and Micah in the seat, teething on a cracker. The phone connection was crackly. "What did you say? . . . What about blood?" I asked, covering one ear to hear her.

"There is blood running down my leg," she repeated in a shaky voice. "I'm miscarrying." She couldn't make the visit today.

"Okay, no visit today. Got it." Then before hanging up, I threw in, "I'm sorry for your loss, Jennifer."

Later that night, after the groceries were put away and the kids were tucked into bed, "I'm sorry for your loss" rang in my head. I processed with Luke. "Was this an overused and insincere thing for me to say?" As we talked, it felt increasingly appropriate knowing that there is loss coiled around her past, in her present, and likely in her future.

Ever since I had started spending time with Jennifer, well-meaning friends, family—even other foster parents—made stinging comments about "Jennifer's choices" that led her to her current circumstance. Once, while I was speaking in a prospective foster parent training class, sharing a snippet of my fostering journey up to that point, a woman brazenly called out from the back of the room, "Ya know what I think?

I think that girl should be sterilized for only thinking of herself!" As others nodded in agreement, I felt my inner defensiveness rising. Yes, Jennifer had choices—things only she could do that would determine the outcome of the future. But choices are not made in a vacuum. Jennifer's background story provided a complicated context of hurdles—both visible and invisible—that she had to overcome. Trauma is a beast whose ugly roar can reverberate for a lifetime.

Jennifer would have to traverse the hurdles in her way, before even beginning to climb the mountain of life, where the weather conditions of trauma and constant poverty meant she would be doing it in a continual downpour. She wasn't starting from flat ground at the bottom; she first had to climb out of the pit of addiction, her coping mechanism to numb the wounds of childhood wrought with suffering. The terrain at the bottom was extra muddy, and she would need sturdy boots with good traction—along with people linking arms with her—to attempt to walk up the steep incline without sliding back, but it was as though Jennifer were climbing through life with flimsy sandals, unable to grasp the few footholds offered to her.

When I first got the call for baby Micah, Jennifer was defined by her struggle—"She's a meth addict," I was told. It was a true statement, said matter-of-factly, not maliciously. While not minimizing an iota of the immense, lifelong ripple effects of substance abuse, the quiet reality is this: Whether it's overtly labeled harmful or not, most of us are addicted to *something*. We all have moments when we fear being unloved or unworthy, and we resort to less-than-healthy ways to cope with the swirling complexities of life. That can look like a needle in an addict's arm, gluing ourselves to our phone screens, or my mindless binge-eating handfuls of goldfish crackers that I don't even like.

This journey had exposed my labels too: Jillana "the people pleaser," Jillana "the emotional eater." The sustained emotional intensity I was experiencing stressed me out so much that my "I'll try harder, be better, eat healthier" goals fell flat as I spooned ice cream right out of the container into my mouth.

My relationship with Jennifer had exposed me to the myriad ways we *all* miss the mark. As I walked alongside her, she was continually teaching me that the answer isn't as simple as cupping our hands around our mouths and calling down from a privileged mountaintop, "Just make a different choice!"

The reality that I know in my bones is this: If I had been dealt the same cards Jennifer was holding and suffered the same unquantifiable losses, there was a very good chance I would be standing in the same place she was.

"I'm sorry for your loss" was appropriate to speak hundreds of times over her entire life. The grocery store nicety turned into an increased sense of understanding the tempest of her life. I wanted to be a part of uplifting her in ways she's always deserved but never received. I wanted her to succeed in having a healthy, whole life, even though since the beginning she had been left scaling an extra-steep mountain with the odds stacked against her. I was still rooting for Jennifer, even when—*especially when*—the stakes were high, with the boy we both loved right in the middle.

5

THE PROLONGED WAIT

Surrender

THE TEETER-TOTTER OF WEARINESS was setting in. I had no guidebook for this path with Micah and Jennifer. Friends and family would ask me for updates, and it was a perpetual "We're waiting to see what will happen and trying to stay grounded in the meantime." I needed someone outside my circle to intentionally accompany me in the wait.

I'd heard of others meeting regularly with a spiritual director at the InterFaith Institute. Of the four people I interviewed, I was drawn to Sister Mary, a nun in her mid-seventies with short wavy white hair, to help me process this tangly mess of desire, hope, and surrender blended together in this time of waiting. Initially, Sister Mary didn't appear to be the most likely fit as there were other spiritual directors who were mothers. However, when we discovered we had both lived in the same city in Guatemala in the past, I took it as a sign that she was the one. Plus, even if I got nothing out of it, getting to hear her soothing British accent for a whole hour every other week would be worth the money.

Sister Mary had a keen sense of how I could keep delving deeper into God while experiencing the "everyday gift of Micah." I told her that eighteen months of being in a connected relationship, hoping the best for Micah while simultaneously rooting for his mother, had taken its toll. Watching Jennifer ride the roller coaster of health, addiction, and codependency while her son was in my care felt like a free fall out of an airplane at times.

"Jillana," she gently reminded me during our session one week, "you have responded to God's call with Micah in faith. In faith, if you jump, there *will* be a net."

The picture of what my family would look like a year from now rested completely on the actions of others, namely Micah's parents and an utterly overwhelmed state foster care agency. The mirage of having control over my own life had vanished, and yet it was a gift to lose the illusion that the good life does not have hard things. This is the very core of foster care—welcoming in, loving, and then returning. But I had underestimated the immense toll of adoring a child and giving him my all, while simultaneously and authentically desiring the best for his mother.

• • •

Five-year-old Sophia piped up from her top bunk, "Mom, can you tell me again about Jennifer?"

I repeated the well-worn script once again. "We are caring

for Micah because his mama, Jennifer, wasn't making safe and healthy choices for herself or Micah. We are keeping him safe for now while Jennifer is learning to make safe and healthy choices. If she can be a consistent safe and healthy mama, the judge and the caseworker will say Micah can live with Jennifer again, which will be happy for the two of them."

Sophia pulled the sheets up to her nose and said, "I'm praying that Jennifer makes bad choices, Mom, because I want to keep him here with us."

I understand completely, Sophia. At that moment, my mind was filled with images of the baby brother I once had and all my pleading bedside prayers when I was my daughter's age. Heartache is a part of life. Foster care gives you a head start in understanding that. I was trying to model for my daughter what it looks like to hope for the best in *all* people at *all* times, even when hope for redemption on Jennifer's part means heart-wrenching loss for us.

I told Sister Mary about Sophia's statement at our next session. She leaned back in her faded pink armchair, her hazel eyes twinkling. She was quiet for a moment, the sound of a decorative tabletop waterfall filling the small room. Sister Mary held her hands up to her lips and reminded me that my daughter's name, Sophia, means wisdom.

"Jillana, it is perfectly okay to pray, 'God, if Jennifer is going to fail, have it be in this critical period, for the safety of this child, so decisions can be made accordingly.'"

"But that feels selfish to me to even utter the word *fail* as I pray, Sister Mary. I want Jennifer to do *well*. I genuinely want her to succeed. And I also want Micah to have a healthy, stable life so he doesn't suffer through childhood like his mother did. I hope the best for *both* of them," I said. "But it's hard to know if that path is in two separate directions, or one path that merges together. It's foggy."

Sister Mary nodded, then quoted Father Richard Rohr: "The path of prayer and love and the path of suffering seem to be the two Great Paths of transformation. Suffering seems to get our attention; love and prayer seem to get our heart and our passion."

The homework she gave me that day was to go home and plant flower bulbs. The assignment's symbolism is that there is always growth and transformation happening underneath the surface. Even in the midst of a bleak winter, there is the possibility of growth. The evidence will emerge in the spring.

I loaded up all three kids and took them to our local nursery to buy bulbs. I bought the largest bag of multicolored tulips I could find, buckled the kids back into the car, and on the five-minute drive home I looked in the rearview mirror to see red and blue lights flashing.

I can't believe this! Am I really getting pulled over for speeding? I was doing my spiritual homework!

As the officer approached my car, my kids were wide-eyed. Suddenly, Micah broke out in a bloodcurdling wail followed fifteen seconds later by the girls. I tried to shush and reassure them as the officer looked at my license. "Mommy is totally okay, kids. We are all fine." But they turned up the volume tenfold. The more I tried to reassure them, the louder they got.

"Ma'am, I'm going to let you go with a warning. Just be mindful of your speed," the officer said. I thanked him and was on my way. I suspected the reason I didn't get a ticket that day (other than my skin color not working against me) was that the officer couldn't stand the noise emanating from my car long enough to write me one.

On a Saturday morning in September, I planted tulips in my front yard. It was the perfect fall day, sunny with crisp blue skies, puffy white clouds, and birds chirping, like a scene from a movie where the protagonist doesn't have a care in the world.

I had never planted flower bulbs in my life. I was armed with a trowel and the bag of twenty-five multicolored tulips. I looked at the directions on the bag to make sure I didn't plant them upside down. Then I knelt down. *No matter what, I am consciously choosing to view these flowers as a symbol of divine goodness.* By the time they bloomed, Micah would have been with us a very long time and things may very well remain undetermined.

As I was digging and thinking about the possibilities, my heart began to sink into a mire of fearful what-ifs. Overhead, as if sensing my emotions, clouds rolled in and the sky turned dark. In a matter of minutes, the weather went from blue skies to a torrential downpour. I was halfway through my bag of bulbs and got positively drenched. For a moment I was tempted to call it quits for the day. *No, I need to see a physical reminder of new life in spring, no matter the outcome.* I continued planting, my hands encased in mud and permanent mud stains forming on the knees of my gray sweatpants. I didn't care. I kept digging.

Six months later the tulips were popping their heads through the earth. They were fully sprouted, and buds of each color promised to bloom soon. Each day when I pulled in and out of my driveway, my eyes were immediately drawn to them, anticipating what was to come. "Thank you, God, for bringing life out of the unknown," I whispered under my breath. And "Thank you, Sister Mary, for your wisdom in my life!"

In the meantime, Jennifer hadn't shown up for several visits again recently nor responded to any communication. I was genuinely worried about her. One day in early spring, as I walked out the door to take the children on an outing to the children's museum, I realized I'd forgotten my purse. I asked them to wait while I dashed upstairs to retrieve it. When I returned, Eleni and Micah—just seventeen months apart—both greeted me with "Look, Mommy!" while proudly opening their pudgy fingers. Most of my unopened tulip buds were cupped in their hands.

I drew them close and gently explained how we don't pick the heads off flowers and how sad it made me. "But I love you so much more."

Actually, that's what I *wish* I'd done.

Instead, I shouted, "What did you DO? You've RUINED EVERYTHING!" I hurried them inside the house, and then stomped upstairs.

A minute (or two) later, I came back down and apologized to my stunned children. Sophia, who hadn't touched the flowers, was crying in the bathroom.

For the rest of the spring, every day I saw my headless tulip stems standing up tall in my front yard. I was aware that my window of stress tolerance was becoming smaller as the days passed and weariness set in. The symbols outside now represented something I didn't want to see; sometimes we plant and wait and hope, straining our eyes to see beauty that never comes or is plucked before our very eyes.

Life went on. I changed diapers, poured milk into bottles, read books, lovingly reprimanded Micah for climbing up on the table, and rocked him to sleep. I sang him his special song while lifting one hand into the air as I rocked him, a gesture that reminded me that the direction of his story was not mine. I only had this present moment in front of me. I needed to believe that everything was part of a divine plan that this particular boy was in my particular home for a specific season.

That evening, after Micah was put down for the night, an email from the caseworker popped up in my inbox:

> Hello Luke and Jillana,
> The DA has officially accepted the case, and we are actively moving forward toward a termination or relinquishment of parental rights; however, if the parents make considerable progress prior to the trial, the case may be dismissed, and a return home plan may be ordered.

I showed it to Luke, who nodded with a resolute calmness that seems ever-present with him, and he embraced me in a warm hug. I resisted playing out scenarios like a chess game. At times, it's easier to try to look further down the road and tease out the hypothetical rather than calmly engaging the here and now. Nothing really changed with this email. I still loved this boy, and so did his mother. While he was one step closer to legally becoming my son, I cringed with a sense of loss for Jennifer, a loss I wouldn't have felt so acutely if I hadn't seen her nuzzle him, tenderly hold him, play with him at the park, tickle him, talk with him, love him. I had a front-row seat to her attempt to overcome massive hurdles to become safe and healthy enough to parent her son. Jennifer's presence was a gift to Micah, and also an unexpected one to me, even though it landed me in Sister Mary's office. I reread the email, took a deep breath, and lit a candle. The bittersweet wait would continue.

• • •

If I'm not purposeful with engaging the practice of waiting, especially for things that profoundly matter, my default is to overfunction and pile high the to-do lists, clamping down on the precious little I can control. I find things to keep me occupied, or I buckle down on my own flimsy self-sufficiency. Distraction comes more easily to me than intentionally embracing the unknown through taking time to be still, pray, read, journal, or walk, in order to center and prepare myself for what is to come.

If this were a luxurious version of waiting, I'd hole up in a cabin in the woods for some reflection time with a citrus candle burning, cozy pillows, and a blank journal. I'd rejoin the bustle of my household, refreshed, and be able to slowly release the calm, as if taking the cap off a perfume bottle for a sustaining whiff. But my real life is a hubbub of emails that need answering, errands to be run, and minor daily irritations such as opening a clean dishwasher to discover a few dirty dishes and a yucky spoon haphazardly placed amongst the pristine.

Still, in the midst of the ebb and flow, when I first started my parenting journey with Royal, long before Sister Mary came into my life, I started writing down prayers or quotes on index cards and taped them in various places I happened to be each day. These gentle reminders of truth transformed my kitchen windowsill, my car dashboard, and my bathroom mirror into sacred spaces. I considered them my breath prayers to God—"You are a light unto my path," "Be near as I wait," "I claim peace"—to be inhaled and exhaled as I scrubbed a sticky pot, sat at a traffic light, or washed and rinsed my face.

On my kitchen windowsill is a quote from Joseph Campbell I had quickly scribbled down because when I read it, it immediately resonated with me.

> We must let go of the life we have planned, so as to accept the one that is waiting for us.

Some of the inked words are blurred from being splattered with water when I wash dishes, but I can quote it by heart. Beside it sits a stack of five small gray stones piled on top of each other, a tiny replica of what the Israelites constructed as a permanent memorial, remembering how God led them safely on a dry riverbed into the Promised Land. Without a tangible sign, humans are fickle creatures, prone to forget. For the Israelites, the stones of remembrance served as a physical reminder of God's faithfulness during forty years of wandering and waiting.

My index cards with words, prayers, and quotes get soggy and are switched out regularly, but that tiny tower of stones stands firm on my kitchen windowsill, where it's been for the past fifteen years. I look at it and am reminded that even in the midst of our weariness, we do not journey alone. Surrender—in the planting, in the hopeful anticipation, and especially when staring at bare stems—was shaping me.

6

AS LONG AS THERE'S BREATH

Hope

I PICKED UP THE PHONE; Jennifer was over the moon. She was enrolled at Mt. Hood Community College, where I taught ESL night classes. She had a contagious enthusiasm in her voice that *this* was step one in moving forward in health and a better life for her and Micah. Although the plan for Micah had been switched to adoption a few weeks earlier, I knew if Jennifer did a 180 and sprinted in a new direction, Micah would go back to her. When we finished the call, I couldn't help but smile at the hope I heard in her voice.

I knew the odds were against her, but perhaps this— *this!*—would be her turning point. I wanted Jennifer to flourish.

Relishing a few minutes to myself in Portland's trendy Hawthorne neighborhood, I walked into a store looking for a gift for a friend. Immediately I noticed colorful letters mounted to the wall. They spelled H-O-P-E. The shop owner told me they were made by an artist in Haiti, using recyclable materials from a garbage dump. The H was fashioned from a flattened can of Raid ant spray. I was instantly taken with the artistry and the symbolism of something beautiful created out of the mundane. But when I asked how much it cost, the practical side of me decided it was too much to spend on a whim.

Later that evening, I found my way to my assigned room in the community college building. I unlocked the classroom, set down my bag, and stood outside the door to smile and shake each student's hand as they arrived. When the last person filed in, I closed the door behind me, glancing across the hall through the large window in the door. And there she was! Jennifer was sitting in the front row, pencil in hand, her eyes on the instructor.

I couldn't believe it! What were the chances that out of the hundreds of classrooms on this large college campus, which serves more than twenty thousand students, we would be assigned rooms directly across from each other on the same evening at the same time? As I taught my class, I had the perfect vantage point to see hope personified across the hall.

When I let my class take a short break, Jennifer's instructor also opened the door for a break. Jennifer was surprised to see me in the hallway. We talked briefly about Micah and then headed back into our classrooms.

As I walked to the parking lot that night after class, I wanted to surrender and be at peace, but I felt panic! *Jennifer will persevere on this new trajectory and get Micah back*. I was sure of it. On the ride home, I was overwhelmed with the thought.

• • •

A week later, I drove back to the gift shop on Hawthorne. I *needed* those letters, to see them and claim them every day. I envisioned them hanging in my stairwell; they would remind me that love *always* hopes. It hopes for the best for people. It's not conditional or self-serving. I determinedly walked to the counter, pointed at the letters on the wall, and told the woman at the register that I'd like to purchase HOPE.

"Just a minute. I'll get it from the back."

When she returned, she said simply, "I'm so sorry. We're all out."

"You're out?"

"Yes."

"You're out of hope?" I clarified.

"Yes."

"You're completely all out of hope?" I asked again, trying to will the instant tears pooling in the corners of my eyes not to spill over.

"Yes," she patiently repeated for the third time.

I gulped. "Okay, thank you." I was out the door and two steps down the sidewalk when I heard the store owner's voice. "I have a feeling this means something to you. If you wait a minute, I will sell you the display."

I bought the HOPE I needed to hang on to for Jennifer, knowing that if she was successful, I would lose the little boy—her son—whom I loved as my own.

I saw Jennifer a half dozen more times on campus, exchanging little waves when our eyes met. We chitchatted a bit during our breaks. Then, just as quickly as she showed up across the hall, she disappeared. I tried calling her. No answer.

The following week, I showed up at the sterile DHS lobby for a pre-appointed visit. I had cupcakes for her on the off chance she showed up since this visit fell on her birthday. I sat watching the clock tick as Micah uncharacteristically sat calmly in my lap. When I was given permission by the caseworker to leave, I handed the cupcakes to the receptionist to give away to someone else and drove home. It didn't take any intuition to know that Jennifer was not doing well. Later that night, when the kids were all tucked in and the house was quiet, tears fell down my cheeks as I stood at the kitchen sink scrubbing dishes.

• • •

On a rare drive alone with Luke a few weeks later, I looked out the window at the Willamette River and said, "You know that feeling when you're talking with someone on the phone and you're just about to say goodbye and then for some reason or another, you get disconnected? You don't know if you should call back and formally say goodbye or just skip it and go on with your life. I feel like I need to say goodbye to Jennifer, but not on the phone. I want to take Jennifer to lunch and read her the letter I wrote to her. I feel like I've been hung up on, and I need some closure to this particular chapter. What do you think I should do?"

Luke drove for a while in silence, a steep terra-cotta-colored terrace on one side of the road, a glistening river on the other, evergreen trees spiking into the cloudless afternoon. Then he calmly said, "I know how important every relationship is to you, and this one in particular. I know you will have a hard time letting go and moving on unless you are able to speak the things in your heart to Jennifer. You should get together with her."

Even though I heard his reassuring words, my mind sped through reasons not to go through with it. *Is this too risky? What if she's out of her mind on drugs and acts crazy and reaches across the table and stabs me with a piece of silverware?*

My dear Mr. Rational said I should give her a call to assess the situation and go from there. "Your chances of being stabbed in public at a restaurant with a dull knife are slim," he said with a smile. "Just go ahead and call her."

"Like right now?"

"Sure."

My heart began to pound, and my palms were instantly sweaty as I rehearsed what I would say to her. I took a deep breath, tapped her number on my phone, and heard Jennifer's voice for the first time in months. She instantly said she'd be up for meeting with me.

"Where?" I asked, biting my nail.

She suggested a truck stop on a side of town I wasn't familiar with. I'd never eaten at a truck stop before, and this didn't seem to be the day to be piling on new experiences.

"Could we meet someplace else?" I asked, biting my nails.

"Let's make it the Burrito House then."

I called Jennifer on Friday, we confirmed on Saturday, and we met on Sunday. I'd never been to that part of Portland before. It's not that where we live in the city is so pristine, but taking this route with dilapidated buildings and abandoned businesses felt completely unfamiliar. I followed Sister Mary's suggestion and purposely drove without the radio on so I could focus on being totally present in the moment through silence. That is until I saw a billboard with faces and names of people who had been murdered with the tagline "COLD CASES—WE DON'T EVER GIVE UP." I quickly switched on the radio.

I pulled up to the Plaid Pantry convenience store right on time and texted Luke as he'd requested: **I'm here. Waiting.** A few minutes later, I recognized Simon's car as he drove into the parking lot, dropped Jennifer off, and pulled a fast U-turn back onto the street.

We had bought a new minivan since Jennifer and I had last met in the DHS parking lot, so I rolled down my window. "Hi, Jennifer."

She got in, smelling like cigarettes. As she'd told me previously, she was pregnant again and showing.

"How are you?" I asked.

"Good."

The Burrito House was located about a mile away. Our conversation wasn't stilted so I began to feel at ease. We walked into the restaurant and were seated at a table next to a water fountain. "Does this table location make you want to run to the bathroom? It would for me if I were pregnant," I said with a smile. And that was all it took to ease into the conversation. After spending so many hours together, we actually had some memories and experiences to draw from that made for a free-flowing conversation. Anyone in the restaurant would have guessed we were old friends catching up as we ate our Mexican food.

"Could I order a takeout meal for Simon?"

"Of course."

I was able to ask some questions regarding family medical background that I had no idea how to answer when filling out forms at the pediatrician's office. For the most part, however, I leaned forward and listened.

Toward the end of our meal, I reached into my purse and pulled out a little white box tied with ribbon and handed it to her. She opened the lid. It was a pendant I found at our local artisan market that said LOVE in Chinese. She had Chinese symbols of her older two kids tattooed on her wrist. I told her I remembered her saying she didn't have a tattoo for baby Micah, but I thought this pendant could work in the interim. She put it on right away. I shared I had a letter I wrote when she stopped showing up at school and I wanted to read it to her now. I asked if that was okay and she nodded.

With a calm voice and slightly shaky hands, I unfolded the paper. Here is part of what I read:

July 2010

Dear Jennifer,

When I first met you, I had no idea what this journey would look like or where it all would end.

Jennifer, the past eighteen months have undoubtedly been a roller coaster. Throughout the ups and downs,

I have always rooted for you. I hope you know that and have felt that. Like all people, you've made some mistakes and gone down some roads that you're not proud of, but I sincerely thought when you signed up for community college in December and seeing you at school in January, it seemed like you were certainly on track to get what you wanted—baby Micah and working toward your degree.

Jennifer, with no hint of judgment, I ask what happened to these dreams and aspirations?

*Sometimes I'll wake up in the middle of the night and think of you—**you, Jennifer**. I think there will be a part of me that will always wonder about you and worry about you. I want so much for you to be okay— more than okay. I want you to have a life filled with love and healing. You are a good person with a good heart, Jennifer. I want the best for you. I will never give up hope that you will find a life direction that will bring you contentment and wholeness in your life.*

A happy childhood, loving family, and fulfilling life is exactly what we desire to give Micah. We love him with all our hearts! I hope you've been able to see that. There's nothing we wouldn't do for him. My mother's heart is overflowing with love for him. And raising him will be one of the best and most important things I ever do in my life.

I know that legal terms like "relinquishment" or "termination of parental rights" do not mean that you don't love him. And he will know that, Jennifer. Luke

and I are committed to always speaking respectfully
of you. You are Micah's starting point in life, and
we would never try to erase that.

I folded up the letter and handed it to Jennifer, who was wiping tears off her face with the brown restaurant napkins. The waitress brought the takeout box and the check. Jennifer and I drove back to the Plaid Pantry parking lot.

I knew we had a post-adoption mediation coming up in a few days, but I did not want to talk about legalities of the case—the case which was our *life*. That would all come soon enough. I turned the car off for a moment, and we both looked straight ahead at the convenience store windows and said nothing.

"Did you know that my friend stole a candy bar from Plaid Pantry once and got arrested, and that my stepdad molested me and my sister and nothing ever happened to him?"

"No, I didn't know," I said quietly.

"How is it fair for him to do that to me without a minute in jail, and my friend who stole a candy bar ended up with a record?"

I silently shook my head, then said, "I'm sorry."

"I've never met anyone like you before, Jillana. I haven't. Your life is a f—ing fairy tale." She said the expletive in the kindest of ways. "And I'm glad my son is being adopted by you and Luke. I think it's the best gift I can give him."

As I drove home, I marveled at how this intense and emotionally exhausting chapter in our relationship seemed momentarily to be wrapped up with a bow. I treasured the goodness of connection but knew the next time we connected, there was a chance it might all unravel.

A week later, Luke and I took a seat in a circle at the mediator's office. Jennifer, Simon, and the mediator took their places. We were there to work out details of our post-adoption agreement. We had an open, welcoming posture toward Jennifer, but since she and Simon were viewed as a couple (and Simon, due to previous criminal charges, couldn't be around children), we legally agreed to very little. There were parts they clearly did not like, such as our not promising them a minimum number of visits per year, as evidenced by Jennifer walking away crying and rejoining the circle with puffy eyes. The mediator wasn't a particularly skilled communicator and made things more awkward. Jennifer and I had done better talking to each other in the restaurant.

The next day, I was at a red light, and Jennifer's car turned in front of mine at an intersection. My heart suddenly pounded. *Am I going to run into her all the time now?* Then I remembered I actually had some maternity clothes for her.

Back at home, I sent Jennifer a text: **Do you still want the clothes? I can meet you at 5:45 in the Payless parking lot.**

She texted back: **Yes, but I was thinking earlier.**

I couldn't help but wonder, *Why are you picky about the time? You seemingly have no responsibilities.*

I called Jennifer to set up a meeting time. It turns out it takes extra gas, which meant more money, to get across town in rush-hour traffic. I felt immediately humbled because I hadn't ever had to think of a thing like that. I told her I couldn't meet anytime earlier that week, so I suggested Saturday.

"What time?" she asked.

I glanced at the calendar on the kitchen cupboard. "We're taking Micah to the fire station open house in the morning, which I think he's going to love. How about three o'clock?"

"Okay."

When I hung up, it hit me full force. I had unintentionally rubbed in her face the fact that I was parenting her son, doing fun things with him.

"Why did I just tell her that?" I wondered aloud. I knew it was my feeble attempt to reassure her that Micah is going to be okay, but that wasn't necessarily how it was received.

At the appointed time, I pulled into a parking space right next to their car to give Jennifer the maternity clothes. The passenger car door was swung wide open and I could see Jennifer with her head resting on the glove compartment. She wasn't moving. I stared for over a minute. Why wasn't she moving? Suddenly, she looked up with a cigarette in her mouth and got out of the car. *Okay, she's alive!* I was beginning to fear the worst.

Jennifer was wearing shorts and a tank top even though it was a damp, dreary November evening.

"How are you doing, Jennifer?"

"Fine. The baby is four pounds now!" she said jubilantly, pushing hard on her bowling ball belly as if trying to smooth out a stubborn wrinkle.

She told me that she and Simon were renting a room in a trailer "with some guy and his mother." They were fifteen minutes over the border in Washington State now, and she was getting public housing assistance.

"That's good," I said politely. "I'm glad you don't have to live in your car."

I opened the back seat of the minivan and pulled out the clothes while her phone buzzed. "Simon wants to know if you brought the baby."

"No, not this time." I pulled up photos of Micah on my phone. She smiled scrolling through them. When she saw a photo of him with a bottle, she said, "What? You're still giving him that? How are his teeth?"

"His teeth are fine. We're working on a sippy cup," I said reassuringly, feeling a bit sheepish.

I began showing Jennifer some of my thrift store finds. "So, I thought this was cute and cozy and could go with this . . ."

Just then, Simon approached the car with a grocery bag. Jennifer pepped up. "Look, honey, we don't need to buy me sweats no more."

Simon didn't respond. He got in the car without acknowledging me and began eating Wheat Thins. I got the message. It was time for me to go.

"It was nice to see you, Jennifer. Be good to yourself," I said and handed her a bottle of prenatal vitamins. "Goodbye, Simon." I got a slight head nod and a low-toned "Bye."

As I pulled away, I was thankful Jennifer wasn't sleeping in her car, yet a trailer with "some guy and his mother" didn't sound encouraging. This was beginning to have a familiar ring to it. I couldn't help but feel like I was standing in line for a ticket on a wearisome merry-go-round that I didn't want to ride again.

•   •   •

Jennifer's son Elias entered the world on New Year's Eve. Our family was in the midst of hosting our annual East Coast New Year's Eve party when I got the call from Oregon Child Welfare. We weren't actually on the East Coast, of course. But for the last decade, we have made it a festive, family-friendly tradition to stuff our house with family and friends, kids included, then watch the televised ball drop in Times Square, blow noisemakers, and shout "Happy New Year!" at 9:00 p.m. in our time zone and midnight in New York. By 10:00, our friends are gone, the house is quiet, and there are hundreds of streamers hanging down from the ceiling for us to clean up the next day. Everybody loves it.

The call, however, came in the middle of starting the chocolate fountain. I took my buzzing phone from my back pocket and stepped into our home office. I learned that baby Elias would be released from the hospital in Washington in three days and was asked, "Could you foster him?" I said I needed to talk to my husband and our certifier first. As I hung up the phone, I took a deep breath and headed back to our guests.

We were just months away from officially adopting Micah, and Luke and I were both well aware that our hands were full. On January 2, 2011, I called our certifier and asked her if she knew of a dynamite, local certified foster family who could foster the newborn and would be willing to let us engage with him and offer a strong, supportive role.

"I wish I could say yes," she said. "But there are so few foster families available, and I'm not impressed with the potential candidates." I've always appreciated our certifier's honesty.

I called Luke next. His response was uncharacteristically emotional.

"Who else loves this baby? Loves his mother? Is raising his brother?" he asked.

I called the certifier back and said we would foster baby Elias.

I told our children, ranging in age from two and a half to six, that Elias would arrive the very next day, which made them giddy. "I need to go to the store to buy some outfits for him, and I would love for you to help pick them out."

The kids and I found cozy newborn outfits and a soft attachment blankie, just like the one Micah had the day he entered our home.

When we got home, I checked my email. It said an Oregon judge made a "left-field" decision and ruled that since Elias was born in Washington, the case would remain in Washington. He would not be coming, at least not now. The state of Washington would be taking Elias into protective custody, and getting him across the border (a mere fifteen minutes away from our house) would be a "long, complicated process."

My heart sank. Micah, now two and a half, woke up from his nap saying, "Baby, mom? Baby? I wanna hold it. Hold it, Mom?"

Classic to the world of foster care, I waited until the last minute to share this update with my children and there was *still* another last-minute change to come.

I talked with the new caseworker in Washington, who told me Jennifer was entering treatment "any day now." I wrote a letter to be placed in the baby's file: If Jennifer did not follow through on what she needed to do, Elias had a family in Oregon who would care for him.

· · ·

A few days later, I was in court again, for Micah. Jennifer was not present. The young, dark-haired court reporter said, "All rise," and the judge said, "Be seated" a millisecond later. We all watched him in silence as he shuffled papers for a moment. Then he pronounced that Micah's adoption date was set for spring of 2011. One piece of good news.

As I pulled into my driveway after court, Jennifer's number was buzzing on my phone. "It's time for me to grow up and not be a kid, Jillana," she said confidently. "A bed has become available at the treatment center. I'm headed there now."

"I believe in you," I said sincerely.

At that moment, Micah came roaring down the driveway on his Big Wheel. He flashed a big grin at me and asked enthusiastically, "Did you see that, Mom?"

I nodded.

"I talk on phone, Mom. It Yaya?" (Yaya is my mom; Greek for "Grandma.")

"No, sweetie, it's not Yaya. It's Jennifer. Would you like to talk with her?"

I handed him the phone. "Hi, Jennifer," I coached softly,

with Micah's singsongy voice repeating the words. "Hi, Jennifer."

He scrunched up his forehead listening to her and then said, "I play outside. I big boy. Bye-bye," and he dropped the phone.

Jennifer and I talked for a few more minutes, before I said my parting words: "Take good care of yourself."

And take good care of yourself, too, Jillana, I exhorted myself. This journey had exposed me to something I'd never identified. I'd never operated at this sustained emotional intensity before. My "I'll try harder, be better, become healthier" promise to myself fell flat when I was stressed.

Jennifer texted me the one picture of Elias she had taken before he was taken to a foster home in Washington. Jennifer still saw me as an ally.

Perhaps not having baby Elias in my care right now was merciful for us both.

• • •

On the day of Micah's adoption ceremony, I got a speeding ticket. I saw a police van parked on the side of the road flash its "gotcha" bulb as I passed. In a move that I recognize oozes with privilege and would be downright dangerous for some, I actually turned around and pulled behind the van and approached the officer with Micah in my arms. The officer was eating a sandwich and looking at his phone. I knocked on the window and startled him. He cautiously rolled the window down.

"Hi," I said in a friendly way. "Did I just get a ticket a minute ago? I'm in the green Volvo."

"Let me see . . ." He paused, scrolling through the screen.

"Yes. You'll get a ticket in the mail and information about a court date, if you want to contest it."

"Okay," I said. Then I bubbled, "I'm actually on my way to court later on today because we're adopting this li'l guy." On cue, chubby Micah, tucked on my hip, reached out and gave a little hand wave to the policeman.

"Congratulations," he said, still chewing his sandwich, not appearing impressed.

"Thank you *so* much," I said, beaming as if I were accepting a Grammy on the sidewalk of that busy city street. Nothing could steal my joy that day.

That afternoon, twenty-six months after Micah was brought into our home, I sat with my family in court. I watched the judge's countenance be transformed from heavy decision maker to someone who more closely resembled a delighted grandfather. He insisted on holding Micah in his seat on the bench, letting Micah play with his gavel. He even folded up paper airplanes and launched them around his elevated seat at the front of the courtroom! We cut the cake with dental floss because no sharp objects were allowed in the courtroom. The girls passed out magnets we'd made of flowers with HOPE written in the middle of them. I said a few words to our gathered friends and family, closing with a request. "And please remember to pray for Jennifer's and Simon's health and healing."

A month later, I called the social worker to check in on Elias, who was now five months old. The caseworker dryly told me she was now "a few weeks away from retirement and had a lot on her plate." This was why she never informed me that Jennifer didn't go into the treatment center and Elias was lingering in foster care in Washington.

The social worker gave me the family's phone number. When I reached the foster mother and identified myself, I asked her how she was doing and listened as she talked about her family, including the "joy" this baby had brought them. I gave her an overview of our history, including that we had just adopted this baby's full biological brother. I gently asked if she'd be willing to have a relationship with us if Elias were to stay with them.

"No. We don't want that," she said. I respected her honesty and knew I needed to be honest too. I kindly said that since we were now considered relatives to this baby via Micah's adoption, we were going to start the process of requesting that Elias come live with us.

She immediately began crying. "My family loves him, and this will break everyone's hearts."

When I called the Washington caseworker and told her I'd like to initiate the interstate transfer process, she sighed loudly. "This is going to mean a lot of paperwork."

An hour later, Jennifer called me in a panic. Fear twisted her voice as she said, "Jillana! I know you're getting Elias! I know you're taking him!"

Striving to be calm and direct, I said, "This little boy is ultimately either going to end up with you raising him or with me raising him, Jennifer. There's no reason he should be . . ."

Jennifer hung up on me before I could finish my sentence. ". . . with a stranger."

She had gotten her tubes tied immediately after Elias was born.

Elias was Jennifer's last-chance, salvation baby.

He was not saving her.

• • •

Since the clear foster care policy preference is for a child to live with relatives, the request was approved for the baby to live in Oregon with his brother. Elias's foster parents traveled fifteen minutes from their home in Washington and arrived at our home in Portland distraught. They cradled him in our living room with tears spilling down their cheeks and talked about how much their kids loved him. He'd been with their family for several months, and they had hoped he would stay forever. As they were leaving, I gave them a letter and a basket of items I'd carefully put together for them, thanking them for their sacrifice and explaining it was never my intention to break their hearts. When they pulled out of the driveway, I wiped a few tears from my cheek on their behalf. I snapped a picture of Micah cuddled up next to his brother, then another photo of us as a family of six.

The following week, an unknown Washington number came up on my phone. It was Jennifer.

"I wanted you to know that I've left Simon for good and checked myself into a drug and alcohol treatment facility."

I needed to get something off my chest immediately, so I boldly said, "Jennifer, the last time we talked, you hung up on me. I was not okay with that then, nor will I ever be okay with being hung up on in the future."

"Okay. I understand."

"So where is your treatment program located?"

The next week, under court order, I made the hour-long

drive to bring Elias to the lockdown treatment facility in Longview, Washington. I chose to bring Micah along as well.

Jennifer hadn't seen Micah for thirteen months and Elias for five months. When she saw us through the window of the security door, she buried her head in her hands. Tears were streaming down her cheeks. When the door opened, she and I gave each other a long, silent hug. Peering into the stroller, she exclaimed, "Wow! My baby has blue eyes!"

Though we kept framed photos of our family and Jennifer together around our home and had reminded Micah of some of the items she'd given him over the years, Micah looked at her as if she were a stranger.

As we toured the facility, Jennifer beamed while holding Elias, calling people over to meet him. She showed me the day care. "This is where Elias will stay from 9:00 to 4:00 when he comes to live with me," she said proudly. Elias started to fuss, and Jennifer seemed perplexed.

I was just about to scoop him up when I stopped and said, "That's his cue he's getting sleepy. He'll fall asleep if you hold him this way, put the pacifier in his mouth, and pat him."

A few minutes later, Elias dozed in her arms, and I covered him with a blanket. Jennifer asked me to take a picture of the two of them together, which I later sent her in a letter.

"The way I see it, I have two choices," Jennifer said, "to be a recovering addict or an active user. I'm fighting to be in recovery every day. I'm happy Micah is with you and Luke. But I'm not giving up on Elias."

I nodded. Just then Micah wandered over and asked, "Do you want to wear my necklace?" He held out the blue plastic beads he'd been holding in his pudgy hands.

"Sure, honey," she said, then looked at me. "Maybe *Mommy* can help put it on me." As I put the plastic necklace around her head she realized it was the first time she'd referred to me as Micah's mom. "It's kinda crazy for me to say that!"

In the kitchen a woman asked, "Jennifer, are these your boys?" Jennifer froze as she glanced over at me. "This is Micah's mom, and the baby is still mine." Later in a private moment I told Jennifer that we are *both* Micah's moms.

Jennifer got special permission to walk the boys and me out to the car and handed me a tiny gift bag. I opened it to find a deflated Mylar "It's a boy" balloon from the hospital, Micah's hospital bracelet, and his first bib, along with a handwritten note saying she wanted me to have those things now. Throughout all the moves and the instability of living out of her car, she'd held tightly to those remembrances of her son.

The ride home was undramatic except for Micah dumping out his snack of apple slices and pulling the gallon-size Ziplock over his head, happily exclaiming, "Mom, look at me!" The plastic bag was sucked tightly around his head. I could have rivaled any stunt driver as I reached back and swiftly snatched the plastic bag off his head while going sixty-five miles per hour down the freeway. This heart-jumping scene was apropos on the drive home as I considered the rapid carousel of hope versus reality I'd been on with Jennifer for years.

Later that night, after the other three kids were tucked in, Luke and I snuggled up on the couch with Elias sleeping between us. Exhausted, we talked about the dizzying world of foster care, and how doing the next right thing in love can take a toll.

. . .

Two months later, my friends held a "blessings shower" for Elias in a restaurant's private room. Elias slept with his head on my shoulder, unaware of the prayers for peace and protection being said over him. There was also a pile of gifts brought for him. The next day, Jennifer was present by phone for court, and Luke and I were present in the courtroom in Washington in person. With summer vacations planned and Elias beginning to meld into our family, we expected a cautious "wait and see" approach from the judge. Instead, in yet another unexpected move out of our control, Elias was mandated to be returned immediately to the recovery facility to live with Jennifer a few days later. It made sense on paper. Jennifer had gotten a "fresh start" at getting her life together, and if she was going to get Elias back, this was the time to do it. On the drive home, Luke's uncharacteristic tears accompanied mine, stemming from a protective, exhausted caution.

As Luke and I drove Elias there a few days later, we passed a faded church marquee with a few letters askew and not properly spaced apart. Still, the message was clear, as if placed there for me to read at that very moment:

AS LONG AS THERE'S BREATH, THERE'S HOPE.

I stared wearily out the window at it. And yet, if I were ever asked to identify a specific moment where peace passes understanding and drives out fear, it would be the actual day of returning Elias to live with Jennifer, mere months after finalizing our adoption of Micah. There was still a well that wasn't totally dry from which a genuine "I'm rooting for you" could be poured.

But it wasn't a naive love. The odds were clearly stacked against Jennifer. She'd have to *quadruple* her longest consecutive amount of time clean to parent Elias clean and sober until he was eighteen. Even with that knowledge, somehow I wasn't panicked and riddled with fear. I gave Jennifer a professional picture of Elias with our family, including all four kids. She hung it up on the wall in her humble room, which now included a crib beside her bed.

"I'll keep in touch," she said.

"I will too" I assured her. I left all the wrapped gifts at the check-in station. Even though this was her fourth child, Jennifer had never had a baby shower before. I wanted her to experience that. I kissed Elias, gave her a hug, and walked out to a group of women surrounding her, exclaiming over both her baby and all the presents.

When we got home, Luke and I promptly took Elias's car seat inside and took apart his crib in the nursery. For a short season I took down the framed professional photo of the four kids together that had been on our bedroom bookshelf because, even with a sense of prevailing peace, I felt an inarticulate ache every time I looked at it and heard my children, especially Micah, inquire about Elias.

"Where's my brudder, Mama?"

I replaced the photo with lines from Mary Oliver's poem "In Blackwater Woods," in which she writes of loving, holding something close, and then ultimately, releasing it with open palms.

. . .

It was in the midst of the hubbub of this particularly challenging year when my kindred spirit and "I've got your back and I understand your life" friend, Bethany, and I were asked to be keynote speakers at a conference for hundreds of foster and adoptive moms. For the past two years we'd done workshops together, and now we were taking the mic on the main stage. The theme this year?

Hold On to Hope.

What could I possibly share about holding on to hope? Even the H-O-P-E letters I'd purchased years ago suffered from an unfortunate accident when Micah had pretended to "go fishing," and his wild cast had knocked the "P" off the wall. Our family had been trudging up and down the stairs for months to the inspiration of H-O-E! Need I say more about how equipped I was to be a main-stage speaker on the topic "Holding On to Hope"?

Our human tendency is to wait to share publicly about hard things until we're squarely on the other, tidier side of our story. We want to share when there's an outcome more acceptable to us and a sound clip that's more palatable for others. We want to share the hard stuff and in the next breath, skip to the blue skies when we can wrap a tidy bow called "God's faithfulness" around it.

Sometimes, however, vulnerably sharing our real stories when we're right in the mucky middle is the best gift we can offer others. There is something to the collective leaning in and searching together for God, realizing Divine Love is always with us, even if we have to squint to catch a glimmer, even if we strain our eyes for something that never is fully realized in front of us.

Despite knowing that outside perfection and the right backlighting for Instagram photos doesn't equate to a happy, healthy, fulfilling life, the allure of "having it all together" is extremely tempting. Expectations of how the story of our life *is supposed to go* can rip us away from walking in humble expectancy. There may be double-rainbow days where we exclaim over God's faithfulness, but many days there's no overt sign of promise in the sky. There's merely a pebble of hope on the path. On days when life's troubles are too cumbersome to even glimpse the pebble, I lean in and borrow someone else's hope by listening to their story. Other days I hold hope in the palm of my hand, a smooth blue rock with the word painted on it, that sits on my kitchen windowsill. In whatever form hope takes, I don't want to miss it.

Hope is substantial, not something superficial served on a shiny platter and passed around like an appetizer to be consumed in one bite, or like a magazine cover promising a whole new you in thirty days. Hope is gritty and acknowledges that sometimes losses are so deep that they will always be felt in the marrow of our bones and will be with us forever. Yet, we are still invited to be people of hope even when we are weary.

Standing off to the side of the large auditorium, I looked at the hundreds of women at the conference getting settled in their seats for this talk. I was digging around in my purse, searching for a tube of lip balm when I saw my driver's license. The weight it claimed I was when I renewed it was in the rearview mirror by a good thirty pounds. I'd spent the last year wearing the largest pants size I'd ever bought, the "too-much-ness" of life directly transferring to the "too-much-ness" on my body. And yet in the midst of the heaviness of many things I would never have chosen, a gravelly hope was still present on my path. In a year that felt especially pummeling with no quick, easy fixes, I humbly took one microphone, Bethany took the other, and we walked onto the stage. I decided it doesn't matter if H-O-P-E hanging on my staircase wall is missing a critical letter—as long as there's breath, there's hope. I don't have to defer talking about hope until a tidy bow is wrapped around the story. I can share about the pebble at my feet.

7

STEADFAST

Attachment

"WE HAVE A NEWBORN WAITING AT the hospital to be discharged, and we need a certified foster family to *pick him up for the weekend.*"

It was just three months after we returned Elias to Jennifer, when I saw the familiar Oregon Child Welfare number buzzing on my phone. I hesitated before answering. Our family wasn't on the list to receive calls that weekend to welcome children in need, but I knew the agency had an age-old depressing math equation working against them: too many children and too few foster homes.

You can do anything for a weekend, right?

Little did I know that this precious child, this "weekend baby," would expose me to levels of joy and grief I'd never known before and would consistently stretch and grow me in what it means to be steadfast. I didn't yet understand how a parent's capacity to endure stretches when our children require our tenacity.

Steadfast (adjective): resolutely or dutifully firm and unwavering

I am drawn to that word. It resonates in my core. If one day I ever succumb to the culture of Portland and get a tattoo, it will be those nine letters artistically inked in scrolling script onto my body.

• • •

When I first became a mother, I wouldn't have admitted to harboring any expectations for my family life. I would have likely been breezy about it: "I'm open. I don't have any preconceived notions of how I envision my family." And yet, if you had pulled me aside in the hospital lobby when Luke and I went to meet the baby and asked me if I felt well suited to take care of a child with significant, lifelong needs, I would have looked at you blankly. If you had given me binders to fill with information on therapies and a slew of diagnoses that needed both hands to count, the heaviness may have caused me to drop them. If you had questioned whether I had the grit to endure meltdowns in public places stemming from a child's brain that works differently, I would be the first to admit I didn't. If you told me that I would go five years straight without sleeping through the night for more than three hours at a time, I might have fallen over right then and there. If you'd told me I'd be a persistent liaison for a child whom the world would not understand but still judge harshly, I would have uttered a soft and somber, "I'm not capable. I don't have what it takes."

And I would have missed out on parenting a child I fiercely love who has significantly shaped my love-stretched life.

Life does not always afford you the luxury of knowing, processing, and answering real-life capacity questions in real time. This, after all, was a *real* baby in *real* time who needed *real* people to pick him up from the hospital and take him to a *real* safe, loving, and temporary foster home.

I walked next door with the phone, keeping the person from the agency on mute awaiting my response, and interrupted Luke playing NBA Jam with our neighbor. "Babe, would you be up for us taking care of a baby who is about to be released from the hospital and needs a short-term foster home? It would just be for forty-eight hours."

"I guess we could do that," he said, barely looking away from the screen.

I immediately unmuted my phone and gave her an enthusiastic *yes*.

Soon Luke and I were in the NICU, holding a swaddled, healthy baby. We took lots of photos holding him against our chests, admiring his perfect little nose while he slept. Wherever he went after the weekend in our home, we wanted to be sure his life was well documented from the beginning.

But he needed a name.

"He looks like a Rob," Luke said, smiling and studying his perfect, delicate face, a light blue cap perched on his tiny head. I lovingly informed Luke that no baby ever shoots straight out of the womb and enters this world looking "like a Rob."

"You're right, J. How about Charlie?" This suggestion seemed meant to be, at least for the time being, until he was given a legal name.

On the third day of his life, we brought Charlie home from the hospital. Our family held him, rocked him, and sang to him. Our three kids and our village of friends oohed and aahed over Charlie and folded him in with such a loving welcome, as though we'd all been waiting for him our whole lives.

Later that week, the caseworker called with an update. They were working to find a safe relative who might be able to care for Charlie long term, but the agency needed more time. We didn't need any arm-twisting to keep caring for him ourselves.

• • •

I unbuckled Charlie from his car seat and headed to the sterile child welfare lobby where his mom and someone supervising the visit met us. I gingerly placed him in his mom's arms. She was bundled up in layers of clothing and didn't say much. I took multiple pictures of them together that I printed and gave her at their next office visit together.

I was bathing Charlie on an early November afternoon when the caseworker called. She explained his mom got confused and showed up at the wrong office on the wrong day at the wrong time, but was asking to see her son. She understood if I couldn't make this work, but was there *any* way I might be able to bring him to the office right then for their third visit?

I made a mental note of my bustling household and all

it would mean to corral everyone into the car unexpectedly and drive twenty minutes to an office across town. Then I immediately thought of Charlie's mom navigating Portland by bus and walking in the rain, her multiple layers getting soaked as she tried to get to the office to be with her child. I could have easily said no, and no one would have batted an eye. But something in my spirit convicted me that I needed to accommodate this afternoon curveball.

I dried Charlie's hair and put him in a freshly laundered outfit, buckled up all my kids, parked, walked into the building, and placed Charlie in his mom's waiting arms. The staff member supervising their visit gave me a nod that told me, "My eyes are on this."

My kids and I played puzzles and read books in the waiting room. Then Charlie's mom emerged sooner than expected and quickly placed a fussy baby back in my arms without saying a word.

She handed me two blankets from the dollar store and a pink onesie still in its unopened package. I thanked her and said I would keep them for her baby.

"Okay," she said in a flat monotone voice and walked out of the office.

That was the last time I ever saw the woman who gave life to Charlie. He was five weeks old.

• • •

A few weeks went by, and there was still no relative stepping forward to care for Charlie. Life went on. Without visits or any other family involvement, life seemed relatively uncomplicated. Even our court proceedings were simple and straightforward. His plan was eventually changed to adoption. Our hearts swelled and grew to include Charlie. He was our chubby, non-sleeping, always-wanting-to-be-held weekend baby, whom we had all fallen head over heels for. Now he would be with us for life.

But then, the day before the one-year mark of folding Charlie into our family, I was standing tiptoe on a chair, aiming to get a pushpin in the wall at just the right height for Charlie's "Happy Birthday" banner when our caseworker called. Charlie's maternal grandma from out of state had responded that she'd adopt him.

"I'm so sorry, Jillana. I know how attached you are to Charlie. You've given him the best possible start to life. She's a relative, though, and you know what this means."

Yes, I knew what that meant. The goal of foster care is to reunite children with their biological parents, and when that can't happen, the next goal is to reunite them with relatives. I am on board with this goal. There is research that says children do better when they are able to be placed with their biological relatives. I am on board with this research. But research doesn't always account for the unpredictability of *attachment*. (It's a delicate equation, no doubt, and one I'd been on both sides of with Elias and now Charlie.)

It's hard to reconcile cognitive research, policy, and procedures, and be comforted when my heart slowly and steadily beats attachment. I'm referring to my own attachment to this chubby, adorable baby, yes—but also to his attachment to our family, the only one he had ever known. I was openhanded, but when none of his relatives stepped forward for an entire year, I had begun to see this as our norm. I had mothered this child for 364 days with everything in my being, and he was thriving. The rhythm of our current family of six felt like the natural, steady rhythm of our life.

Being steadfast by attaching and engaging when things are sunny is a breeze. But knee-jerk reminders for foster parents can come at any minute. Kids who live under our roofs, sleep in our beds, sit around our tables, and are loved with every fiber of our being, may have their life course altered by state policy and procedure. In a five-minute phone call, a child and a family's life direction may pivot away from its previous trajectory. Hearts still remain resolute and beat with attachment, however, even in the midst of anticipating loss.

With my voice cracking, I told our caseworker this was news I was not expecting to hear, but I thanked her for the call. I hung up and looked at Charlie in his high chair, making soft cooing noises, happily shoving Cheerios in his mouth. My mind felt simultaneously on overload and hollow. *Why now? Tomorrow it will be one year since we brought home our "weekend" baby.* I stared at the birthday banner dangling down, still needing to be tacked onto the other side of the wall for the big celebration.

After a short call with Luke, I parented my four children for the remainder of the day in a daze, wanting only to flop into bed, curl up into a fetal position, and pull the covers over my head.

The following week, our caseworker called again. Charlie's grandmother wanted to speak with us. We had no idea what to expect. It turns out Charlie's grandma, recognizing our mutual attachment, wanted to get to know us, and to our surprise and delight, she gave us her blessing to become Charlie's forever family.

I crumpled onto the bed in relief and happiness. Later, when Charlie's adoption was finalized, my children gained another loving, attentive grandmother who sends them gifts for Christmas, and cards for every holiday with crisp dollar bills inside. Charlie's grandma has shown me a benevolent example of what it looks like to engage with her grandchild and hold the unspoken tension of grief. Throughout the years, she has shared heartfelt remarks of gratitude to us for raising her grandson and yet I know there's still a yearning for it to be another way, wishing her daughter could have parented the child we are now raising.

•   •   •

I first started noticing milestone gaps and delays in Charlie when he was around eighteen months old. He was late to get his teeth, late to crawl, late to talk, and late to walk. If he was not being held, he was inconsolable. Luke and I took turns rocking him multiple times a night because of Charlie's fragmented sleep. His head was measuring small and he could not self-soothe. All of this fell into an ambiguous "global developmental delays" diagnosis. The professionals and caseworker acknowledged this but didn't express any concern, just encouraged a slow and steady "Let's keep tracking this."

Between years two and four, Charlie's general global developmental delays turned into a multitude of diagnoses that all felt like fuzzy pieces, not connecting to form a clear picture of the puzzle of Charlie. I pored over books. I stayed up late reading journal articles. I made appointments with specialists and arrived with long lists of questions. I was a sleuth with a big magnifying glass, looking for clues.

It wasn't until I did a deep dive into the vast and life-long effects of brain damage from in utero alcohol exposure that the bullet points of Charlie's behaviors, strengths, and struggles came into crystal-clear focus. When I presented my research to the team of professionals and pointed out how every other diagnosis he'd already been given was a classic, common diagnosis that often missed the bigger picture, they agreed. Charlie was on the spectrum of having FASD (Fetal Alcohol Spectrum Disorder), a group of conditions that occur when a baby is prenatally exposed to alcohol. There are several risk factors for FASD, such as the amount consumed, the frequency of consumption, and the points in pregnancy at which the alcohol is consumed, but this much is clear: There is no known time during pregnancy when it's safe for a mother to drink any amount of alcohol. FASD is the single most common *preventable* cause of intellectual and developmental disabilities, is more prevalent than autism, and is much more prevalent in foster care than in the general population.

For a split second, there was relief. Some of the mystery with this child had been solved! Charlie would be eligible for a new one-on-one aide through developmental disability services. The prognosis is better for children diagnosed at a younger age. Charlie has significant brain differences through in utero alcohol exposure. This helped provide clarity for why he didn't sleep for more than a few hours at a time, is highly anxious, and has a quick fuse and short-term memory, amongst many other challenges.

After the initial relief of a formal diagnosis of Fetal Alcohol Syndrome, under the umbrella of FASD, a big, black spiral of grief quickly encapsulated me. My precious Charlie had *lifelong, irreversible* brain differences! The best thing we could do was help him engage the world around him through accommodating him. Because we cannot peer into someone's brain, our main clues of neurodiversity come from how someone looks, talks, and engages. Brain differences for those who experience FASD may be overt or subtle. The brain differences often cause external behavior that *seems* willful. This becomes problematic because it's easy to judge how we see someone acting on the surface, when in fact, we do not understand.

If I was still under the guise that I didn't have preconceived notions of what my family was supposed to look like, this changed it all. The first domino of my subconscious expectations tumbled. My family life was going to have no other choice than to press into a *new normal*—a norm that would look markedly different from that of other families and at times feel intensely isolating. Because of Fetal Alcohol Spectrum Disorder, we were living in a whole new reality:

- Many with FASD operate in a way extremely different from their peers. Social differences and life skill struggles make growing up tough. Due to their brain challenges, some may behave in a manner that severely lags behind their chronological age. This discrepancy won't be readily apparent to those interacting with Charlie, leading people to unfairly judge him.

- Development for those who experience FASD can be typical or high in one area and very low in others. The brain is complex, and those with FASD often have a mishmash of abilities that make life for them and others confusing. (For example, Charlie can put together amazing LEGO creations, do his grade-level math, and has a great sense of humor, but at age ten, even with posted visual cues, he still needs help getting dressed and serving himself a snack, and he is completely taxed by writing his name.) A typical cruel combination of these skills areas is that Charlie has high verbal communication skills and low receptive communication skills. This means he processes everyday conversations as if they were bad phone connections where voices crackle and cut off. He grasps enough of what's being said or asked of him to *seemingly* be able to hang with the conversation verbally, but not enough to process with full clarity in real time. Despite us doing our best to accommodate the extra processing time needed, this gap of skills, along with sensory issues and memory challenges, leads to a volcano of exasperation for Charlie.

- Charlie, like many who experience FASD, has no obvious physical signs that readily identify him as having a brain-based difference except for perhaps his cute Coke-bottle glasses. When he verbally or physically lashes out due to misunderstanding or frustration, people attribute this to a choice he's actively making and not a reaction stemming from his invisible brain-based disability.

- Those who experience FASD are like a pot at a constant simmer. All it takes is one little pebble thrown in to make it boil over. This can be as simple as hearing a "not right now" answer or something unexpected happening. For instance, this morning Charlie had a full screaming meltdown of frustration when his treasures—which today were a fistful of hot sauce packets combined with a Christmas ornament—wouldn't fit in his cargo pants pocket. It was a supreme disappointment to him. This was the pebble thrown into the pot which led to screaming, crying, and objects being flung around the room.

- The bright and true essence of Charlie is someone unique, curious, loving, smart, funny, and creative. Due to FASD, he also experiences anger, explosions, aggression, impulsivity, and perseveration (hyper-focused, looped thinking) that threaten to cloud the joy of who he is. With Charlie, we rarely have full days solely comprised of good or bad. Our days are a constant intermingling of highs and lows, like riding a daily roller coaster of unpredictability. We know there will be dips and turns, but we can't pinpoint exactly when moments of tenderness ("I love you, Mom. You're the best, Mom!") will be immediately followed by moments when he says something offensive ("I hate you, you idiot!") and vice versa. While Charlie does not intend this and it is not his fault, there is a bone-weary-exhausting emotional whiplash that comes with it. In order to have compassion for this, however, we must only think of how *we* would respond to others in situations if everything we thought internally spewed out externally, going from zero to sixty in a flash with absolutely zero filter!

- Over 60 percent of individuals with FASD experience school disruption (detention, suspension, expulsion). Ninety percent of those with FASD experience mental health issues. I am intimately familiar with both of these statistics. Fifty percent of those with FASD will be incarcerated, often related to an inability to connect actions and consequences.

I'm not sharing this for you to pity me. I'm not sharing it because I have regrets about saying yes to my just-for-the-weekend baby. I would say yes to him again. With his approval, I'm sharing this because I want others to see my son and recognize the obstacles he has to scale. This invisible disability, one I had zero knowledge about before parenting him, will affect every moment of his life, forever, with intense ripple effects for him and for our family. FASD is more common than most people realize. I want increased awareness to lead to increased compassion for my son and others like him. Life with Charlie is one where steadfast love *has* to be the anchor. Charlie has invited me to continually adapt and to rumble with joy and grief on this parenting road-less-traveled.

"When does it go away, Mom?" he asked me calmly one night while we snuggled together, reading a pile of library books. "When does the alcohol get all out of my brain?"

I am well-versed in talking matter-of-factly about the brain. In fact, I must keep the focus on the brain or else the conversation shifts quickly to blame. But if you asked me to name a gut-wrenching parenting moment, it would be looking into my son's eyes and telling him the honest answer.

"That's such a good question, bud. The answer is you're smart *and* your brain will always be affected by Fetal Alcohol, but we will always keep learning and growing." He responded matter-of-factly that he was hoping it would go away soon, and then turned his attention back to our book.

I attended a workshop for parenting kids with FASD in which the presenter started the session with "Welcome to the Navy SEALs of parenting." *Navy SEALs?* I had zero idea, holding the little bundle of Charlie in the hospital, that my parenting life would now include military references.

This life now includes calmly and assertively saying, "Go upstairs" to my older three children for safety while a small but powerful child was trying to hit and chuck hard objects at them. I can certainly tell you, when I envisioned my family life, I never once envisioned needing to comfort my middle-school-age daughter because, while she was watching TV on the couch, a stealthy ninja named Charlie came up behind her with scissors and snipped off a portion of her hair. My notion of family never included needing to keep a child in my line of sight at all times, or hiring an aide to help shadow him around the house, so I can do ordinary things.

And yet, despite the inescapable teeter-totter that simply *is* in utero alcohol exposure, the essence of Charlie shines through. One day not too long ago, he sat at the kitchen table for a merciful three minutes and wrote me a note. "Mommy, I love you 10,000,000 times. From Charlie." His Valentine's Day bag from school came home with "I love my mom and dad. BFF" written all over the hearts. And while he doesn't like much physical touch, Charlie will unexpectedly give monster hugs on his own terms. If you ask him if you can hug him, he will look at you and likely shout, "No!" and run away. But when Charlie is able to handle the sensory input, he'll cup my head in his hands and gently kiss a faint scar I have on my cheek.

"I love you, Mommy. You're the best and prettiest mommy."

"I love you too, Charlie."

• • •

Many years ago, I pulled up to Charlie's preschool, a supportive environment with teachers well-versed in handling kids who struggle. The class was sitting on the steps of the preschool dutifully waiting for their parents to come get them, wearing their backpacks with their hands locked around their knees. At the top of the stairs was Charlie, lunging like a rabid dog trying to throw himself down the stairs while his teacher held on to the hood of his jacket. Charlie was yelling, "Shut up! Shut up! Shut up, all you stupid people!" (A few years later, this kiddie language would be replaced with the profanity of sailors that he heard from classroom peers and soaked up like a sponge.)

As I walked up the stairs to claim him, I thought about how I never considered myself a judgmental person. In fact, I prided myself on being accepting. But the truth was, before Charlie came to me, at times I did have an internal monologue playing in my head about other kids' behaviors.

Had I seen Charlie before walking this humbling path of parenting him, I would have likely reasoned, "If a child this young is so out of control, his life clearly lacks structure," or "If a child is talking this way in public, imagine how he is talked to at home, to be repeating such things!"

That child is now *my* child. I'm well aware of the goodness, love, and intentionality we're pouring into him. But what I'm continually astounded by is how Charlie has helped me to erase all the critical internal monologues I've ever had in my head when I only see a sliver of the story.

At a recent eye doctor appointment, despite me holding anxious Charlie cradled in my lap like a toddler, my seven-year-old son tried to kick the ophthalmologist as he shone a light in his dilated eyes. Charlie started swatting at him, spewing expletives. He meant, "I don't like this. I'm uncomfortable. I'm scared," but it sounded like a drunken man's berating tirade. We weren't able to get a good read on his eyes.

The doctor looked at me and said, "You're doing an awesome job, Mom. Seriously. Keep up the good work." It could have been dripping with sarcasm, but instead it was sincere. I thanked him, then had to look away to keep tears from spilling down my cheeks.

Mercy will always triumph over judgment.

• • •

One night when Charlie was seven years old, he commanded me to lightly tickle his arms, as I do most nights while he drifts off to sleep. It takes him an incredibly long time to fall asleep each night, so I lay next to him silently, until he politely requested in his high-pitched voice, "Sing me 'Amazing Grace,' you little f—."

"I'm sorry, Charlie, what did you just say to me, sweet-heart?"

He repeated it. Clear as day. Innocent as ever.

Here's the dance. If I respond in a way that he knows is edgy, he'll repeat it despite the short-term memory loss associated with his disability.

So I simply tell him in a casual, roll-off-me-like-rain manner, "Charlie, we don't say this word."

Despite my best intentions, Charlie retains this piece of language and starts repeating it, loudly, anywhere and everywhere, as if speaking a long-awaited prophecy over people.

If I can distance myself for a millisecond from the fact that I do not want my child continually repeating this word and that this doesn't reflect the way we talk to one another in our family, I can recognize that what Charlie said to me when I was putting him to bed was a rather striking combo. While I'll never see having this word tumble out of my child's mouth as acceptable, the fact that my child is commanding me to sing "Amazing Grace" to him most every night is not something that escapes me.

Amazing grace is, indeed, the only way I'm going to make it.

8

EXPECTATIONS

Adjustment

WHEN CHARLIE WAS SIX, he told me he wanted to play an instrument, so I signed him up to take a class at the community music school. I called the school in advance, explained our circumstances, and asked to be present with him the whole time. We were invited to show up thirty minutes beforehand to walk around the school and the classroom to become familiar with the surroundings and ease Charlie's nerves.

On the way there, Charlie was a chatterbox, expressing his utter excitement about music class. He held my hand as we walked from the parking lot to the building, and he patiently waited while I checked us in at the front desk. The classroom on the third floor had natural sunlight streaming in and was decked out with flags and ribbons. Drums and shakers lined the perimeter of the room. My son's eyes widened as he slowly made his way around it all in a jovial mood.

I asked Charlie where he wanted to sit. He pointed to the very back corner of the room, and we made ourselves comfortable on the carpet. When the teacher walked in and greeted us, Charlie looked down and went mum. When the first student sat down close to us, he made a kicking motion at her and demanded, "Sit over there!" pointing across the room. When she went to look at the instruments, he shouted, "DON'T TOUCH THOSE!"

As more children filled the classroom, Charlie's agitation grew exponentially in seconds, and he tried to spit at the kids. It was time to act. I scooped him up, with his limbs flailing and Charlie yelling, "Shut up!" and I headed out the door. I found an open area on the first floor where Charlie could run around in circles in an attempt to become regulated. After five minutes, he seemed calmer, so we slipped into the class again and reclaimed our spot in the corner.

Charlie sat rigidly in my lap. When the teacher brought him a bead drum, he took it and threw it down. When the teacher invited him to join the other kids in a circle, he refused. In the middle of a song, Charlie jumped off my lap and sprinted out the open door. He was already a flight ahead of me on the stairs as I grabbed my purse and ran after him. Thank goodness there was a push door with a handle slightly taller than Charlie that stopped him from bounding out of the building.

Catching my breath from the unexpected aerobic workout, I said, "Charlie, I need to keep you safe, and running away from me isn't safe."

"I want to go HOME!" he shrieked. I picked him up and carried him back to the car, adrenaline still pumping through my body. He did not fight me as I strapped his little body back into his five-point harness.

We drove in silence for the first few minutes before Charlie, in his loud, one-volume voice, said from the backseat, "I was scawed, Mom. It was so scawy in der, but I yike music scwool, Mom. I want to twy again tomahrow. I will be bwave."

It was a rare gift for Charlie to actually articulate his anxiety. I affirmed that this sounded like a good plan. I silently wiped tears spilling down my cheeks at the red light as we headed home. They expressed the ever-present tension of exasperating behaviors due to his disability and the tenderness of his essence; the recognition of the gigantic obstacles he will always face to engage in life in contrast to the smooth pavement many of us walk and take for granted.

• • •

I have come to accept that many questions I have about Charlie are like balloons being released into the sky that will forever have an element of mystery. Organic brain damage through in utero alcohol exposure, trauma, and mental health are all in play, but it's impossible to know when one balloon will collide into another. Just like we would never tell someone who is blind to "just try harder" to read the blackboard, we do what we can to accommodate Charlie for success with his brain-based disability. We have modified our environment to strive to reduce his many triggers. We "show" and not tell Charlie as much as possible. We have laminated visual reminders posted around our house for things like hygiene and getting dressed.

But here's our reality: We can't always anticipate every little wrinkle and iron it out before Charlie stumbles across it. A wrinkle could be running out of BBQ chips, misplacing a LEGO piece, or wanting to drive to a river, right that second, to go gold mining. It's whims, inklings, and impossible desires that can whip up physical and emotional hurricanes.

My reality of never quite knowing what the next fifteen minutes will hold with Charlie makes me stop—and dare I say, *celebrate*—what before I would have mistaken as a purely low-level expectation. I notice when Charlie has the capacity for a brief moment to join us at the dinner table even if he stands while the rest of us are sitting. *This is a gift.* If the bus driver says he stayed buckled on the bus today, *high five!* When he actually pets our Labradoodle, Theo, without attempting to yank his tail, *I appreciate that.* If he uses his words and doesn't hit, *I'll take it.* When I get a report home that says, "Minimal swear words today," *hallelujah!*

Even our other children have to constantly adjust. I wish I could say it was always without resentment, but it's not, and that's understandable. Luke and I create space to intentionally check in with Sophia, Eleni, and Micah, both collectively and one-on-one about FASD's (unquantifiable) effects on them. One of my girls told me through quiet tears how unfair it is for Charlie to be showered with prizes when he makes his bed for a few days or gets dressed himself, and when she brings home a report card with straight A's, we say, "Good job, sweetie." I wince inside—*ouch*—and acknowledge her hurt.

It is not always balanced, I know. I strive to be present and celebrate her by the two of us going out to dinner before we take in the school play, or by hitting the Starbucks drive-through when we're running errands around town, transforming the minivan into a haven of mother/daughter connection. But I sometimes wonder if it's enough. The attention pie in our family is not sliced evenly.

When you have a family member with a brain-based disability, things may always seem off-kilter, a precarious teetering of the family's equilibrium. It will never be perfect. There is nothing seasonal about Fetal Alcohol Spectrum Disorder. This is forever the ebb and flow of our lives. What can I do but name it, grieve, pray, process with Luke, go for a walk with a friend, talk to a counselor, wash my face, adjust my expectations, and look reality in the face. Rinse. Repeat. I try to remember what a dear friend and mentor told me long ago: "Strive to be intentional with all your kids and pour into them in ways they can receive love, but don't buy into the lie of perfection and be named by failure."

One day when a happy moment quickly turned into an unsafe one, I closed Charlie's door behind him as his shrill screams echoed through the house. I heard a tornado of toys and books being flung around the room, taking chunks out of the bedroom wall and pelting the door. I sat slumped outside his room and closed my eyes, monitoring my breath.

The dominoes of my unnamed expectations fell with every jarring crash.

The first domino represents the belief that what you pour into a child will be what comes out of a child, if you stay the course consistently and patiently.

The second domino holds the myth that love and nurture will somehow outrun the effects of in utero substance abuse.

The third domino represents the fact that there will be occasional intense *seasons*, not a lifetime of varying degrees of intensity.

It feels surprising at times, even to me, that I've never struggled with blaming Charlie's birth mom in this preventable disability. I can only imagine the chaos in her life that may have led her to not know she was pregnant, not understand it was unsafe to drink during pregnancy, or not be able to stop drinking because of her own trauma-filled life. What's done is done. My tears have never been in anger toward her, but rather in heartbreak over the exorbitant amount of effort and energy it takes for Charlie to function in everyday life.

We are *all* broken, striving for wholeness, with different starting lines in life handed to us.

After what felt like an eternity of listening to Charlie scream, he was quiet. I softly knocked on his door and whispered, "Char, I'm coming in." I saw his small body in a crumpled heap lying on his bed. I slowly sat down next to him, mindful not to talk, and silently rubbed his legs, glancing at the walls that needed to be patched and repainted—again. I walked downstairs and promptly let my short fuse of exasperation explode with one of my girls after seeing the disaster they'd created in the kitchen. My response had much to do with my stress tolerance being worn down by the storm upstairs and less to do with the flour covering every surface of my countertop.

In retrospect, I have learned that "the body keeps the

score"—meaning the trauma, heartache, and emotional intensity we take in has to *go somewhere*. It is challenging to take it in every day and not see it come out in some unintended ways. But at the time, I just felt awful and hypocritical—how could I rub the legs of one child who dented the walls and lose my temper with the one who was making cookies for the family?

After giving myself a little time-out in my home office to take a few deep breaths, I came out, hugged my daughter, and apologized. I've gotten a lot of practice over the years in apologizing.

There is goodness in this too.

• • •

I love how Charlie slaps his leg and does a genuine belly chuckle when he thinks something is funny. I love when Charlie affectionately tells us he loves us. I love how Charlie will let us read to him on the couch for an uncanny amount of time, despite all his hyperactivity. I love the way Charlie says "geen gasses" for his green glasses and the way he invites his siblings to play with him. When they say yes, I could burst with happiness. Just as quickly as we have an enjoyable moment, however, Charlie will start punching or kicking, unprovoked. The enjoyable "normal" moment becomes safety management mode, trying to keep him and others safe. If I can't get him to calm down, I will have to pick up his small, thin body, knowing I'll have scratches and pinch marks on my neck to accompany his flailing limbs.

I'm keenly aware that I won't be able to carry Charlie like this forever.

A few weeks ago, I scribbled Leonard Cohen's words onto an index card and placed it on my kitchen windowsill.

There is a crack in everything.
That's how the light gets in.

As if on cue, I stood on my tippy-toes and stretched out my fingers for a crystal vase on our top kitchen shelf. It wobbled and then plummeted off the shelf, hitting the counter and breaking into four big pieces before tumbling to the floor and breaking some more.

This reminded me of what Sarah Thebarge writes in her book *Well*, describing the Japanese art form called *kintsugi*. The artists intentionally break pottery and use the pieces to create a new piece of art held together with lacquer containing flecks of gold, silver, or platinum.

A piece of pottery that has been shattered and then repaired with expensive lacquer is far more valuable than a vessel that has never been broken. . . .

Something inexplicably beautiful appears in the brokenness, not despite the cracks, but because of them.

Our bodies and our souls and our hearts break as we go through life. The hope we can hold on to is not that we will remain unbroken, but that when we inevitably do break (and we all do), God will restore us as only a Kintsugi master can: carefully, artfully, beautifully—with extravagant, glimmering grace.

My life will never be symbolized by an intact crystal vase sitting on a doily, carefully protected in the middle of a pristinely set table. My daily life resembles more a broken vase with blobs of glue oozing out in some places, little chips missing, with exposed rough edges and hairline cracks. As I swept up the shards of glass on the kitchen floor, I felt an anchored, inner contentment that cannot be taken from me, a gold-flecked lacquer of grace holding the broken pieces together, grateful for the life that is mine.

• • •

The huge floor-to-ceiling screen behind the stage had bold, purple capital letters declaring, "YOU ARE ENOUGH!" I was seated in the audience at yet another parenting conference with my journal open and my pen ready. The speaker had the audience repeat "You are enough!" several times after her and asked us to turn to our neighbors and encourage them with this message. The speaker's gleaming white teeth and shiny black hair made me think she'd be perfect as a model in a slow-motion commercial for Pantene Pro-V. She paused on stage as the audience repeated the phrase after her again, looking at us approvingly, before pointing to the audience and saying, "Yes, you are ENOUGH, Mama! Believe it!" With that, she confidently walked off the stage with her perfect, springy hair.

Even though everyone around me was applauding loudly, I wasn't feeling it. I wasn't inspired. Despite knocking on every door and being as well-resourced and well-researched as I could be, despite the praise of specialists saying, "Good for you for all the work you've done to educate and advocate and get a diagnosis for your son so young," I felt inadequate. Quietly mouthing the words "you are enough" intensified my loneliness.

I imagined the speaker's pep talk punctuated with invisible pom-poms and supposed her intent was to say that, despite our inadequacies, we are who our children have, so let's give ourselves grace. But I missed it in the hollow hype.

Out in the community, usually after an intense public meltdown (pick a venue, any venue—it's happened in all of them), I'm usually told something like "Wow! He's so lucky to have you. I could never do it, but God gives *special* children to *special* people."

Some people throw in the well-meaning but misquoted proverb "God never gives you more than you can handle" for good measure.

I am not encouraged when I'm told this because I am *not* a special person, and any child who lands in foster care is *not* holding a four-leaf clover.

I am just a person who said a simple "yes." The reality is that I *have been given* more than I feel equipped to handle—often—but God has also given me lavish grace, strength, and a sense of humor.

Charlie may often come across as a prickly porcupine due to his disability, but I love him with a fierce, loyal, and protective love with every single fiber of my being.

The truth is, I am *not* enough, but Divine Love is with me in the midst of my own inadequacy and reveals to me the ugly sides of myself, when exhaustion and pride mix together. In moments when I'm worn down, pride can coil around me like a snake and hiss, "You shouldn't have to spend twenty minutes of your morning trying to console your third-grade son who is trying to cram all his 'gold mining tools' into a tiny backpack that clearly isn't big enough." When I pull out a different, bigger backpack and calmly suggest to Charlie that this one will have room for the ever-important gold mining pan that he "needs" to go about his day, I'm met with flailing-on-the-floor frustration because *these* tools need to go into *this* backpack. In engaging the countless instances where Charlie wants things a certain way that are just downright impossible to accommodate (such as a meltdown when it's Tuesday and he wants it to be Wednesday), exhaustion and pride can hiss at me, "This is beyond you. This isn't worth your time." As if parenthood comes with a checklist with boxes marked "worthy" and "unworthy."

I know I'm promised new mercies every morning, yet sometimes I wake up with residual trauma lingering like a dark cloud, residue from what happened the night before when immediately after Charlie told me, "I love you, Mom," in the next breath, he did a 180 and called me a b— because he didn't want to brush his teeth.

The speaker's puffed-up-but-hollow exhortation of "You are enough!" in huge backlit letters on a stage didn't speak to me. But believing that in the midst of my "not-enough-ness," Divine Love is walking alongside me encourages me to keep going, find humor, apologize often, and embrace every nook and cranny of contentment that doesn't depend on the stars aligning with circumstances.

• • •

We'd never taken a family vacation just as a family of six without other adults to help us with Charlie, but we felt ready. (True confession: The last time we had gone to a beach house as an extended family, everyone was helping to watch Charlie in the house, which meant nobody specifically was assigned to him. This is precisely why a plumber driving down the gravel road in front of our rental house spotted my thirty-five-pound son with a tiny shovel hoisted on one shoulder, confidently strolling to the beach alone. I was grateful for the knock on the door, but Charlie was not so appreciative.)

Two summers later in 2017, our family was gifted with a week's stay at a beach house on the southern Oregon coast. We were all looking forward to it. Charlie does well in wide-open spaces, a far cry from our home in the heart of the city.

After a day of building sandcastles, fresh out of the bath, Charlie was cuddled up with his king comfort item, the blanket we wrapped around him when we picked him up from the hospital on that drizzly October day for "the weekend."

As he often does at night, Charlie snuggled up to me and said in his high-pitched, squeaky voice, green glasses pushed up on his nose, "Mommy, pweez tell me again the stowy of how you and daddy 'dopted me and gave me dis blankie to keep me whoorm." It's a script he knows by heart, as old and worn as his blanket, and as always, Charlie enthusiastically shouted out the answers.

"Mommy got a _____ (CALL) that there was a _____ (BABY) born at the hospital [usually at this point he starts shouting, "It's ME! It's ME, Mom."] that needed a family to be kept _____ (SAFE) and healthy. So we brought you home from the hospital and we loved you. You grew inside

_____ (biological mom's name) tummy and she gave you life and we will always respect her for that. The _____ (JUDGE) decided you needed a forever home and we were able to _____ (ADOPT) you and have you become a part of our _____ (FAMILY) forever. We _____ (LOVE) you, Charlie!"

Charlie's pure exuberance shouting the details of his adoption story could rival any million-dollar winner on any reality game show any day. It's in these treasured moments of self-regulation where the joyful essence of Charlie shines bright.

The next day when we pulled up for our hike at the state park with ocean views, Charlie refused to get out of the car. Once we cajoled him out, he seemed content to be carried in my arms, pointing out various things we were seeing, especially looking for birds. Then Micah flung a stick he'd found into the middle of the forest. Charlie hadn't expressed an iota of interest in the stick beforehand, but suddenly that stick was the most important thing in the world to him. He wanted it back.

We offered him all the other sticks we could see, but Charlie couldn't recover. Our hike was cut short. I literally carried Charlie back to the car as he flailed about, completely dysregulated, while Luke tried to redeem a few more minutes in nature with our other kids. A compassionate bystander, understandably not accustomed to this commotion, asked me if I needed help. Once inside the minivan, with Charlie safely buckled in, I examined the scratches on my face and neck.

As my family piled back into the car and we journeyed down the road to the tide pools, Charlie was now quiet but on edge. Our entire family is well-versed in the hyper-vigilance of riding in silence, willing that pin in a behavioral grenade to not be jostled. When we pulled up at some tide pools, Charlie hid his face and refused to get out of the car. Luke offered to stay with him, but I encouraged him to go with the other kids.

"Will you read books to me, Mama?" Charlie asked sweetly a few minutes after everyone left. I climbed into the back row of seats with him and read until the rest of the family returned and we made our way down the coastal high-way for a picnic on the beach.

After the usual umbrella, towels, toys, and picnic sup-plies were all strewn about on the sand, we went for a walk. Charlie, with one hand straight behind him as if he was to be handed a baton in a relay race, was happily running along the shore, looking for "twehzure."

I stopped, picked up a stick, and wrote all my family members' names inside individual heart-shapes in the sand before the kids excitedly shouted that they had found a cave and to come quick. They had discovered a lone, welcoming cave with a giant boulder inside that looked straight out onto the ocean. We all climbed onto the rock, but soon the kids scurried down and ran down the beach, with Luke following closely behind. I didn't want to move. I stayed in the deserted cave and relished the solitude, watching as the waves lapped up the names of all my family members I'd written with a stick. Charlie's heart and name was the last to get erased.

Gazing at the ocean, I thought about how sometimes I can talk about my Charlie boy and his lifelong, invis-ible disability of Fetal Alcohol Spectrum Disorder in a very straightforward manner, the way I'd read the menu at a restaurant. Other times my chin quivers and tears spill down my cheeks. Grief from fiercely loving my son and the domino effects of my many subconscious expectations of "family" is not linear. It is circular. It is rarely a tidal wave anymore. It is simply the waves of realization and re-realization of how life looks different for our family as we strive to both accommodate and stretch Charlie in a world that doesn't understand him and is often not a kind, hospitable place.

I am continually learning and relearning that how I am doing personally is not tethered to how Charlie is doing. While my exhaustion level may naturally ebb and flow from his struggles, and how he's doing affects me significantly, my well-being isn't inextricably bound to his. Parenting Charlie continues to teach me that looking for joy in life isn't a cutesy suggestion you glean from a magazine cover while standing in the express checkout line. It's planting your feet and being committed to searching, even if it feels at times like I'm squinting to catch a glimpse of it.

As I climbed off the boulder to go rejoin my family, a splash of unexpected color caught my eye. Toward the back of the cave, violet and golden wildflowers were bursting through the side of the rock wall. It looked like a florist had arranged the lavish bouquet and showcased it there.

Through practice, I've grown accustomed to pivoting my expectations and exploring the natural accompanying emotions that surface with the regular adjustment needed in parenting Charlie. Few things surprise me anymore. But this image of splendor impossibly bursting forth through unyielding rock overwhelmed me in the best of ways.

There is often beauty dangling where I least expect to find it.

9

ASKING FOR HELP

Intentionality

I WAS WASHING MY FACE IN THE MORNING at my bathroom sink, looked down at my ring finger, and gasped. The small center diamond was missing. Luke and I checked to see if it got snagged on the sheets and gingerly looked on our bed. Luke took apart the drain. We didn't empty out the vacuum bags before first sorting through the dust for *weeks* to no avail. Six months later, after spending the weekend away with our daughters, I came home to Luke, who was smiling like a Cheshire cat. He handed me a gallon-size ziplock bag.

"Look, Jillana!"

"Look at what?" I teased. It was clearly empty.

"Just feel it." he said eagerly.

At the very bottom corner of the baggie was a small diamond.

"You found it!" I squealed. I had accepted a long time ago that it was gone forever.

"Well," Luke hedged, "I *think* I found it. I was vacuuming the minivan and something told me to search through the dust-buster bag after I got done with the floor mats." At the very bottom in the midst of the grime, there it was.

"But," he informed me, "it could also be a fake from here," and with that he held up Sophia's hairbrush covered with dozens of rhinestones the identical size as my diamond. Also, he wanted me to know that he knew a snack-sized plastic baggie would have been much more appropriate for the situation, but we were all out.

The next day I walked into a jewelry store, holding the ridiculously oversized bag. When someone asked what brought me in, I acknowledged this was an unusual request, held up the baggie, and asked, "Can someone please tell me if this diamond is *real*?"

A quick look under a jeweler's loupe and a man with salt-and-pepper hair replied, "Oh, it's *real* all right!"

Against all odds, my wedding ring was restored! Despite the shine of my ring, at year ten in our marriage (a year before Charlie entered our lives), Luke and I were getting a bit dull and off-kilter in our communication. We were still learning that being fully united in purpose with the holistic picture of our lives—striving to love well and show up in the world in meaningful ways—did not inoculate us from difficulties or make the smaller things that bug us go away. In fact, sometimes the lived-out reality of the larger picture invites those hard things to waltz right inside our door and cozy up on our couch.

We were in an extremely busy season of life. The demands of work, leadership, parenting, foster care, and walking alongside some friends struggling through their own tough challenges left little time for Luke and me to be present with one another, let alone ask questions and listen to one another.

I decided to be intentional and plan a surprise dinner date with Luke. He knew something was up when my parents arrived out of the blue to take the kids out for ice cream. Still, Luke feigned surprise that made me glad we were getting away. The meal was delicious, but even more satisfying was the evening's conversation. Each of us was genuinely captivated by every little word the other one said. Turns out, when we actually spent intentional time together—like this rare date night—we actually still very much liked each other, to the surprise of neither of us. When we were getting ready to leave the restaurant, I announced the second revelation. "We're spending the night in a friend's luxurious guest cottage. I packed strawberries and chocolate to enjoy in the hot tub."

"You're wonderful," Luke said.

Forty-eight hours later, elated children welcomed us home. They were emotionally satiated from good grandparent time. Luke read the girls their bedtime stories while I rocked and read to Micah. Luke then stood in the hallway, serenading the girls on his guitar with his standard set of U2 classics. I put Micah in his crib and began to fold laundry, while the girls screamed, "Just one more song, Dad!" U2's "With or Without You" was followed by a special request of "Twinkle, Twinkle." We gave our kids their second round of kisses and soon they were asleep.

But the euphoria of the romantic getaway vanished the following night with a reality showdown in the kitchen.

"Jillana, why did you leave the colander in the sink?"

What?

Luke takes care of the house just as much as I do, so this had nothing to do with stereotypical gender roles. In fact, he prefers to cook while I'd rather take out the trash and mow the lawn any ole day. Luke is wired to be methodical and linear—finish A, then start B—while I, more prone to being relationally interrupted by the kids, circle around the task.

I looked at him in hurt and disbelief. "The colander? Really, Luke? I can't believe you're saying this."

So when Luke and I sat down in the marriage counselor's office a few weeks later and the therapist asked each of us, "What brings you in today?" I replied dryly, "The colander in the sink."

We saw the therapist for several months on Saturday mornings. We realized we were aligned with the larger picture of life, but in the absence of having consistent time together, the smaller annoyances were adding up and taking a toll. We learned that when we spend an exorbitant amount of time discussing something seemingly petty, it may have everything to do with what's *not* being talked about. It's easy for relational threads to unravel with apathy. And yet when I look at my best friend, it's not one huge tidal wave of stress or weariness in the background that I fear would take us out. If anything, the thing we must proactively guard against is simply trudging along in the sand and letting life circumstances dull our joy. Luke and I are partners in this life; he is with me through it all. We are committed to respecting how each of us is innately wired—to find, dare I say, genuine delight in one another's many (many!) differences, and reach for each other's hand along the way.

•   •   •

Once, Luke and I stole away for a couple of days to Bainbridge Island in Washington, a few hours north of us. Everything there is so picture-perfect it doesn't seem real. We welcomed this break from our reality. We zipped around town in my parents' green Mini Cooper. We arrived at a quaint hotel whose advertising hook exalted its sumptuous linens. Before dinner, we took a short walk on the dock, where we encountered a fiftysomething woman with cropped hair, laboriously walking with a cane.

As we passed, her eyes locked with mine. "Never get cancer!" she blurted out, leaning heavily on her cane.

"I'm so sorry," I said. "Do you have cancer?"

"Yes, and I'm walking around here because everyone keeps telling me to get some fresh air because that will be good for me, but . . ." She paused, leaning on the wooden dock railing, and sighed. "I was walking to the store to get something to eat, but I don't know what I want to get, because everything tastes bad. Just really bad, you know. Like eating a penny."

Standing on the dock for the next fifteen minutes, we learned the woman, named Cathy, had a brother who told her to "snap out of it" because he didn't believe she was really dying. She had a boyfriend who dutifully drove her to all her chemo appointments, but she wasn't sure he really wanted to hang in there with her anymore. He didn't want to talk about her pain.

"What more do I have to talk about other than pain?" she asked me pointedly.

Talking softly, I asked if she had found a local support group. She told me she tried and didn't like it for various reasons.

"Do you have any kind of religious faith to rely on?"

"Faith doesn't really help when it comes to stuff like this," Cathy said.

"I'm sorry you're going through this, Cathy. I will remember you in my prayers."

"I'd appreciate that," she said. Then as abruptly as she had started the conversation, she announced. "I have a craving for oatmeal."

"May I give you a hug, Cathy?"

She accepted, then bid us goodbye.

In a town that looked like it was straight out of the movie *The Truman Show*, reality had found Luke and me through a random conversation with a stranger. Luke gave me the raised eyebrow and boyish grin that had captured my heart back in college.

"Of all people, Jillana, *of course* it would be you who Cathy would engage."

He took my hand as we continued along the dock. We were there to focus on one another as the undeniable main thing. Yet when a stranger initiates an out-of-the-blue conversation and needs someone to acknowledge her reality, if only for a few minutes, when we have capacity, this squarely fits within the larger picture of who we are and what we want our life to be about. Luke and I went on to have dinner at an outdoor table right by the water. We stayed up way too late watching a movie and eating chocolate. Before falling asleep, I silently prayed for comfort for Cathy.

Nothing is ever truly picture-perfect despite manicured lawns and sumptuous linens.

• • •

Maya Angelou says, "I've learned that people will forget what you said, people will forget what you did, but people will never forget how you made them feel." The roads of our lives are full of intersections, on-ramps and off-ramps in which we both shape others and are actively formed by the presence of our partners, mentors, and community. It gives our lives enduring structure and direction, whether for a short season or sustained over a lifetime.

Around our fifteenth anniversary, Luke proposed we discuss the "centering questions" our counselor encouraged us to ask of one another—"What's going well for you? What do you hope for? How can I help?"—over a game of Frisbee golf. We each continued answering those questions over a rare game of pool. While we were working on our bank shots, we dreamed up something we—and the other families who participate—now lovingly refer to as "Family Feast."

For years we hadn't been able to participate in our weekly small group gathering because it was too late in the evening and often too overstimulating for our youngest. But we wanted to find a way to journey with other families as much as possible within our family framework. We decided to host a monthly Family Feast dinner with others who share some of the same barriers our family has experienced. We provide the main dish and others bring whatever they can. For six years strong, we've kept the gathering simple, but the result has been a meaningful, restorative, consistent-over-time connection. We celebrate with one another, we grieve together, and we tangibly and emotionally show up for one another.

Recently, a friend who's a single adoptive mother in our group and has back issues, asked if some Family Feasters could drive across town to help her unload a large storage bin of heavy items. She was apologetic and said she hates asking for help, but the thing is, those of us who had capacity to show up were genuinely glad to do it. I, too, still occasionally buy into the deception that asking for help is equivalent to showing weakness, but I'm debunking this myth with practice.

Though rugged individualism is one of our highest American values—always wanting to be the one who lends a helping hand and never the one who needs one—interdependence is not something to recoil from. Interdependence is actually a beautiful inspiration. It sheds light on the shadowy truth that running through life, claiming we can do it all on our own, is just plain exhausting and lonely. It's not how we're created to be. Dependence on God and interdependence on our neighbors and our community is the soil in which we flourish. The vulnerability of being "in need" allows others to expose *their* true need, allowing people to be real and rooted. Those who experience disability are often one step ahead of the rest of us because the facade of not needing one another is dropped.

"I can do it all and give all that my children need of me all the time" is a prime parental myth rooted in our shiny view of parenting self-sufficiency. In my case, this lie avalanched down the parenting myth mountain by the sheer fact that I need someone every weekday to help me watch and care for my youngest child, who requires "line of sight" supervision. Those I have in my home as aides for much-needed help have offered connection and belonging (among life's simplest yet greatest gifts) not only to Charlie, but also to me! It's pulling up a front-row seat to a picture of interdependence for both of us.

Not buying into this "be all/do all" lie of parenting, I signed Micah up at age seven for a mentoring program called Faithful Friends. It took nearly two years for the program to find him a match, but for the last four solid years and counting, Jake and Alli, a young, hip couple full of fun and energy, have faithfully picked him up on Monday afternoons. Sometimes they go out in the community to go bowling or play mini-golf. Other times they head back to their house to watch a movie, play a board game, and make dinner together. You've never seen a kid so thrilled for Monday afternoons!

This mentoring program looked at the circumstances of our lives instead of just a few bullet points of how our family appeared on paper. I needed support, and I asked for it. And I've appreciated them coming alongside our son in ways that were beyond my capabilities with all the dynamics under our roof. Jake and Alli are radically generous with their years of consistent relational investment into Micah; an intentionality that is treasured so greatly that Mondays are priceless and by far the best day of the week.

. . .

Despite both my grandmothers now being gone, I am grateful for growing up with their intentional presence in my life. Their presence was as dependable as knowing there would always be orange jelly candies thick with sugar sitting in a glass dish on Grandma Helen's coffee table. Grandma Helen would ask me questions about softball since I was an "expert" who played. She taught me how to play a ruthless game of dominoes, and she also understood that I found worms slimy so when we went fishing, she babied me a bit by baiting my hooks with mealworms *and* taking the catch off my line.

My other grandma, Lorna, was always decked head to toe in colorful outfits, scarves, hats, and pizzazzy jewelry to boot. With Grandma Lorna, I went to the performing arts theater and traveled, and she professionally framed my not-so-inspiring middle school artwork and hung it on her walls. Though my two grandmas were completely different from each other, their presence indelibly shaped my life for the good through their loving interest and devotion.

Every now and again I take a whiff of the few remaining drops of Grandma Helen's White Shoulders perfume bottle still in my bathroom drawer and inhale the memory of her. I now throw my earrings on my bathroom counter in the glass ashtray Grandma Lorna used to keep her house key in. She'd bought the ashtray decades after she gave up smoking, but she couldn't resist the allure of a beveled purple ashtray, glistening in the sunlight. That presence permeated my life in ways that will always be with me.

Mentors also have indelibly shaped me with their intentionality of presence. It's amazing to have friends who share the same life stage as you and can relate to what you're going through now. But it's equally precious, if not more so, to spend time with women who have the layered seasons of time and perspective to reflect alongside you.

I have several older women in my life whom I revere and with whom I spend time regularly. These cherished mentors—some of whom I have formally asked to mentor me and others who have just ended up that way—exude grace and humor, and listen with a depth I want to give back to them. I am privileged to listen to their stories of situational curveballs thrown at them: traversing the mountains and valleys of a difficult childhood, a strenuous marriage, unjust treatment before retirement, the death of a spouse, or the mental illness of a middle-aged child. Through the sharing of their decades of stories, they remind me of the truth Anne Lamott writes about—that the complexities of life are usually summed up by the simplicity of these three essential prayers: Help, Thanks, Wow.

I draw encouragement and strength from their lived, one-foot-in-front-of-the-other perspective. And unlike the culture of social media, where one feels something and immediately puts it out into the universe ten seconds later, they have earned wisdom from living their experiences and thinking about them over time, often from many angles. They offer me perspective, and sometimes I draw strength simply from knowing that they're still standing after parenting a gaggle of teenagers like the three I delightfully have under our roof right now.

• • •

A few months into the spring pandemic of 2020 when Oregon schools and businesses were completely shuttered, Eleni asked her older sister to give her a hair trim. Sophia, with exactly zero haircutting experience, obliged. Had Eleni been paying anything, she would have immediately requested a refund for her choppy, way-shorter-than-a-trim new look.

Eleni's immediate, emphatic response after she looked in the mirror was: "Well, nothing to do now but shave my head!"

"I'll take you to the salon when it opens," I offered.

She shook her head. "Nope, it's okay. I always wanted to shave my head."

I looked at my girl, adorable with her pierced thirteen-year-old perfect button nose, and who always inches toward edgy. I asked her to give me a week to think about it.

She argued that not needing hair to look beautiful was about female empowerment and that it was important to her. I could get on board with this reasoning, though it still felt a bit rash in response to a home haircut gone awry. Getting a buzz cut to match her dad's created a hurdle in my mind about what others would think seeing a teenage girl with a shaved head. I prickled, wondering about assumptions they'd make about her. *Is she ill and on the verge of a breakdown? What assumptions would be made about me?*

A few days later, Eleni sat Luke and me down on the couch and gave us a compelling PowerPoint presentation as to why she wanted to shave her head. She even passed out clipboards with paper for us to write down our specific questions and concerns so she could address them after she concluded her presentation, standing up next to the TV in the middle of our living room. This impressive girl meant business! At the end, Luke and I looked at each other and nodded. I told Eleni that it's not what I would choose for her, but that I could tell this meant something to her. I recorded the shave-off and tried to sound as positive as possible as I watched her, with the help of her dad, take an electric razor to her gorgeous hair.

I'm in plenty of relationships with mentors and friends of various ages and in various stages of parenting to position this no-big-whoop into clear perspective. Yet it gave me an opportunity to reflect on the ways I am tempted to make something important to my *child* erroneously become something that reflects on *me*. It also was a decent family life lesson in being intentional about who's holding the scissors around here. After a year of awkward hair regrowth that only could be described as a mullet, I let Eleni make the salon appointment when she was ready. She bounced out of the salon with the original haircut she had requested from her older sister.

• • •

I have a friend who sends me a Christmas card each year with a photo that looks like it should hang in a gallery or appear on the cover of a magazine. In this year's photo, her daughters are wearing monogrammed denim dresses with real daisy chains adorning the tops of their heads. The four family members are holding hands, looking lovingly at one another as a soft sunset glows behind them. They are not just proverbially running through a field of wildflowers. They are literally in a field of wildflowers!

On year three of being too overwhelmed to send out family Christmas cards, I felt both inspired and perhaps a bit jealous. I decided I could either sit and look longingly at a photo shoot that doesn't seem feasible with the needs of our youngest or intentionally go with a "good enough" philosophy. I decided on the latter. With the camera on a timer, our family snapped one photo of us all cobbled together in our living room to capture Christmas. The bookshelves were messy behind us and the picture frames of our kids held a bit of dust. There was nothing staged. Charlie was lunging halfway off Luke's lap, his head blurred by his motion, and my three older smiling kids had glares on their glasses. I'm fairly confident Micah had been wearing the same mismatched outfit for two days straight. The Christmas tree wasn't centered behind us. We barely captured a lone branch in the corner but voilà—it was, indeed, our wonky family Christmas photo. I didn't send it out to everyone on my Christmas card list, but I did choose to be brave and send it to some people to acknowledge "Here's a little snapshot of our very real life."

The following year, I decided we needed professional help, so we hired a photographer. Charlie refused to look at the camera in our family shots. Instead, he insisted the photographer take a photo of only him standing on the sidewalk, arms down at his sides, looking straight-faced at the camera, with a teeny-tiny LEGO figurine placed in front of his feet. After one click of the camera, despite our best bribes, Charlie was done with the photo shoot. Today this perfectly captured moment in time stands framed on our piano right next to the professional photo of the other five of us. I'm learning to just take the photo and roll with it, regardless of the outcome. While it is a far cry from a field of wildflowers, I am grateful for the photos, nonprofessional and professional alike, because they intentionally capture our family's reality in all its glory.

What you can't see in the background of our family photos are the people who have stood behind us and alongside us, propping us up along the way—the steadying presence of our grandmothers, our marriage counselor, our parents investing time with us and their grandkids, the friends who walk through our door for Family Feast, our child's aide, and the mentors both in my life and in the life of my child.

Contrary to our culture's highest value, we did not get here by pulling ourselves up by our bootstraps. We got here by intentionally leaning into those around us, both asking for help and offering it. We got here by listening to many voices with varying life experiences, those who have gone before us. None of this is apparent, looking at our unpolished family photos, but it is nevertheless present.

10

SHOWING UP

Paying Attention

"BUT WHAT ARE THE KIDS GIVEN? What do they do?" I asked my trusted foster care certifier, Anna, as she sat on my living room couch in 2011. She was there for her semi-annual home visit to inquire if there was anything new going on in our family, to look through our closets and to make sure we had a properly working fire extinguisher in order to remain a certified foster family. I held Micah, who had been part of our family since he was six months old, in all his squirmy three-year-old glory.

We'd been foster parents for eight years, but the day before Anna's visit, I'd witnessed something at the child welfare office for the first time. A set of siblings with solemn expressions were traipsing inside with an equally somber staff person. Someone whispered to me that the children had just been removed from their home.

As Anna finished the required biannual inspection of our house and sat down on our sofa, I asked the questions— *What are kids given? What do they do?*—that had been circling my brain after witnessing that scene.

"There is no standard protocol for the children in this time," Anna said. "To be honest, staff always have to scramble to keep the children occupied with whatever they can find in the office. Sometimes they use their own money to take kids through the McDonald's drive-through."

"What do you think would help occupy the child during this time of waiting? What would staff want to know they could always count on to give to a child awaiting a foster family?"

I took some hasty notes while we brainstormed.

Anna unhesitatingly went through some essentials: something to color/write on, coloring book, journal, activity book, construction paper, pencils, markers, crayons, toothbrush, toothpaste, flashlight, and night-light for the child's first night in a new bedroom. And definitely a plethora of healthy snacks!

Over the next few days, I met with more people and asked additional questions, my pen poised to capture the comments of those who worked at Child Welfare. Their answers were both enlightening and alarming.

"How many children are in foster care in Portland?"

"Approximately two thousand five hundred children on any given day in our metro area."

"What do kids usually bring with them when they enter foster care?"

"Many of them have nothing except the clothes on their

backs. Others might have a garbage bag of belongings, things they grabbed quickly in a sometimes unsafe situation."

"How many offices do children wait in?"

"We have eight offices that serve the three counties."

"Approximately how many children per year are waiting for a foster home at the child welfare office closest to me—the one where I took Micah to visit with Jennifer?"

"There are approximately three hundred children at that office alone."

I asked more questions, and I listened.

When I had compiled my ideas, I sat around a table with child welfare leaders to present my thinking. "We'll use stackable and sturdy 4 × 8 photo storage boxes—the kind you buy at any craft store. They're not too cumbersome for a child to carry. Each box will be filled with age-appropriate items and clearly labeled. In addition to the essentials, the box will be filled to the brim with books, toys, games, socks, water bottles, LEGOs, and anything else that a child of that age would enjoy. There could also be a simple note of encouragement inside. We'll call them Welcome Boxes. Something to call their very own in a time when there are more question marks hanging over their heads than answers."

When I shared the concept with Jennifer, she was excited to help me craft the messages.

"Are you sure a handwritten message inside the lid of a box isn't too cheesy?" I asked. She assured me it wasn't because these were messages she hadn't heard growing up in foster care. Together we came up with these affirmations.

You are worthy. You are important. You are unique. You are cared about. You matter.

• • •

After getting things off the ground, I applied for a grant from my church, Imago Dei Community, to propel "Welcome Boxes" forward. The money for the grant came through my church's participation in an international movement called Advent Conspiracy, whose stated purpose is to bring a deeper meaning to Christmas by avoiding getting caught up in holiday consumerism. Participating congregants are encouraged to take a portion of the money they would have spent at Christmas and contribute it toward international clean water projects as well as local initiatives that serve needs in the community. While the actual Welcome Boxes would be made by community members, the grant would go toward printing brochures with instructions on how to assemble them as well as buying cabinets each child welfare office can use for storing their Welcome Boxes.

I put together teams to create drop locations, where boxes would be sorted and then delivered to a specific office, which would inform the team of the exact amount they needed to serve children coming into their care. Our goal was to make three hundred boxes for our local office.

Grandma Lorna came to visit and was delighted to go shopping with my girls and me to pick out items for a range of toddler to teen boxes. She outdid herself on the affirming messages, making them pop with her colorful, artistic flair. My young girls buzzed around like little worker bees, taking items off the kitchen counters and dining room table and packing them in a box that would delight the child who opened it.

As word got out, more and more of the community got

involved. On one weekend, a Sunday school class put together Welcome Boxes; on another, bank employees did the same.

Soon our garage became a makeshift warehouse full of Welcome Boxes. Micah opened up the lid of a Welcome Box, saw something cool inside, and asked if he could have it.

"Sorry, bud. That box is for another little boy your age."

"Awww, man! I wish *I* was in foster care. Those kids get it all!"

Ugh, the irony! It was an opportunity to gently set the record straight and to realize he was so young during his nearly three-year stint in foster care that Micah didn't internalize the stigma that most kids suffer in state custody.

One day I called a child welfare office and offered to drop off a storage cabinet bought with Advent Conspiracy funds. The supervisor was grateful, but then she said, "Jillana, Welcome Boxes have been helpful, but can I share with you something else we could use?" She invited me to come to the office and see the state of the rooms where kids visit with their parents and siblings when they are separated in foster care. I took her up on the invitation and also invited a photographer friend to join me. At my request, we ended up seeing all four of the child welfare offices in my county that day.

During each of the tours, I was paraded through rooms with worn furniture, murals that had seen better days, broken crayons, and tables of puzzles with missing pieces. I was told repeatedly, "There is no funding to invest in these spaces," which is why they did the best they could piecing things together. The shabby rooms were certainly not communicating the dignity, worth, and value that families involved with Child Welfare deserve for the precious little family time they get to share together. What if these dark and depressing spaces could communicate something different; something to aspire toward, where a parent could genuinely say, "When my family is reunited, I hope to create a warm and inviting space like in this room."

Norene, Anna's supervisor (whom I barely knew at that time), would become one of the first major champions on the inside of Child Welfare to uplift and propel what would come to be a wave of community momentum investing in the foster care system. Norene gave me a friendly wave in the parking lot of the local office, where I'd started the tour that day. "How were the tours?" she asked. My chin started to quiver, betraying the poise I wanted to have, as I stood in the hot sun of the parking lot.

I told her my conviction. "Over the years, I've walked into this very building to do drop-offs and pickups dozens upon dozens of times so my child could visit his biological mom, and I had zero idea of the condition of the rooms down the hallway. And if I, as a foster parent, had no idea, how much more in the dark is the general community? They need to know! More people need to understand that *this* is where families are spending sacred time together in an effort to stay connected during their time apart in foster care."

I invited my church and a few non-profit organizations to join me on another tour to see what I saw, to meet the people working inside the building, and to connect staff working within the foster care system with the outside world. Terms like "community" are buzzwords easily tossed about as "values" in child welfare, but at the end of the day, there needs to be a connection between the actual people inside the building and those outside of it. Faith communities, non-profits, and local businesses all want to be responsible neighbors. There was opportunity here.

In this specific instance, the ninety-minute tour, the first of many to come, was eye-opening to the people who had never been inside the facility. The areas had harsh fluorescent lights, the staff lunchroom was dark and dreary with an old microwave, and the hallway had several drab and sterile "visitation rooms" where interacting families are watched through a one-way mirror.

The end result was what I hoped for—a commitment from several community partners to do a "makeover" of the visitation rooms and staff lunchroom. Community members worked alongside child welfare staff, and in two days, a group of around fifty volunteers transformed the lunchroom into a place a person would actually want to take a breather and eat their lunch, and provided new couches, lighting, a fresh coat of paint, and brand-new donated toys for the visitation rooms. A total of ten thousand dollars' worth of items were donated from a local paint store, toy shop, and a business specializing in framed art. In addition, a sandwich shop down the street provided food for the work crew of volunteers. And the rest was donated by the churches and businesses who participated.

These tours, which often felt like Christmas Day to me, became the backbone for making relational introductions, which led to all eight child welfare offices getting a significant makeover where lobbies, visiting rooms, and staff break rooms were visibly transformed. It was an investment with faith communities on the front lines. But I knew we weren't done yet. There was so much more beyond boxes and make-overs to come.

I organized a new community liaison who would receive needs and requests for children in foster care and get those needs funneled out to faith communities and businesses in the surrounding neighborhood of that particular child welfare office. At first it was a mom-and-pop-shop approach (now it's much more sleek and streamlined), but it pulsed with relationship. *Community* wasn't a vague term; *community* was an actual person.

Kelly, the local community liaison volunteer at the Gresham child welfare office, could listen to what staff needed to serve kids in foster care well. They called her, emailed her, talked with her, and were genuinely happy to see her. She was known inside the office for getting needs met for kids, and by those outside it as someone who connected them to real needs for kids in their community.

Who says the tattoo shop down the street can't supply size 13 football cleats to the teen in foster care who needs them, and that the coffee shop down the street can't encourage foster parents with a free shot of caffeine? Who says the florist in the neighborhood can't make things a little brighter for families walking into a child welfare office lobby with a donated bouquet? Or that a financial firm can't sponsor a weight room for the staff? Those whose faith compelled them to help and those interested in the common good could all lean in for the sake of showing up for those impacted by foster care. Having liaisons at every office embodied community outside the agency walls. This changed the narrative that the two choices people have are either (1) become foster parents or (2) do nothing. There *has* to be a menu of options for people who fall in the middle of the continuum. As the momentum increased, a plethora of long-term and short-term volunteer opportunities emerged, many of which had never been done before.

While donating and volunteering are undeniably good things, there was no escaping the fact that there was—and still is—a crisis shortage of foster parents in our community. There are many reasons, but this reality remains: Children whose lives have already gone awry through no fault of their own are doubly punished by having to wait in an office for someone to say yes to them. Having to wait or bounce from place to place until a suitable foster family says yes does not reinforce the uplifting message of "You are worthy." In fact, it communicates the opposite. It was a message that I was determined to start talking about.

Steve Duin, a prominent columnist for the *Oregonian*, caught wind of this momentum via someone inside the walls of the child welfare office. He wrote a feature article with the headline "A Revolution in Portland's Foster Care" that turned this movement from a trickle to a stream to a flood. There was a photograph of me reading to my young children, with a book covering up Charlie's face because he was a toddler still in foster care. Steve mentioned Welcome Boxes, office makeovers, and the momentum to change the paradigm about who gets involved in foster care. With the sharp increase of interest that accompanied that article, it was clear we were at the point where this movement needed an actual name. The two dynamic gentlemen who had invited me early on to come under the umbrella of their non-profit, and to use their considerable community influence to be "all in," agreed that Embrace Oregon seemed like a fitting name.

I did a major life pivot, leaving teaching and the international students I adored in order to devote myself full time to the depths of this burgeoning grassroots movement. Luke shared with me that if we were to splice together all the reels of our lives and every frame seamlessly folded into the next with perfect sense, there *may* have been a missed opportunity to grab hold of faith and live daringly. If my life were a movie, this would certainly be my record-scratch, plot-twist moment. "Wait a minute! I thought she was a teacher! What is she doing leading a movement?"

On paper, this move didn't make financial sense, but when I looked at the landscape of ESL teachers, I saw many good ones. I wasn't urgently needed. When I looked at the landscape of a community movement with a relational heartbeat to sustainably serve those impacted by foster care (including kids, foster parents, staff, and eventually biological parents), I saw a lane wide open for opportunity and response. Also, my husband had a good point when he teasingly affirmed, "When you're 'volunteering' more hours each week to this cause than you are teaching, maybe it's time to take the leap."

We hosted an official kickoff for the launch of Embrace Oregon in 2013. A pre-event gathering was held at our church. Child welfare leaders mingled with pastors, business leaders, and current foster parents. The purpose of the night was to highlight the zoomed-out story, which is that ultimately, our community is better and stronger when we all come to the table and lean into—and not away from—one another, which requires each of us zooming in and examining what is ours to do.

It was time to make our way to the main church auditorium. I stood off to the side of the stage and looked out. This would be my first speaking gig to a crowd this size, and I had butterflies from excitement and nerves. And then came the faux pas that still makes me cringe to this day.

As I was being wired up for my hands-free microphone, I started internally fretting, *How do I make sure this thing is off if I need to run to the restroom? Man! That would be embarrassing if they heard the toilet flush.* The sound guy was standing incredibly close to me, getting the microphone hooked onto my blouse, when without thinking I asked him, "Are you going to turn me on?" The deer-in-the-headlights look clearly communicated to me that he hadn't been a part of my inner monologue. *Eeek! Did I really just say that? Scandalous!* In that moment, I wanted to kick off my heels and head for the hills, lest an even larger disaster awaited me on stage.

This, I reminded myself, *has never been about me.* I took the stage that night, and so did my colleagues. We shared the opportunity before us. Jerry Burns, the senior district child welfare manager for the most populated county in our state, also spoke. Steve Duin was there, too, and would write another article, "Redefining the Shadow of the Church and Aiding Foster Children," quoting Jerry Burns:

> The families we see are beset by domestic violence, criminal histories, unmanageable debt, school failure, . . . and they live in relative isolation.

And that isolation is as fatal to those families as it is to the mission of DHS.

We need to do things differently; this isn't working. . . . We need community-based organizations and nonprofits to get involved in these people's lives when we leave. If not community-based organizations, then faith-based organizations. Or neighbors. Or mentors. There has to be a caring person in their lives, someone they can turn to in a pinch.

That's the tragedy of what happens too often these days. People are so wrapped up in their own lives that they're not reaching out to others. Embrace Oregon represents something that is dramatically different.

•   •   •

Recently a child welfare leader who was admittedly skeptical about this community partnership a decade ago said to me, "I thought you would be here today and gone tomorrow, just another group coming in with their own agenda, but I must admit, when I think about who I can always count on, it's the people your organization rallies that first come to mind. You have my respect both because you have listened and because you have stayed."

What started small grew. Some wondered if this community engagement model developed in the state's largest urban area would hold up in a rural community with markedly different dynamics. Respecting the nuances of each county, the ultimate dream was still the same: a sufficient number of safe, loving, equipped foster families waiting for a child, and not a child waiting for a foster family. The state of Oregon awarded us a grant for a pilot project to see if the flames of generosity in Portland could be fanned out to other areas around the state.

Long story short, it was a success. Every Child is now the branded name of the statewide movement that operates in every county in Oregon. It has drawn interest from several other states across the country, and a top official from the federal Department of Human Services flew out to Oregon from Washington, DC, to meet with our team. With the expertise of many dedicated individuals—those officially on our team and literally hundreds of steadfast faith communities, businesses from the private and public sectors, and thousands of committed volunteers—the effort continues to grow as partnerships form and people dependably show up. With Every Child's dedication to speaking clearly and professionally, and with our signature warm tone, all foster care, adoption, and volunteer inquiries—thousands per year—for the entire state are now routed through Every Child, so the Every Child team can connect those interested to their local child welfare office.

Looking back over the last decade, I recognize that a glossy binder containing a carefully crafted ten-bullet-point plan wouldn't have gotten Every Child to where we are today. It's a mountain-moving, mustard-seed kind of story; one that's allowed me to don a blazer and speak to the state legislature, and to sit around the table with leaders in all sectors. I combine professional poise with my unabashed lens of being a mom and looking at ways various sets of parents (foster/adoptive/biological) can positively influence and engage one another.

I was invited to share about our work on a local TV station alongside Allie Roth—a friend, a mom, and a fellow founder of the non-profit With Love. Walking into the studio together, we had multiple reminders to silence our phones, which we dutifully did, but we learned the hard way, right in the middle of our interview, that silencing doesn't automatically turn off your phone's alarm. Allie's daily alarm to go pick up her child from school started ringing mid-interview. Her alarm tone was the theme song from the musical *The Greatest Showman*, and it kept playing continually. It took everything in us to keep looking natural, smile, and engage the host with this unexpected background music. The producers were able to muffle it somewhat when the program aired, but you can still faintly hear it in the replay, and you can definitely see the split-second look of alarm in our eyes when the song started blaring.

The following week, I received a handwritten note of thanks from the governor for our work, which I appreciated, but what made me smile more was opening up a surprise package from Allie that contained *The Greatest Showman* DVD with a note that simply said, "The show must go on!"

While there are some lighthearted moments, I'm not naive, and I don't sugarcoat the very real challenges of working with a large government agency that is the legal guardian of children in foster care. The work is gritty. This is a field with not many feel-good stories in a land of perpetual, depressing hard knocks. But hard does not mean unworthy.

With the reality of my life and my priority on ending my workday when school ends for my kids, I've scaled myself back from a sprint to a sustainable, energetic walk. As a founder, however, through all the pivots and changes from grassroots to a more polished work, I'm honored to still be on the team.

Today the words of Edward Everett Hale inspire what I and others working and volunteering with Every Child strive to do: "I am only one, but still I am one. I cannot do everything, but I can still do something; and because I cannot do everything, I will not refuse to do something that I can do."

In 2011, the year I was awarded the Advent Conspiracy grant, we met our goal of three hundred Welcome Boxes within a few months. Now, a decade later, thirty thousand have been made (and we've received well over one million dollars in donated goods and services)! But this was never just about a box. It was about getting the community to *see* the children carrying the box. Over the last decade, our family has had the privilege of saying an occasional short-term yes to children in foster care who needed a temporary place to stay until a longer-term solution could be arranged. Every child who has walked through our front door has carried a Welcome Box, and many of them have slept with the boxes on their pillows.

We have a long way to go, and there is still much work to be done. But a box became the humble invitation for the community to ask better, deeper questions: "Why are children from our neighborhood waiting in a government office in the first place? How else can I help?" The answers to those questions became the catalyst for a full-fledged movement; a movement that creatively stepped outside the box to envision a new possibility.

• • •

I picked up the phone for a scheduled conversation with a woman in her late fifties who wanted to run an idea past me. Two minutes into the conversion, I was grateful we were not doing this in person because my raised eyebrows and grimace would have given away my response to her "generosity." She wanted teen girls in foster care to get together with a group of girls from a wealthy suburban high school so the "foster care girls could benefit from the exposure of being around kids who go to Europe for the summer." (Yes, those were her exact words.)

"Interesting. And what do you think the benefit would be for your girls?"

"Well . . ." She hesitated, then said, "My girls would become more aware of their privilege."

Awareness of privilege is not a bad thing, but it was clear to me that the roles of who was to be the giver and who was to be the recipient were predetermined. I politely passed on the opportunity to make this connection.

When we have the opportunity to widen our circle, there is no galloping in on a white horse to share our one-sided experience and claim to save the day. There is no set-in-stone labeling of roles. It's about listening and being humble about all you do not know. Learning from and walking alongside those affected by broken relationships and fallible systems help to save us from ourselves when we're left to our own devices, especially our literal ones. That's different from setting up situations to pat ourselves on the back because we decide to engage with people who are different from ourselves.

Even if our hearts are in the right place, we won't always see the "results" that we hope for and that others can point to and applaud. I love how my husband, Luke, sums up our nearly two decades of personal fostering experience: "Our calling is to love above all else, not necessarily succeed."

This can be hard to unravel and accept.

Luke expanded on the idea of relationship versus rescue:

If we approach foster care like our culture teaches us to approach other aspects of our lives—work, family, education—in which we create our own success, we are doomed to burn out and fail. Children who have experienced the trauma of abuse or neglect or have been exposed to alcohol or drugs in utero may never live up to our conditioned understanding of "success." Similarly, their parents, who in many cases have established lifelong habits of unhealthy behaviors, may never "get their act together" in the ways we might hope. If we approach the milieu of foster care with a results-oriented mindset, we will experience nothing but frustration.

Instead, we need to recognize that "Where there is love, God breaks in." That truth allows us to do all we can to pursue wholeness and health spiritually, emotionally, physically, and socially in the lives of children and families out of love, without it being measured by results, change, or success. Viewing our interaction with children and families through the lens of relationship instead of rescue allows us to weather the ups and downs of growth, change, and failure, while not being discouraged from our divine calling to love.

•   •   •

Our daily reality mixes the significant and the ordinary. We strive to embrace "I'm living life to the fullest" each day, and yet we hold the tension that there are many days when piles of dishes stack up in the sink, bills come in the mail, and smooshed goldfish crackers on the car mats dim our "Carpe diem!" The inspirational moments in our lives collide with the mundane; the glorious possibilities become intertwined with the daily to-dos.

In certain seasons, it's easy to get caught up in the daily goal of simply outrunning the tidal wave of the urgent from overtaking us. Let's be honest: An image of trying to outrun a tidal wave isn't an inspirational Etsy print we want to frame on our walls—"Carpe diem!" is so much sexier.

If we consider most aspects of our world for any length of time, we see things that are not as upright as they should be. The world is alarmingly slumped. So we wrestle with what is ours to do in the midst of holding the tension that God doesn't need us to do things. Yet we are invited to participate in the restoration of things that aren't right in our world by both *doing* and *being*—simultaneously.

A sibling group of four stayed in our home for a week in an effort to simply keep them together while the agency searched for a foster home. What these children needed and deserved was an ocean of care and support. What was within our capacity was to pour in just a few drops through one week's worth of togetherness. Toward the end of the week, when the kids were feeling more comfortable, Luke put on music in the kitchen as we were clearing dishes after dinner. One person started dancing and then another. Pretty soon the majority of us, including all four of our guests, joined in demonstrating the simple-yet-difficult sway of both *doing* and *being*.

What's happening in the world can be daunting, and daily life can be overwhelming. When we see injustice, our natural tendency usually comes down to three responses: (a) We become paralyzed by the enormity of the issue, questioning our ability to even make a dent in the solution; (b) we wait for X, Y, or Z to happen before getting involved; or (c) we believe that unless we can wholeheartedly fling ourselves off the high-dive and into the deep end of justice work, our small offering will not be worth it.

But here's the thing: We don't have to have it all figured out or go all in to start walking toward others, paying attention and discerning what is ours to do. There's beauty in the simplicity of showing up. Showing up to help your older neighbor fill out a tax form. Showing up by joining your school board. Showing up by noticing the new person at small group and inviting them out for coffee. Showing up to your child's classroom to acknowledge and support the teacher. Some people show up with funds, others march and use their voices, and still others may volunteer with enthusiasm. There is no "one way." There is no predetermined script. The world has no shortage of ways—big and small—in which we are invited to creatively show up and pay attention.

• • •

My favorite comfy sweatshirt proclaims in big letters "LOVE ANYWAY." I'm preaching to myself when I wear it and look in the mirror. My desire to use my life and my voice is measured against the backdrop and capacity of my very real life. Everyone's backdrop looks different. The succinct prayer "Dear God, be good to me. The sea is so wide, and my boat is so small" is one that has always resonated.

There are days when what we are facing in front of us will take up every single ounce of all we have within us, and we cannot do one speck more. That's nothing to be ashamed of. And when we engage more deeply, it doesn't give us permission to have a puffed-up sense of self-worth. The reality is this: We cannot—nor are we meant to—do it all.

Energy is required for every yes. It is easily possible to become physically and emotionally depleted, withdrawing more than you have in order to give to those under the roof of your home or outside of it, *even if what you're giving is a good thing*. It is not wise for us to zealously serve others if our families—ourselves included—are left constantly nibbling on the leftover crumbs of our own capacity.

Sometimes we pay attention and show up in the world in one small way, and it remains one small way. At other times, it exponentially becomes something greater. What matters most is the heartbeat with which we offer it.

A friend and mentor, Miriam, whom I initially crossed paths with in my non-profit work (and who devoted thirty years of her life to working in child welfare before retirement) gave me a handmade clay tile of a short poem that speaks to the importance of not letting the world pass us by without a sense of wonder. It sits prominently on my home office desk, a reminder that we need not parse out life into distinctly separate categories of "personal" and "professional" to open our eyes to see and engage who and what is in front of us.

I don't know what makes you come alive and what is uniquely yours to do in this world. You and I, however, are continually extended an invitation to show up and move toward love, knowing we have infinitely more to learn than we could ever teach.

11

NEIGHBORING

Beyond the Surface

WE LIVE IN A RAPIDLY GENTRIFYING neighborhood in south-east Portland. On one side, we're located a few blocks from 82nd Avenue, known for used car lots and being a prostitu-tion strip at night. By contrast, a few blocks on the other side of us are multimillion-dollar homes nestled on a hill, next to one of the city's prized forested parks. Our home sits in this in-between space. Sitting in the hammock that hangs from the big tree in our small front yard, I see new mothers push their babies in expensive buggies around our neighborhood. On Monday nights when our recycling is hauled out to the curb, cans and glass bottles are snatched up like treasure by those with worn shoes pushing ragged strollers. It's a section of the city where both realities coexist side by side.

Luke and I were both raised in the suburbs, but we've lived

the two-plus decades of our married life in the city. Before moving to our current home, we briefly lived in a home on a quiet cul-de-sac that was still within the city limits but had a cookie-cutter suburban vibe. I loved the idea of a place where the kids could safely ride their bikes, but this home left much to be desired in terms of being known, getting to know others, and building community. Our neighbors opened their doors cautiously. Instead of taking a one-minute walk to retrieve mail from a locked communal mailbox, neighbors would pull up in their cars, open their keyed mailboxes, and then disappear into their three-car garages.

When we moved into the heart of the city, I baked cookies, and our family went around to introduce ourselves to everyone on our street, a gesture that had been treated with a sprinkling of suspicion in our former neighborhood. Here, people flung open their doors and welcomed us to the neighborhood. We learned who had lived on the street for sixty years and had raised their families there, as well as the stories of other, younger families, like ours, moving into newer homes. Despite the location of this house having an unmistakable darker color on the crime maps than my previous "safer" suburban-like neighborhood, I felt safer here because of the simple truth that people talked with one another. They looked out for one another and their homes. My neighbors across the street and on both sides of our home represent four distinct cultural heritages different from my own.

Soon after we moved in, Luke built an epic tree house in the massive black walnut tree in our backyard. A rope swing dangled off another branch. We got a netted trampoline and placed it in the corner of our small yard. We set up a basket-ball hoop and tetherball pole along our long driveway and a Ping-Pong table in our garage. Without any official sort of declaration, our house became the hub. To this day, all the neighborhood kids come in and out of our backyard and in and out our front and back doors, especially when the Portland sun peeks through. We wouldn't want it any other way.

There *is* one aspect of city life that is hard to get used to: noise.

A few summers after we moved in and became well established, two people moved into a rental house nearby. Although Charlie was six, he was still on a newborn's sleep schedule, never sleeping for longer than three hours at a time during the night. On a particular three-night stretch in late June, Charlie was awakened double the normal amount of times by the neighbors' loud conversation, piercing laughter, and occasional arguing between the hours of midnight and 3 a.m. When I peeked through our bedroom shades, I could see the source of all this noise was the woman in the rental house, sitting on her front porch with several others. Unlike with my other neighbors whom we befriended, my attempts to engage with the occupants of this house had been minimal. My greetings had been met with curt head nods or distant smiles before the neighbors shut the door.

In the late afternoon, I vented to Luke. Charlie and I couldn't survive this unneighborly noise and the havoc it was wreaking on our already minimal sleep!

"I think I should be a grown-up and go engage in bit of friendly conversation rather than smolder with resentment," I announced to Luke. I glanced out our window and saw the neighbor on her front porch, smoking. This was my opportunity to take the high road. Though Luke expressed some hesitation about this turning out the way I was envisioning it, I walked out the door and headed her way.

"Hello there. I'm Jillana," I said, smiling, taking a step off the sidewalk and onto the path leading up to her front porch. "What's your name?"

"What does it matter?" she replied, unsmiling. She came down the porch steps, arms folded across her chest, a half-smoked cigarette in her fingers. She looked to be in her early thirties, thin with a pretty, freckled face and greasy black hair pulled up into a bun.

Inwardly I was taken aback but I tried to conceal that outwardly. "Okay . . . hi. I was hoping to have a friendly little conversation with you about the noise level at night. We have a child who already struggles with sleep, who has been woken up the last few nights, and I just wanted to make you aware that the sound carries. I was hoping you could be mindful of this." I tried to keep my tone friendly and positive, to let her know I wasn't upset.

"Okay, JuJuJuJu—whatever," she replied, mocking my name. Instantly I felt my eyebrows raise and my forehead scrunch up, surprised. "I have lived here for two years and other than you asking me if I'd seen that neighborhood kid you were looking for, this is the first time you've ever talked to me." As she spoke, she pointed her cigarette at me. I found myself retreating back to the sidewalk. "How DARE you come over here and talk with me about MY noise level when I have to listen to YOUR kids running around the neighborhood and tearing down the sidewalks on their Big

Wheels all day long! How DARE this be your first inter-action with me!"

I knew I should have said, "I hear that you're offended. I didn't mean to offend you. I'd like for you to hear my concern so that we can both move forward with a mutually satisfying resolution." Although my brain told my body to model a peaceful stance (which I did), that message didn't get fully translated to my mouth. Sleep-deprived and on edge, I defended myself, dripping in sweetness but with a tart tone.

"I'm sorry. I introduced myself to the *other* person living in this house when you moved in. And I'm sorry I didn't bring you a plate of cookies when you moved into the neighborhood."

"Get off my property."

I took one giant step backward, as if I were playing Red Rover. My heart was thumping.

To end the exchange with a smack, she added, "And I hate having to navigate all your stupid orange cones! Talk about having a 'friendly little conversation' about inconvenience."

I looked past her to her porch littered with empty alco-hol bottles. I wish I could tell you that my heart broke with compassion for her, but that would not be the truth. This is when I internally fell apart. She hit a nerve, and I wanted to heap shame on her. I wanted to scream that I needed those cones because my son was prenatally exposed to alco-hol and now he is unable to anticipate consequences, even obviously dangerous ones. When we show Charlie visual cues and say, "Don't go in the street, Charlie," he understands it to mean at that exact, literal spot only, not six inches from the spot. A few weeks before, I saw yet another car speeding down our street when the neighborhood kids were engrossed in a game of tag that zigzagged from one side of the street to the other. I immediately went online and ordered $227 worth of neon orange safety cones to place along the side of our street. I couldn't care less what this neighbor thought of my "inconvenient" fluorescent orange cones. The wine bottles on her porch were not pushing my compassion buttons.

I said nothing other than a subdued, "Sorry I took up your time" and walked back to our house.

Three of my children were waiting inside the front door. "What did she say?" they asked in a chorus.

"It didn't go so well. She wasn't so nice," I replied dryly and headed upstairs where Charlie was waiting for me to begin the long process of rocking him to sleep. I sat down in our tan micro-suede rocking chair facing the window, my heart still pounding. I couldn't believe that now I had to stare at the woman's house, a stark reminder of a neighborly conversation gone awry. As I replayed our words in my mind on a continuous loop, my sense of security in helping to build a caring, collaborative neighborhood took a nosedive. I'd never in my life had a social interaction spiral downward like this one. I wasn't appreciative of anything she was adding to the neighborhood.

Suddenly, my girls excitedly bounded up the stairs. "Mom, the mean girl is here, and she wants to talk with you."

I went downstairs and opened the front door, feeling perturbed but trying not to show it.

"Look, I'm Pam-e-la." She said her name in staccato syllables. "I don't want things to be bad between us. I'll try to keep it down. I'm going through a hard time right now. And you talked to me in a condescending tone."

"I didn't intend to do that. I'm sorry."

And with that, she said, "Okay," pivoted, and walked away.

The following week I was getting the mail from the box on our front porch and looked up to see Pamela sitting hunched over on her stoop, her purse around her neck, wine bottles cascading down her porch steps. As I sorted the mail at my dining room table, I looked through our large window and saw an ambulance pull up in front of her house, no lights flashing, no siren blaring. An EMT opened the back doors and Pamela stoically climbed in.

The compassion I might have felt earlier, if I hadn't been seething, rushed over me.

Because there's always more to the story.

A few weeks later, I looked out our front dining room window and again saw Pamela smoking on her porch. With the same inhale/exhale "don't overthink it" mentality of the first sour encounter, I grabbed some wrapped peonies, dahlias, and lilies I had bought at the farmer's market earlier that week and headed toward her house, careful to stop at the sidewalk and not cross the line onto her property.

I stuck my arm out straight with the bouquet and simply said, "These are for you."

"You can come up," Pamela said flatly.

I walked a few paces as she came off her porch, and I handed her the flowers. "I'm sorry we got off on the wrong foot. I didn't mean to be rude."

"Okay," she said. And that was that.

It's been two years since that exchange. I hosted a neighborhood chili night to bolster some neighborhood camaraderie, and while distributing invitations, I was tempted for a moment to skip Pamela's house. Instead, I walked up her front porch, while her two dogs barked wildly inside, and slid the invitation into her already full mailbox. I didn't expect Pamela would show up (she didn't) but inviting her was important to me.

Pamela is still aloof. I still feel a tad cautious around her, but I'm no longer uncomfortable in my own neighborhood. Pamela has further exposed me to this foundational truth: We often have no idea at what point we're intersecting with someone else's story.

On the days when the sun is peeking out, I see her painting on a canvas and smoking on her front porch as I put out my orange street cones in the afternoon and dutifully drag them back into the driveway in the evening. Every once in a while, when I feel her eyes on me, I give her a reserved smile, and she responds with a slight head nod.

The neighborhood is bustling. Rain or shine, we have countless people walk in front of our home every day on the way to the forested park sitting atop the hill on our street. Some pause and peruse books in the small free library box Luke and the kids built and put up in our front yard. Our neighbors, through their different cultural lenses and their sharing of life's ups and downs, continue to shape me. Pamela invited me to peer beneath the surface, discover where our raw spots rubbed up against one another, and realize that absent of any grand gestures, there is still a way to unearth reconciliation.

12

TODAY

Surviving vs. Thriving

THE CHILDREN WERE PLAYING IN the backyard when the police officer pulled up to our house.

I felt like I was floating above the scene. Just two weeks earlier, I had been in this same driveway, talking with Jennifer as she picked up four-year-old Elias from our house after he had spent the day with us. Even though Elias hadn't lived with us since he was a baby, we still saw him and Jennifer frequently. They had regularly been coming over for Sunday lunch the last few years and celebrated holidays with us. We had several framed photos of our families together displayed around the house.

On the occasion of that particular visit, before Jennifer left with Elias, I perceived something was off. I spoke with Luke about it briefly upstairs in hushed tones. Without having time to overthink it before she walked out the door with her child, I asked, "Jennifer, could we talk privately for a moment?" The two of us stepped into the home office, and I closed the door. I asked her some gentle yet direct questions about how she was doing. As she tried to reassure me that she was fine, I sensed she was hedging. The feeling was nearly imperceptible, yet I couldn't shake it, the way you can sense a distant storm coming from feeling the wind and looking at the sky.

"Jennifer, leave Elias here with us if you're struggling."

"I'm fine. Just tired, that's all," she said, wiping away tears.

Days later, I found out that after our conversation, Jennifer had dropped Elias off with someone whom Jennifer *thought* would be safe, but Elias was hurt there. Despite someone from Child Protective Services telling her she had to return to pick up her child or risk her child entering foster care again, Jennifer didn't come back. Elias officially entered foster care shortly after our home office conversation. We stretched our already tattered capacity to say yes once more. We were his relatives, shoulder-tapped by the state agency who stepped in as his official guardian. He was now safely with us, but I was both concerned about Jennifer and also furious with her.

A neighbor stood gawking at the police car in my driveway as I filed a missing person report on Jennifer at the encouragement of Child Protective Services. *Where was she? Was she dead?* I described her tattoos and the make and model of her car. The officer scribbled the information in his tiny notebook. The sounds of my kids and several neighborhood friends bouncing on the trampoline in the backyard filled the air. The front door opened, and Elias enthusiastically called out, "Auntie, can I have some juice?"

"Sure thing, Elias. I'll be there in a minute, okay, sweetheart?"

Elias stared at me and the police officer for a full twenty seconds before shutting the door without saying a word.

Suddenly the stack of books I had dutifully checked out of the public library years earlier containing facts and snippets of stories about lives forever altered due to substance abuse felt extra cumbersome. It was one thing to read about this when caring for an infant and toddler, and quite another when you have a child who's asking point-blank, "Where's my mom, Auntie?"

The officer handed me his card with the missing person report case number written on it. Before he pulled away, he commented that he's seen it all before. Meth screwing up people's lives and making them neglect their children.

I flashed back to less than a month earlier, when Jennifer and I had stood up and shared our collective story with new foster parents seeking certification. Everyone applauded and praised her for the courage it took to share her story.

And now, presumably the same substance and the same man pulled Jennifer away—again. *How could this be happening?* Jennifer and I had had a crystal-clear agreement for years: If she was struggling and couldn't parent Elias for whatever reason, she would bring him to us. But when it came time to enact the plan, she abandoned it and her child. Despite the concerned conversation I had with her, nothing was going according to plan, even our mutually agreed upon plan B.

I was losing my ability to hope for her. I was losing my ability to care.

• • •

We never used the term *foster care* with Elias. He was family, after all. Luke and I carefully explained that he would be staying with Auntie and Papa for a while until his mama could be found and become safe and healthy. We put bunk beds and an extra dresser in Micah's room. Jennifer's roommate dropped off Elias's things, including a framed professional photo of him and his mom together that we put on top of his dresser.

I pulled into the familiar juvenile court parking lot several weeks later. I put my purse on the security conveyor belt and walked through the metal detector. I trudged up the stairs to sit outside that familiar courtroom. At the first court date with Micah seven years earlier, I told Jennifer I was rooting for her. Today I was tired right down to my bones, and my body seemed too heavy to move. Jennifer, who had been found by police a few hours away with Simon, huddled and whispered with her attorney, while I sat with the staff from Child Protective Services. We did not exchange eye contact.

I took my place on that familiar front-row bench of the courtroom. The last time I was in that very room was when the same judge was flying paper airplanes around his courtroom for Micah's adoption. When the judge asked dryly, "Foster parent, any update?" I gave a short factual update about how Elias was doing, but quickly into my second sentence, I had a catch in my voice. I had to pause so a tidal wave of emotion didn't overcome me. I drew a deep breath and said, "We are committed to Elias and care for him deeply. We were not expecting this. Thank you, Your Honor." I sat down and gripped the bench as hard as I could, willing my eyes not to tear up.

The stark contrast between being a general foster parent and now a relative foster parent struck me. The first time I found myself sitting in court with Jennifer, I didn't know what the journey would look like, but at that time, I had voluntarily raised my hand and said yes to a child in foster care. Yes to capacity. Yes to desire. Yes to loving a child for however long was needed. Yes to openhanded wonder with where this all would lead.

This time, as a relative, I didn't go in with natural capacity, innate desire, or a sense of wonder. I was here at court out of dutiful love and commitment, knowing full well that with the critical lack of foster homes in our community, Elias's best option was with us. But I wasn't naive. What's best for one child does not mean it's best for others. While uplifting one child to keep them afloat, others may drown. We were flirting with ramming our family right past dutiful love and commitment and sinking them with resentment.

Unlike the first court date, there was no "I'm rooting for you" and hugging.

This was my fourteenth court date.

I was exhausted.

I didn't want to be there.

• • •

The truth was, our family was running on fumes.

Sophia, our eldest, had attended a struggling charter

school in which there was one teacher per grade. Her teacher appeared to be an uninspired novice, content with assigning perpetual busywork. When we later met with the principal to see how we could support this new teacher, she surprised us by admitting that it would probably take about six months for the teacher to get up to speed, and that because Luke and I both had a teaching background, Sophia might be best served at home. So quite unexpectedly, we began to homeschool her.

Soon after, a relationship with close friends went awry, and the lingering emotional aftermath loomed like a dark cloud. Additionally, an adult friend, who had grown up in foster care and shared Thanksgiving around our table the first year Jennifer and her other kids joined us, overdosed and died. We were emotionally drained.

Then Elias arrived. There was an unquantifiable toll on daily life with our new addition as Elias adjusted. Even though he'd lived with us as a baby and we had been a consistent presence his whole life, it was still the first time he was living with us that he could actually remember. His room was new. His preschool was new. His routine was new. Not living with his mom was new. Having a caseworker visit him was new. Also, he wasn't accustomed to living with siblings around his age, so when a huge bin of his toy cars was dropped off from his previous apartment with his mom, he confidently said, "Nobody ever touch my stuff, okay?" This is reasonable for items of special significance, but not exactly how things work with a bin of hundreds of Hot Wheel cars when you're folded into a family with two other boys who are close in age.

Almost simultaneous with Elias's arrival, Charlie officially received the daunting diagnosis of Fetal Alcohol Syndrome. Luke and I were still trading off waking up every two to three hours a night because of Charlie's unsettled sleep patterns, just as we'd done for the past four years. We were exhausted.

Then Micah's behavior majorly regressed. Despite our one-on-one intentionality with him, he was as confused as Elias. It was his first time sharing his room. And the framed photo of Elias and Jennifer, sitting on top of Elias's dresser, was something Micah saw every day. The "mom" talk in our house had previously meant me. Now his brother was talking about his "mom," and his mom was also Micah's first mom, but Mom was also me. This wasn't new information, as we'd always been open with Micah, but it was literally in his face and as a result, dysregulated his emotional stability.

The swirl of life all felt like too much. It all *was* too much!

How did I cope? I woke up before the kids and had some daily quiet time with a steaming cup of tea on the couch. I journaled. I exercised. I signed myself up for counseling. And I went to bed at a reasonable time.

Actually, that's the list of what I *wish* I had done!

Instead, I responded by emotionally eating my feelings of being overwhelmed. I know that when I'm palming goldfish crackers into my mouth, it's never about hunger. It's about the overburdening. My growing physical weight mirrored my emotional heaviness.

Luke coped mostly by going to the gym and investing in his work. He actually turned down an alluring job offer that would have meant more time away and more stress, so he could offer a consistent, stabilizing presence to our family.

We were surviving but certainly not thriving. The amount

of pressure we were dealing with wasn't sustainable. We were weary. We had no margin emotionally, physically, or spiritually. Our pads of grace for one another were razor thin.

And with no end in sight, I didn't know how to turn it around.

• • •

Though the preschool where our older three kids had attended made last-minute room to include Elias, he struggled at school. Many times, Luke and I fielded phone calls from a desperate preschool director asking us to come immediately because Elias was under the table throwing things, shouting, or intentionally spilling the paint supplies. When I would arrive, Elias would passionately tell me about whatever preschool injustice had just occurred to trigger the big feelings, and then he would collapse into my lap.

"Auntie, I just want to stay with you! You keep me safe!" he'd repeat. I'd hold him and reassure him. When he was calm, I told him I'd be there right on time to pick him up when school was done, and then I'd return to my non-profit work. The desperate phone calls still happened from time to time but subsided in frequency.

Elias was excited to have one-hour weekly visits with his mom at the child welfare office, which now looked exponentially more inviting. I couldn't help but remember the countless hours in the past I had brought Micah to the same office to be with Jennifer. This time, Jennifer didn't ask for me to supervise the visits between her and Elias, and I didn't offer. A transporter would pick up Elias from my house in the afternoon and drive him to see Jennifer. Oftentimes, after their time together, Elias would come bounding in the house, proudly proclaiming in a sing-songy manner, "She's becoming more safe and more healthy, Auntie!" But as much as he wanted to see her, I could see the emotional storm brewing inside of Elias as he anticipated these visits with his mom. Occasionally, he would cheerfully say, "Okay, let's go," and other times he would cry beneath the dining room table.

One week, when a transporter came to pick Elias up for his visit, Elias ran upstairs and hid under his bunk bed. The transporter stood in my front hallway and said the visit might have to be canceled if they didn't get going soon. I knew Elias would be devastated if he missed this visit. He had expressed excitement in his bedtime prayers the night before about seeing Jennifer.

Barely above a whisper, I asked Elias if I could crawl under the bunk bed with him. He nodded. I wiggled my body beneath the bedframe and took his hand. The two of us lay there silently, looking up at the wooden slats so close to our noses. Thirty seconds later, he whispered, "I'm ready to go see my mom, Auntie." I gave his hand a little squeeze, and we crawled out from under the bed and walked down the stairs. Elias got his coat and dutifully got in the car with the transporter. He came back two hours later from his visit a happy boy.

Another evening, much to Elias's dismay, I agreed to let Micah fall asleep in our bed instead of in his bunk bed. Elias was a nonstop chatterbox at night, and Micah was having trouble falling asleep. Once he was asleep, Luke would have to heave Micah back up into the top bunk, but Micah desperately needed a break from the continual talking from his younger brother in the lower bunk.

Elias was not happy with this arrangement. To show his displeasure, Elias, in his newly turned five-year-old glory, wrote *pew* in permanent marker all over the slats and sides of the bunk bed. He meant *poo*.

Pushing down the minor annoyance and stifling a slight smile when I discovered the marker the next morning, I asked Elias why he wrote that. "Because sometimes things just stink, Auntie," he answered sincerely.

I couldn't have agreed more with that simple truth.

● ● ●

A few years ago, I was given some succulents in white pots. These are my favorite kind of plants. I am drawn to their shapes and spikes and clusters and all their different Crayola shades from sea green to Granny Smith apple green to forest green. I have always admired succulents—big and small, planted outside or potted indoors.

But my fondness grew exponentially when I discovered that succulents are often found in environments that would be too harsh for other plants. They're adaptable to less-than-ideal conditions. They store water in their leaves, their stems, and their roots so they don't have to be planted in good soil, or even *any* soil for a period of time, to survive. Succulents can live uprooted. And while this time of being uprooted will leave them bedraggled and certainly not thriving, they will still survive. Succulents seem to embody what artist Frida Kahlo, who lived in intense physical pain, wisely observed: "At the end of the day, we can endure much more than we think we can."

The longer we rode the emotional roller coaster of

Jennifer's addiction and Charlie's daily teeter-totter of unpredictability, the more I realized that I was living an uprooted succulent life: surviving, but in no way thriving. I was bedraggled and struggling.

To deal with the stress, Luke took up triathlon training with a buddy for six months. I'll admit, at face value, it seemed like a healthier coping mechanism than mine of eating peanut butter and chocolate chips off a spoon after the kids were in bed, but in the end, it was *his* healthy outlet that nearly killed him.

The day came for Luke's race. As the kids and I dropped him off at the staging area, the temperature was already reaching record-breaking heat. We wished him luck. Around the time we anticipated he'd finish, we gathered by the finish line to cheer for Luke as he completed the final leg in his triathlon. But he never made it. Luke collapsed, unconscious, minutes away from where we were waiting.

Though my insides were racing, I calmly made arrangements for a family friend to meet me in the hospital parking lot as I followed the ambulance. We switched keys as she took the kids home in my minivan and I walked through the automated doors that opened to the ER. The doctor pulled me aside. "We almost lost him in the ambulance," he explained. Almost *lost* him? Luke hadn't suffered dehydration—he had hydrated the whole race and took his normal glucose packets in addition to his prerace nutrition. Instead, he suffered from "exertional heatstroke." His internal body temperature had risen so high that his muscles, heart, lungs, and liver began to shut down and release deadly toxins. In such cases, the central nervous system shuts down out of self-protection.

I was told this was a "wait and see" situation to assess whether there was any long-term neurological impairment.

"Mrs. Goble, are there any external stressors in your home?" the doctor asked me.

I gave a slight nod. I felt numb. *Where to begin?*

The doctor said he'd be back shortly and pulled the curtain back for me to go in. Luke was lying on a metal table, naked, eyes closed, packed in ice, with tubes and wires everywhere. I immediately wriggled my hand into his and stared at him. My mind was frozen, unable to take in the contrast between the children munching on granola bars, eagerly awaiting him at the finish line just thirty minutes before, and now seeing him here with his eyes closed and machines beeping. As ice melted off the table, it dripped to create puddles on the tile floor by my feet.

I just stood there staring at his face. After what seemed like an eternity, he opened his eyes. They squinted hard at me and then, without moving his head an inch, frantically followed the shape of a rainbow, scanning the ceiling of the room from one side to another.

"Where . . . . . . am . . . . . . I?" The pauses were so long between words it was as if he were retrieving each of them individually from a dusty filing cabinet in his mind.

Because he asked me the question painstakingly slowly, I thought I would answer in kind.

"You . . . . . . are . . . . . . in . . . . . . the . . . . . . hospital, ... my love."

"Am . . . . . . I . . . . . . going . . . . . . to . . . . . . be . . . . . . okay?"

I truly didn't know the answer to that question, but I

instinctively said, "Yes, Luke, ... you . . . . . . are . . . . . . going . . . . . . to . . . . . . be . . . . . . okay."

A few tears spilled down his cheek. Though my exterior showed calm, my inside was rattled.

It didn't take long for our community to start pouring in, praying in the waiting room and standing with us, watching Luke manage a few words before drifting in and out of sleep. When I got home around midnight, a friend who had driven across town with wine and ice cream was there to sit with me and our babysitter.

Five days later, all five of the kids went with me to pick up Luke. We huddled around him and walked him slowly to the car. The doctor's orders were still ringing in my ears: Get plenty of sleep at night, rest during the day, and keep the stimulation low.

The doctor clearly had never been to our house.

I kept plugging through the next tumultuous week, head down, determined to keep our household flowing with as much normalcy as possible for the kids. But once Luke was home, and his follow-up appointments and tests showed he was going to eventually make a full recovery, I felt the rush of sheer and utter exhaustion in the marrow of my bones. Also, once Luke's speech cadence was completely back to normal, he was able to teasingly share with me that it was frustrating that I talked to him at a snail's pace. He could, in fact, keep up with comprehension, despite his measured, deliberate words as he lay on the table packed in ice.

Our friends, family, faith community, and countless staff from our foster care agency rallied around our family.

They paraded through our house, stuffed our fridge with food, gave us hugs and words of encouragement, and hired a much-appreciated house cleaner. In our deepest moments of vulnerability, we were upheld by generosity, lavished with encouragement, and rooted in interconnection.

In a short season, we were hit with taking an unexpected educational detour for our oldest daughter, saying yes for the second time to folding Elias into our family, experiencing tension with Jennifer, processing a daunting diagnosis, and almost losing Luke on the ambulance ride to the hospital. Amidst my weariness, there was a reverent awareness of how life can pivot in a flash, landing you smack-dab in the depths of the unexpected.

• • •

For the next seven months, I showed up for all court dates and every meeting where the foster parent was welcomed. Jennifer often called to talk with Elias, and after they talked, she and I would connect briefly. Our conversations were more formal than they had been previously, when we let Jennifer borrow our car when we went out of town, for example, or when she sat beside us in church or came over to hang out over Sunday lunches.

One day, Luke and I picked up Jennifer from her clean and sober treatment center and took her to Red Robin for dinner. The purpose was for the three of us to sit face to face and discuss what went wrong, share our accompanying emotions, and talk about how to move forward in health and harmony. Tears streamed down Jennifer's face, just as they had years earlier when we sat together in a restaurant after Micah's plan was changed to adoption. Everything I had hoped would come out of that meal happened without our having to force it. Luke and I both listened, yet shared gently and directly, not sugarcoating the toll. It seemed apparent she had received intentional counseling focusing on the patterns that led her down this path. She expressed regret, earnestly apologized, and said she wanted our relationship to "go back to normal."

With my customary active hand motions, I expressed directly how we felt about her. "Jennifer, our love for you is here—" I said with my hand up above my head—"and always will be no matter what. But we will need to slowly rebuild trust because our trust in you is here," I added, lowering my hand to the table.

"I know you guys love me," she said, wiping her eyes with a napkin.

We walked out of that restaurant two hours later reconciled with a mutual feeling that "things are far from perfect, but our family is back on track." Shortly afterward, while Elias was still in foster care with us, we began inviting Jennifer back into the sacred space of our home.

Nine months after Elias came to us, I stood up in court and gave my last update to the judge. This time I didn't feel downtrodden or experience a sudden rush of emotion walking into court. The judge asked to speak with me privately in his chambers afterward. He acknowledged that our situation was "unique" to see from the bench: a foster mom turned adoptive mom turned relative foster parent, continuing to engage with the same biological mom over the span of eight years with two boys and three separate cases. A few weeks later, it was ruled that five-and-a-half-year-old Elias would live with Jennifer.

Jennifer now had stable housing connected to the treatment facility where she could live with Elias. They were attending counseling together. Things looked promising. They both expressed excitement about being reunited.

As I've done for all the kids who are in my home longer than a few days, I made Elias a photo album, but this wasn't for a goodbye, just a farewell to this particular season. We are *family* and I will be his Auntie forever.

As Elias and I talked about the upcoming transition, he'd crawl into my lap or give me a spontaneous hug. It was hard to know how he'd respond the day he moved back with his mom.

When the day arrived, Luke and I put his belongings in the trunk of the car, the kids lined up in the driveway, and each one gave Elias hugs or high fives. He was unusually quiet on the fifteen-minute ride across town, holding his photo album in his lap. As we passed exits on the freeway, an earnest voice from the car seat behind me piped up. "Auntie, I've just got one question and that question is: Who will keep me safe?"

I took a deep breath and with tired hope and cautious enthusiasm, I said that the judge decided that his mom was safe and healthy enough now for him to live with her. "Keeping kids safe is one job of being a parent, but Auntie and Papa, your teacher, and your doctor also have the job of making sure you're safe, too, because we all care about you."

When we pulled into the driveway of her apartment, Jennifer was waiting for us outside. Elias got out of the car and immediately wrapped his arms around her in a tight hug. As Jennifer excitedly showed Elias their shared room, I unloaded his belongings. I got a quick tour of the new place, then hugged them both goodbye.

There were 287 days between Jennifer backing out of my driveway with Elias and me backing out of her driveway after returning him to her. A lot of life had been lived between those two significant driveway milestones. Elias was returned to Jennifer's care on July 7, 2016. This date felt significant to Jennifer because July 7, 2011, was the day we returned him to her at her treatment facility as an infant. There had been a *lot* of life lived between those two foster care milestones with Elias, and an undeniable amount of twists and turns in life since first telling Jennifer I was rooting for her in the spring of 2009.

This long season had stretched me and reminded me to my core that pouring into others isn't a zero-sum game. Zest and a can-do attitude has to flow from somewhere. There is no flow when the river of energy, margin, and capacity upstream is dry. I had been surviving on air. I was eager to say goodbye to this season.

I needed to remember how to be rooted in down-to-earth practical ways.

• • •

I'm far from having it all figured out. Although I firmly believe that we are made for more than just surviving, there are times when simply putting one foot in front of the other can be a holy act. Hoping to do more than merely survive life means realistically assessing what we need in order to sustain ourselves. That starts with an honest acknowledgment of what we've endured and all we're currently holding.

Rachel Naomi Remen writes about this in her book *Kitchen Table Wisdom: Stories That Heal*:

The expectation that we can be immersed in suffering and loss daily and not be touched by it is as unrealistic as expecting to be able to walk through water without getting wet. This sort of denial is no small matter. The way we deal with loss shapes our capacity to be present to life more than anything else. The way we protect ourselves from loss may be the way in which we distance ourselves from life. . . . We burn out not because we don't care but because we don't grieve.

Because I don't want to live in denial and because I hope to inch closer to thriving rather than surviving, here are a few small practical ways I've found personally helpful to keep me aligned: I keep a five-year journal by my bed, a few lines written every night to help me remember the sacred and the ordinary mixed together in the daily. I fill up my water bottle with ice every morning; I take it with me in the car and keep it on my desk during the day. I write in a gratitude diary. I keep a personal paper calendar and a huge monthly family calendar on the fridge and intentionally write *only* in pencil. It's symbolic of the flexibility needed to navigate our days in addition to the practicality of everyone being able to see their upcoming games and appointments without asking me "when" questions.

Silence and solitude do not come naturally to my personality, nor do they come naturally to my household, but they are essential to my thriving. I meet with a counselor. I have recently started getting acupuncture and massage. I see a chiropractor not just once a decade as a fluffy extra, but as part of my remaining rooted. When I walk alone, my prayers intertwine with my steps. When I walk with friends, there's often nonstop gabbing. Both kinds of walks fill my cup. If I'm headed somewhere with the kids or casually meeting family or friends, knowing there's much that can go awry, I always give myself a fifteen-minute window rather than an exact time. It cuts down on sending the proverbial "**Running 10 minutes late**" texts.

Sometimes thriving looks like carving out early Saturday mornings to have an intentional coffee date with Luke, even when that means pulling up chairs to the same table we sit at every day and pouring our coffee into the same mugs. This in-home connection is actually something I look forward to in the humdrum of normalcy to stay bonded. It's a way to "carpe diem" our time together while our youngest is on the iPad and our older kids are still sleeping. This simple, no-frills weekend rendezvous in this particular season of life helps us connect relationally and avoid becoming business partners navigating logistics with the kids.

I have a solid evening wind-down routine that involves my bathtub and a book. Luke often reads in his overstuffed chair in the corner of our bedroom, and this shared late-night silence is my personal picture to accompany the definition of comfortable coziness. Consistent sleep is something I didn't have for a very long time with Charlie, so I underrated it for years, but sleep is undeniably a part of anyone's thriving and something about which I'm increasingly mindful. While I can write in a journal, talk with the counselor, take a walk outside, and sit in the tub, it's foundational sleep that affords me the ability to notice what I'm feeling, acknowledge the struggle, remember that I'm human, and talk to myself in the way I would compassionately engage a friend. In addition to sleep, there is also the notion of rest beyond simply sleeping.

Dr. Saundra Dalton-Smith talks about the importance of various types of rest. There is *spiritual rest*, which includes prayer, meditation, and being in a community where you feel wholly accepted for who you are. There is *emotional rest* in having authentic, truthful connections with people you trust. There is *social rest* in being mindful of how relationships affect you on the continuum from life-draining to life-giving. There is *sensory rest* with things as simple as lying down in a quiet, dark room, turning devices off, and being mindful of the constant glare of your computer screen. There is *mental rest*, such as doing a brain dump on paper to avoid your thoughts pinging around when your head hits the pillow. And there is *creative rest*, feeling restored by taking in beauty in nature, walking around an art museum, making something, playing an instrument, writing—anything that awakens you to wonder.

Still, even when we're intentional about practices that nourish us, they may not be enough to overcome our innate wiring and/or environmental stressors. We may still feel like a bedraggled succulent living on air and not flourishing in soil. While succulents can adapt to less-than-ideal conditions, we may need help overcoming the harsh environment of our day-to-day reality.

Faith and shame can spin some intricate tangly webs, and I've witnessed one that says someone who takes a pill to help with anxiety or depression makes their faith journey less-than, because you can't believe in God and believe in scientific medicine simultaneously. Hogwash! There's zero shame in taking doctor-prescribed meds—I personally have done so in a season, knowing that along with nutrition and exercise, it's an extra toehold that can increase my capacity to continue climbing to the best of my ability when the slope of life feels particularly steep.

• • •

When Elias rebonded with his mom, he initially expressed fear about coming to our house again. If he came over, would his mom still be at the apartment when he got back? In the past, our house represented fun. Now it represented trauma and separation. The first few times we picked up Elias, he became anxious about his mom and wanted to check on her right away, worried she might not be there when he got back. We adapted to the brief visits—he'd walk in our house, stay for a few minutes, and then promptly walk back out, asking us to drive him home. Within a few months, however, he became confident enough to know he could spend time with us *and* go home to a mother who was waiting for him.

Many years later, a new kid in the neighborhood came into our backyard on a December afternoon to bounce on our trampoline. Elias was there, too, and she looked at him, as if this were her backyard, and asked pointedly, "Who are you?"

Without skipping a beat, Elias pointed to me and said, "I was her foster kid. And my brother lives here. She adopted him."

Since we never use the term "foster kid," I was surprised to hear Elias describe himself that way.

"And who else am I to you, Elias?" I said playfully.

"My auntie!" he enthusiastically exclaimed, beaming with that smile I adore.

Jennifer and her two older teenagers were inside our warm house celebrating an early Christmas dinner with our family. Micah swung back and forth on the tree swing near the trampoline. Elias and I held hands as we steadied ourselves in the middle of the trampoline. We started bouncing up and down, jumping in rhythm. We collapsed in a crumpled heap when we got off balance and then got right back up and continued to jump. It was the perfect picture to illustrate the past decade of Jennifer and me figuring out how to do life together.

With all the chaos, hurt, and anger that had existed between us, having Jennifer and all her kids around my dining room table has been one of the purest forms of hard-fought joy I've ever known. "Joy is the most infallible sign of the presence of God."

After dinner, we gathered in the living room, and Jennifer handed me a wrapped gift. Inside the box was a glass tea-light candleholder with these words written on it:

The Best and Most Beautiful Gift Is Family

Not surprisingly, the tea-light candleholder was broken in a Nerf football incident in the kitchen shortly afterward. But the small glass square containing those words was still intact against all odds. Jennifer and I, despite it all, were still leaning *toward* one another, and not away. If you ever come to my house, you'll see the piece of glass with that phrase tucked in the pot of a succulent on my windowsill, reminding me of the gift of family.

13

FAMILY TOGETHERNESS

Impact

THE FIRST TIME WE WENT TO the movie theater as a family, Charlie happened to be obsessing about exercise bungee cords and cramming countless items of utmost importance into his Dora the Explorer suitcase. The cargo pants he was wearing offered extra storage for a Christmas ornament bulb that he shoved halfway down a side pocket because that's as far as it would go. Before leaving, we had drawn a visual about going to the movies so Charlie would better understand what to expect.

And yet, when we pulled into the parking spot he refused to get out of the car. Once he changed his mind, he walked into the theater with the exercise bungee cord tied around his waist and his Dora suitcase dragging on its side six feet behind him. Leaving both items in the car was a deal breaker. We held our heads high as we all walked into the theater. Luke clasped Charlie's hand and I following behind them like the truck with blinking lights trailing the oversized load, warning people not to pass, or in our case, not to trip.

Halfway through the movie, with his suitcase full of treasures stacked up on his lap, Charlie loudly declared, "I'm done," slid off the big leather seat, and promptly walked down the steps and around the corner toward the hallway, his little suitcase of treasures thumping behind him. In an instant, I caught up to him, and the two of us spent the rest of the movie wandering around the lobby, Charlie delightfully unaware of people staring.

I knew the next time we headed to the movies things had to be different. Charlie would stay at home with his aide, enjoying being able to play and do what he wanted to do, rather than having his will bent to sit still for a movie.

I appreciate watching a movie without distractions as much as the next person, yet it does not feel good to me to do "family time" when one of the family members is missing. I know that leaving Charlie is sometimes what is best for him—and best for the rest of us—but I wrestle with the heart paradox that being healthiest sometimes means family togetherness without Charlie. It's a tricky family tension I feel acutely.

This afternoon, Luke, Sophia, Eleni, Micah, and I settle in the comfortable theater seats with buckets of popcorn to share and watch the movie *Wonder*. It's about Auggie, a boy born with a severe facial deformity, and the ways in which his parents and older sister, Olivia, also navigate their lives in a world where people don't often know how to interact with Auggie. The story picks up when he's mid-elementary-school age, the same age as our Charlie. His parents have devoted a significant portion of their lives to helping Auggie overcome his challenges and engage life. As Olivia watches her mom paint a scene of outer space, she narrates in her mind:

"Auggie is the sun, and our whole family orbits around him."

This line strikes deep within me and breaks me open.

I instantly have tears rolling down my cheeks that won't stop falling.

Tears of unnamed expectations for family life that have fallen by the wayside.

Tears that I can have this afternoon with my older three children.

Tears that they have to duck flying objects and are regularly exposed to Charlie's screaming.

Tears of how Charlie's smile and leg-slapping chuckle bring such life to a room.

Tears for the way my older children have learned to tiptoe on eggshells around such an unpredictable sibling.

Tears for all the daily things of life that are the equivalent of walking down the sidewalk for typical children and are like climbing a mountain for Charlie.

Tears for the ways all of us sitting in the theater with the screen glowing off our faces are liaisons for Charlie in a world full of people who do not see his invisible disability, nor do they understand.

Tears because if I were not living it, I wouldn't have

the capacity to truly understand Fetal Alcohol Spectrum Disorder either.

Tears because our kids do not get an evenly sliced piece of the "parents attention pie" to gobble up for themselves.

Tears because I think our kids might voice the same sentiment as Auggie's sister, only substituting a name:

Charlie is the sun, and our whole family orbits around him.

I know the story line I *hope* my kids will have about the selflessness and tenacity they learned through growing up with Charlie. I also know I don't get the luxury of crafting the narrative lens through which they view their childhood and their youngest brother. This isn't a single "event." This isn't a "Do you remember that one time . . . ?" story to be told around the dinner table in decades to come. This is a family striving to remain balanced with a family member whose unique wiring can easily tip us off-kilter, through no fault of his own.

This is *our life*.

• • •

In her original seventh-grade poem "Raised by a Mess," my daughter Sophia portrays our family well. She describes us belting out Broadway tunes in the kitchen, having family dance parties, and dealing with screaming children. The poem concludes:

> *I was raised by Games that I can't ever stop playing*
> *Books that can be read over and over again*
> *Music that keeps my heart going daily*
> *Togetherness my dream for the world*

Annoyances that will fade away as the years go by
Memories that will last forever
I was raised by that kind of mess.

Eleni, my second oldest, is the one who tapes schedules and charts to our kitchen cabinets and by her own volition, reviews sight words on cards with Charlie to help his reading. He usually enjoys playing school with her for a bit and then will suddenly throw the cards or start screaming, "You're so stupid, Eleni," at the first sign of frustration. Even with this, Eleni is not deterred from lovingly coming up alongside him the next day and saying, "You want to play school, Charlie?"

Regularly, Micah faithfully chooses to get out of bed when Charlie wakes him up before dawn with an urgent request to build a specific LEGO creation. When a child struggles with making and maintaining friendships and you see his siblings modeling faithful friendship, it is tangible, silky grace.

Now obviously my children are not always cherubs, but when someone is sentimental in a movie theater, you don't ruin the moment. Charlie with his invisible disability has given our family a lens through which to see what other families go through in their moments of triumph and struggle.

When we walked out of the theater, my face was sufficiently red and puffy. *Auggie is the sun, and our whole family orbits around him* looped again and again through my mind. As we drove home, I invited instant feedback from our children about how things were going in our household, asking how I could be more intentional with them, eager to hear how I could do things differently and better. I could easily rattle off a long list of things I could improve to up my game of intentionality and to assure them they are loved, no matter what. But I wanted to hear what they thought.

They told me one by one they're okay, two of them even using the adjective *well*. I started to softly doubt, "Really? You're well? With all we have going on day by day under the roof of our home, you'd say you're *well*?"

Luke reached over and said, "Babe, just believe what your children are telling you." He held my hand the rest of the way home.

I struggle to accept our family dynamics that whirl around unpredictability instead of falling into a soft acceptance. I can sometimes surrender myself to the lie that if I could just handle things better, life might look different. But then I hear my inner voice say, *Stop striving and just be*.

I look at my children's faces and embrace what they declared: At this moment, we are *well*.

• • •

A year after Elias was returned to Jennifer, he was at our house for lunch, slumped down dejectedly in his chair, munching on a quesadilla. "Auntie," he said, "Micah has Charlie, but I'm his *real* brother, right?"

This was similar to a conversation Micah had initiated with me about Elias a few weeks earlier as he attempted to rollerblade for the first time. I steadied Micah by holding onto his elbow as he tried to keep from falling on the sidewalk. His jerky movements seemed to mirror the pattern of questions he was asking about who was "real" to who in our family. He got to the heart of the matter: If people are officially related, does that make them more real? Do siblings come with two tiers—siblings and *real* siblings?

As I let go of his elbow and now firmly gripped Micah's hand, his arms flailing to keep balance, I provided the technical terms of *full siblings, half siblings,* and *adoptive siblings.* He has all of them.

"Do you have all of them?" he asked me earnestly.

"I have two out of the three. The most important thing, though, bud," I said with a reassuring smile, "is not the specific title but that we really love each other."

Later that night, Micah and I read *The Velveteen Rabbit* aloud together before bed. In the classic children's story, the Velveteen Rabbit was so loved he started looking shabby, with his hair loved off and his eyes dropping out, but author Margery Williams writes,

Once you are Real, you can't become unreal again. It lasts for always.

Several months later, nine-year-old Micah was meeting with the mentoring program director in our home. This is the mentoring program I signed him up for when he was eight, in an attempt to wrap stabilizing support around him as he torpedoed downhill emotionally when Elias was in foster care and sharing a room with Micah. When the opportunity arose, I wasn't going to pass up the chance to have more caring adults in his life, just because that particular season had passed. In his getting-to-know-you interview, he was asked how many siblings he has and to draw a picture of his family.

"I have *three* sisters and *three* brothers."

As I stood in the kitchen doing the dishes while they worked nearby at the kitchen table, I turned my head at his answer. What he said was totally accurate: Under the roof of our home, he has two sisters and a brother; but he also has Elias and two older half siblings, who often join us during the holidays. I had never heard him include his siblings outside our home before.

If Micah had given that answer before I started walking this relational road with Jennifer, it would have made me feel uncomfortable, perhaps even petrified, as if including his other family threatened to undermine my standing as a mom. At that time I didn't know anyone who was walking this same road, and I'd never seen it modeled. But now, I was appreciative of his answer.

I was grateful Micah was comfortable and confident enough to express his story, the narrative of our two families and our untraditional blending. Grateful that Jennifer and I have built a bridge with no blueprint—rickety at times, no doubt, but it's held us and allowed us to walk alongside one another for thirteen years and counting. Elias and Micah are growing up with a more integrated story. From the very beginning and at each developmental stage along the way, we'd built upon the framework, never shying away from what's real.

One memory of integrating his experience that lives in infamy was a dialogue Micah initiated with Jennifer when he was four years old. Our family invited Jennifer and Elias for dinner at Olive Garden to celebrate her one year of sobriety.

As we were waiting to be served, Micah was coloring his paper place mat. He stopped and looked at Jennifer intensely and said, "Hey Jennifer, ya know something?"

"What, bud?"

"Did you know that I came out of your tummy?"

"I did," she said simply with a sly smile. "I was there."

"Oh!" was Micah's earnest reply as he resumed coloring.

After his mentorship interview, years of conversations between Micah and me flooded my mind, especially the questions he'd asked while processing his story. *Why was I in foster care? Why do I live with you and not my other brother?* I looked at his paper where he had drawn his family. Everyone from both families was included and integrated in the picture. Underneath, in small, neat handwriting, was the finishing touch:

And we are all real.

14

COME AS YOU ARE

Friendship

I HAD STAYED IN CONTACT WITH TERESA, the fellow teacher and native Guatemalan whom I lived and worked with at the compound in her country. A few months after we had started at the orphanage together, she received a surprise letter in English from Andy, an American carpenter who had visited the orphanage and met her.

"Jillana, could you read the letter to me in Spanish?" Teresa asked.

"Of course."

The letter wasn't long, and Andy got right to the point: Meeting Teresa had been the highlight of the entire trip for him. As I translated his words, Teresa blushed and smiled. When I finished, she asked if I would translate her Spanish reply into English, then she eagerly typed it to him on the communal computer available to us and pressed Send.

The next day he replied, and I found Teresa giddily hopping around our small trailer waiting for me to tell her what Andy said. Between teaching, grading, hanging out with the girls in my trailer, doing regular lice checks, and translating ever-increasing lovey-dovey letters between Teresa and Andy, she and I shared some late-night conversations.

Fast-forward two years. Andy and Teresa got married and moved to Washington State. For their honeymoon, they took a long road trip down the West Coast, stopping in San Francisco to see Luke and me. Teresa still was learning English so when they were leaving, Andy asked, "Could you tell Teresa we should be at Disneyland in about eight hours?" I was happy to help. Teresa happily announced her pregnancy to me shortly afterward.

Several months later, Andy called me from the hospital, anxious and distraught. He had rushed Teresa there because she was bleeding. She had miscarried. "Teresa doesn't believe it. She insisted I call you. Could I put you on speakerphone so you can hear what the doctor is saying and then translate it for her?"

I was coming home from a long day of teaching on the crowded N Judah train in San Francisco that was noisily jostling down the tracks. It was not an ideal environment for a sensitive conversation. I cupped my hand around my mouth and spoke with Teresa as gently as I could. She mournfully squeaked out a "thank you" and said something that stuck with me long after I hung up the phone.

"Sometimes something you know in your head just needs to be spoken to your heart through the voice of a friend."

•   •   •

Friends speaking truth can be comforting or stinging. I am continually learning how to gracefully let go of the notion that life should look like a conveyor belt, especially when it comes to the stereotypical ages and stages of family life, like older siblings babysitting younger siblings, for example. A simple innocent sentence is voiced over lunch by a trusted college friend: "Isn't life easier now that our oldest kids can be left home every once in a while to care for our youngest?" It stings me unexpectedly. That typical reality might never be my reality. Discouragement lies in wait, ready to slither and hiss in my ear, "You're moving backward, Jillana, while everyone else is moving forward. It's getting easier for them but not for you."

When these times come, and they do often in various settings, I try not to simply nod and falsely agree, "Yep, totally getting easier." That might keep the conversation going, but it just isn't true. My friends deserve the whole me, the real me. I am learning to share my truth so that shame can't whisper, "Isolation! You're the only one!" It's a dance to authentically acknowledge my reality while speaking of things unrelatable to theirs. There are times when it's appropriate to have all eyes, all ears, all hands on deck in terms of support and focus when a friend is in a particular crisis. I've done that for friends, and friends have done that for me, but there's extra discernment required for those of us whose life circumstances majorly stray from the typical path of what, when, and how much to share.

In the midst of COVID, I was part of a group of eight women who found refuge in our friend Missi's garage. For the first few months of the pandemic, we brought our own lawn chairs and sat apart in her driveway, eager for a rare in-person connection. Right after our first driveway session, Missi was diagnosed with aggressive breast cancer. Although we were keeping in touch via obnoxiously long group texts, we were more determined than ever to meet each month to hear Missi's updates in person and to cherish the time spent in company with friends. Some of us had been good friends for years and others were newer in establishing connections, but with all of us having foster care or adoption as part of our parenting background, there was a certain amount of "I get it" without having to go into details. Our conversations usually revolved around various aspects of parenthood, partnerships, and all the endless rabbit trails branching from those subjects. Missi, who wore a knit cap on her bald head, added an extra level of awareness of the fragility of everything we talked about, griped about, or laughed about.

When winter came and the temperature dropped, we could no longer meet outside in the driveway. So Missi designated her garage as our safe haven, a part of it temporarily furnished with a rug, old couches, and side tables. We all agreed Missi's garage had officially received "college dorm status," as we gathered and practiced pandemic protocol, bringing cups of tea from our own kitchens. We affectionately referred to ourselves as the "Garage Crew." Surrounded by tools, bikes, and bags for Goodwill, it was cozy, inviting, and warm because of the sense of belonging and space for truth-telling.

When I was talking with my parents, who have nearly seven decades of experience in friendship—including relationships with several couples they've journeyed with closely through four decades of life—they reflected that friends accept you as you are, but they also push you. My mom, sitting next to my dad and me around the kitchen table, said, "Friendships can be comfortable, but they can also be stretching, and good friends are often both. They value and show interest in you for you, not for what you have. Friends never approach you with a 'What am I gonna gain here?' perspective."

Loneliness is universal; it was around long before social media, and sometimes we have to be the ones to take the initiative in this simultaneously complex yet simple thing called friendship. We must put ourselves in the position to have friends. Taking another sip of his coffee, my dad quoted the old adage, "If you wanna have a friend, be a friend."

• • •

Today's social media world presents both opportunities and hurdles to a sense of belonging. Through social media, we can potentially encourage one another, share our love of common interests, and perhaps feel less alone. But a lot of the time, if we're not insanely intentional, social media exponentially does the opposite! Even using the word *friend* as a descriptor for the hundreds or thousands of folks who scroll through your life as you scroll through theirs dulls the vibrancy of the word. Social media, while it can be a force for good, puts brittle popularity on a pedestal. It can change the way we see ourselves in relation to others—our "friends"—when we have a steady stream of their highlight reel juxtaposed against our less glamorous reality. Scrolling is a primary hurdle I set myself up to trip over when what I really need is silence or solitude or, best of all, authentic connection.

And more often than not, social media only makes me more lonely.

It's amazing how people who went to the same elementary school can find one another decades later. I was in my late thirties when I accepted a "friend" request from Jade.

I was in fifth grade when I met Jade and a new group of girls. They were the "cool" girls who wore Guess brand acid-washed jeans with the triangle on the back pocket, the ultimate sign of eighties "in" fashion in California. On the school playground, hurdles had been set up. I still have no idea why track hurdles were set up on the asphalt instead of on the grass, but there they were. Jade, the ringleader of the cool girls, breezily said, "Those hurdles look so easy!" and her squad chimed in, "Yeah. Totally." I muttered, "Totally" too.

Suddenly, Jade declared, "Let's run hurdles!" I watched as she ran, easily clearing them. Then the other girls started lining up, and Jade called each one by name to do what she had done. They all effortlessly floated above the hurdles. As I watched and listened, I realized they were all on the school track team. I was not. But I was tall, and I had watched the Olympics, so when my name was called, I lined up because, come on, how hard could this *really* be?

The answer was brutally clear as I hit the first hurdle, fell on the pavement, scraped my chin, and knocked the wind out of myself. When I picked myself up, I acted tough and shrugged it off like it was no big deal, fighting back tears. I don't recall if those girls said anything to me, either kind or disparaging. I only remember silence.

My only other memory of cool Jade was the following year, when we were placed next to each other to sing the quintessential elementary-school graduation song "Lean on Me." In the world of social media, we're "friends," but even in the real world several decades earlier, it was hazy.

• • •

Today I woke up, and before I even turned on a light or exited my bedroom, I felt like I'd had the wind knocked out of me. What happened actually wasn't so out of the ordinary. You see, Charlie cannot embrace paradox. If he tells one parent he loves them, he immediately turns around and tells the other he hates them. The whole concept of both/and is *not* his forte. Despite visual cues trying to teach him this, Charlie is unable to grasp that you can express love to two people simultaneously. Luke and I are well-accustomed to the unpredictability of Charlie's verbal affections and afflictions bobbing up and down multiple times per day.

This morning, he tiptoed into our room to serenely crawl into bed with us for a few minutes. He held out his arm for me to massage it as he's prone to do, and I obliged. I heard him sweetly and gently call out, "Love you, Dad," and then, as if he was shouting at a moving train, I was walloped with a forceful "HATE YOU, MOM!"

This isn't head-shaking. This normally isn't something that consciously fazes me most days because I hear it often, but this morning at 6:30 a.m., I am *done*. Over it. Can't deal with it. I am irritated and deflated.

Still, I went about the things called for in my day that I simply had to do, and let any extra fall by the wayside. I sent this text to two trusted friends in New York:

Not his fault his brain misfires, but I'm allowing myself to just be sad today—to take a walk in the sunshine and try to accompany the grief instead of rush it away.

Then I called a friend whose child experiences the same disability. "Lean on Me" is the anthem of our friendship. There's nothing she can do to fix my situation, but she listens to me as I did for her last week. She allows me to simmer my own pot of tear soup and express deep breaths and heavy sighs as I walk up and down our neighborhood sidewalks. Over the years, she has entered my home, stepping on my "Come as you are" doormat more times than I can count.

As I fix us coffee and we sit on my couch, my eye turns to the bag of coffee beans which proclaims, "Notes of sweetness, paired with complex acidity, all coming together in a satisfying cup." I can't help but notice that our "Come as you are" friendship is a significantly sweet sip of life's inevitable acidity. We share circular giggles and struggles and so much of the mundane in-between. Having a loving friend increases your endurance.

• • •

"Have you seen your son lately?" I ask Renee as we walk uphill, the Portland rain not slowing us down as it beads on our coats. Her oldest child, who is my age, has had a long journey with mental illness and substance abuse. For the past few years, Renee and her husband have gathered around our table in a regular rhythm, and we've collectively sighed with them in hope and heartache. A few Christmases ago she was lifting up sleeping bags on Portland's downtown city sidewalks looking for her son. Then he got into treatment and was doing well, with mental wellness and sobriety aligning to bring him to a higher capacity to engage life. But mental health and addiction is a precarious combination.

Renee puts together brown sack lunches for the homeless every week and passes them out on Wednesdays. She always hopes to see her son, but even when she doesn't, this is her love offering to him and to God. As we round the corner on our walk, she tells me that before last week, she hadn't seen him in months. She couldn't help but wonder if he was still on this earth.

"How do you know even where to begin to look?" I ask.

Renee says she listens for a still small voice inside to literally guide her bicycle at every intersection in downtown Portland, where tents and tarps are stretched out in every direction. Her voice lights up when she tells me she saw him this past week, and he allowed her to hold eye contact with him for a while, and they talked for a few minutes. She was grateful he took her brown bag offering and then at his urging, she moved along.

"Does this give you hope that you'll see him again next week?"

As we huff up the incline of a steep sidewalk, she turns and says, "Whenever I receive flowers or a box of chocolates from someone, I'm delighted and enjoy them. But I don't expect gifts every week."

Father Greg Boyle writes:

The ancient Desert Fathers, when they were disconsolate and without hope, would repeat one word, over and over, as a kind of soothing mantra. And the word wasn't "Jesus" or "God" or "Love." The word was "Today." It kept them where they needed to be.

Renee holds the tension; she faces the daily toll of the unknown without crumbling and still shows up to offer what she has. Of course, she wishes her story were different, but it doesn't change her commitment to living the one before her. I'm in awe of her treasuring the mere knowledge that her son is alive, a reality so many would consider scraping the bottom of the barrel of expectations, let alone receive as a gift. This is not a grown-up version of playing the Pollyanna glad game. Renee is sure-footed. Each Wednesday Renee comes with her humble brown bags, gifts of food from her kitchen. She knows that if she's meant to see her son that day, she will. But even if Renee can't find her own grown child to bestow this love offering, she has an ever-present awareness that there is nourishment given to someone else's child, made in the image of God.

• • •

I met Samuel and Victory years ago, when I was teaching ESL at the International Institute in Buffalo, New York. I was teaching all levels of classes at the Institute, and on this day, I saw a couple and their baby in the front entrance looking a little dazed.

I was on break, so I went out and introduced myself. Samuel and Victory had just come from Sierra Leone. Samuel's English was extremely good, so I knew he would be in the advanced classes. Victory did not say a word. Their baby was wrapped in an oversized toddler coat with the sleeves tied around his tiny body and a doll-sized hat sitting atop his head, not covering his ears. Victory untied the sleeves to reveal her precious son, Maliki, who was wearing only a onesie in the middle of a New York winter. I just happened to have winter baby clothes at home that would fit him, so I got their address, which wasn't far from our house. I made arrangements to drop off the clothes.

When I arrived at their second-story, unfurnished apartment, I was taken aback at the living conditions. The kitchen floor was severely warped, sloping like a mountain range, making it tricky to keep your balance on one side without sliding toward the window. Paint was peeling everywhere. I willed myself not to stare as Victory invited me to sit with her on the floor and hold the baby. As we sorted through the clothes, she uttered a few timid English sentences such as "I like it" as she held up various articles of clothing. I smiled and responded, "I am happy you like it." Before I left, I invited Victory and Samuel to our house for dinner.

That first time at our house, Samuel was comfortable conversing, but Victory was tense. Yet we continued to have regular meals together, alternating between our place and theirs. One night in our living room, Samuel wondered aloud, "Do people have many friends in this country? When we walk in the neighborhood in the evening, no one else is outside. We just see them through their windows, watching television." We affirmed that the glow of TV screens is, indeed, in competition with genuine connection with our neighbors.

A year into our friendship, Samuel called. Victory's mother had passed away, and he asked if I could come. By this time, they were in a somewhat better apartment with a bit more furniture. When I walked in, Victory was on her knees wailing, facedown in the living room with her hands outstretched as far as they could go, her pregnant belly touching the floor. There was something so sacred about her strong outpouring of emotions as her fingertips reached out as if to grasp someone. In the back room, I heard the television blaring cartoons for her son. Victory never apologized for her emotional outburst and wept unabashedly. I sat there with the perky plant I brought sitting next to me, in a mostly empty living room. I wasn't able to comfort her in her native language. I knew nothing of her customs, yet I felt humbly comfortable sharing this space with her. We eventually shared a cup of tea, and she showed me the few photographs she had of her mother.

Years later as we made plans to move to Oregon, Samuel and Victory presented us with a parting gift. Their relatives had shipped clothes for us from their home city in Sierra Leone. Victory had me try on a maroon dress with gold lace edging the bodice. She wrapped my hair in a cloth that matched the dress. I have a photograph of Victory with me in my African dress, holding their daughter, Sally Jillana. (True confession: When I learned they chose the name Sally because they wanted to give their daughter a "real American name," I wondered if they thought it was popular from the overabundance of the name Sally in outdated ESL materials.) Sally Jillana, the strong and beautiful girl she is and who she will continue to be, has been shaped by the resilience of her parents, who carved a new path amidst the unknown. Their outpouring of undeserved friendship and goodness was reflected back to me tenfold from my simple act of noticing and saying hello.

· · ·

I picked up the phone at night and heard someone sobbing. My friend Barbara from college was having a miscarriage and her husband was out of town. I threw an oversized sweatshirt over my jammies and drove across town, thinking of Teresa's words spoken a decade earlier: "Sometimes something you know in your head just needs to be spoken to your heart through the voice of a friend."

I wasn't there to remind my friend that she had two sleeping children tucked in their beds down the hall, or that perhaps someday beauty would come from ashes. As we sat on the couch together, I was there to bear witness to the burning.

In the weeks that followed, I checked in with her as she sifted through the soot of her heartache. I have never personally experienced miscarriage. There are many women who could have connected with her with a deep firsthand knowledge of what she was experiencing. There would come a time in the future for seeking out the profound knowing that comes from someone else sharing a similar experience. In that moment, however, I couldn't do that for her, and I'd

never pretend to. Just as my friend can't relate to my life as
the parent of a child with intense special needs yet still listens
attentively during our last decade-and-a-half of lunch dates,
these differences have not hindered us in growing our friendship. When Barbara called, I could answer the phone, show
up, admit out loud there were no perfect words to say, and
offer to pray and be silent. Whatever she needed, we were
there *together*.

• • •

A few years later, I was at the hospital holding this same
friend's leg in the early morning hours as she pushed out a
baby girl on my thirty-fifth birthday!

Sometimes in life we are privy to a glorious version of
connect-the-dots on the continuum from hopes dashed to
hopes fulfilled! Many times, however, we are simply left to
embrace—or battle—the mystery. I have walked beside other
friends, equally emotional, equally prayerful, for different
matters in their lives that remain unanswered, tenuous at
best. Anne Lamott writes, "This is the most profound spiritual truth I know: that even when we're most sure that love
can't conquer all, it seems to anyway. It goes down into the
rat hole with us, in the guise of our friends, and there it
swells and comforts. It gives us second winds, third winds,
hundredth winds."

With the daily tug-of-war that pushes and pulls on our
time, our attention, and our focus, we need the relational gift
of invested friendship that comes easily in times of joy and
walks softly alongside us in times of sorrow. Friends seek to
understand life experiences and perspectives different from

our own. Friends step on our "Come as you are" doormats as they walk through our front doors and sit on our couches. Friends sit in freezing garages together huddled up in sleeping bags, not caring an iota about ambience, but craving connection.

Whether for a season or for the long haul, the truth that continually echoes throughout life is this: The world becomes more bearable with friends.

15

IN EVERY NEIGHBORHOOD

Grace

IT WAS 4:30 P.M. on a Friday when my cell phone rang. I answered and heard Emily's voice on the other end. I adore Emily. As a caseworker, she works hard, advocates fiercely, and speaks professionally.

With four kids, Luke and I don't regularly accept emergency foster care calls after business hours or on weekends. Our lives are full, and there are countless reasons to justify why saying yes to a child in short-term foster care is inconvenient. Yet we are not naive to the immense (and mostly invisible) need in our community, and so, as Luke and I looked at our calendar and we talked as a family, we decided that being on call the week the kids and I had off for Thanksgiving break was within our capacity. We officially said we'd be open to receive calls on Monday, but this call came right as I finished up work on Friday.

"We really need help," Emily said and proceeded to tell me about a toddler named Grace who had been waiting in a government office in my community for countless hours. This little one had never had a bed or any sort of sleeping schedule and was nonverbal. She needed a safe place for the weekend.

"Emily, when do you need to know?" I asked, eyeing the clock.

"Do you think you could get back to me in twenty minutes?"

As soon as I hung up, I called Luke, who gave his okay, and then I quickly huddled with my children to get their take. I gave Emily the answer in less than twenty minutes—*yes*. The kids immediately started working on a colorful "Welcome, Grace!" poster that we hung on the front door. The caseworker and Grace arrived at 6:00 p.m.

Within minutes of arriving in our house, Grace had cleared our bookshelves, dumped out toy bins, and was running around the room. When she stopped long enough to eat, she sat in a booster seat and pounded down a quesadilla, a serving of pasta, a banana, and two glasses of milk. I suspected food scarcity had been an issue in her previous household.

That evening, when I got out the pack 'n play to put in our bedroom and rocked her in a nearby chair, huge tears rolled down her cheeks as her eyes darted around the room. The caseworker had explained that Grace had been with her mom earlier in the day, then she spent half a day in a government office and now, suddenly, she was here. She couldn't ask questions verbally, but her body language and dark eyes screamed, "TRAUMA!" I sang to her, rocked her, and stroked her hair until she was in a deep sleep before gingerly laying her down. She slept for twelve straight hours!

It didn't take long to see that Grace was incredibly special. The daunting descriptions and high needs the social worker had told me about on the phone proved true in our first three days of getting to know one another. Yet, this girl had such an underlying softness to her. We started teaching her some basic words in sign language such as *more* and *please*, and she picked them up quickly. She had moments of tantrums and also moments of unexpected, loving arm pats. After a day filled with coloring pictures and copying how my girls twirled around the kitchen floor to classical music, her chubby arms raised like a ballerina, she fell asleep clutching her blankie with her fingers wrapped around my hand. Emily called and updated me. Despite many phone calls, she was still searching for another foster family to invite Grace into their lives. Grace was around our table for Thanksgiving, and we were privileged to have her.

By the end of the week, I could've easily filled a small journal on Grace's endearing qualities. For one thing, the girl was crazy about frozen waffles. Once Grace discovered that the Eggo waffles were kept in the bottom freezer drawer of the refrigerator she could pull open herself, she helped herself to them liberally and wanted nothing to do with them once they'd been toasted or buttered or given a side of syrup. She was of the firm belief that a girl shouldn't have to choose one pretty hair bow when five are available, insisting on rocking all of them at the same time. She loved having her teeth brushed with the battery-operated toothbrush that played the alphabet song. Her shoes and her jacket were her comfort attachment items—she wore them nearly all the time, the jacket zipped up to her chin. More than anything, she yearned to learn and soaked up positive affirmation like a sponge.

Every night when I rocked Grace to sleep, I prayed her future family would pour their time, love, and goodness into her to unravel her vast potential.

• • •

The juxtaposition of images in my mind range from the Grace who tried to gouge my eye with her fingers when I first picked her up to the Grace who wraps her arms around my neck, gently pressing her forehead against mine and nuzzling my nose, her big brown eyes staring into mine. In that moment, Grace's communication deficit doesn't seem hindering, because no language is needed to express tenderness.

Grace accompanied me to a child's birthday party over the weekend, quite possibly the first she'd ever attended. The theme? Superheroes.

Grace delightfully decorated her mask with gobs of glitter glue and sparkles. I thought about how this dear girl doesn't need someone who changes into tights, dons a cape, and has a secret identity. Grace needed an ordinary family who finds her *worthy* of their loving attention and would commit to her well-being for however long she was in foster care. The truth was that a government agency could not wave a magic wand for a caring family to show up for Grace. All our family could offer her was a temporary yes for a short amount of time, but our yes allowed divine grace to creep into the spaces of our ordinary, full lives.

People often throw out the *hero* word to describe foster parents, like candy tossed to the masses at a parade. We "heroes" can scoop up the accolades, open the wrappers, and devour the hero sugar, believing there's something special about us. After all, that is a much more alluring picture than ordinary people with strengths and weaknesses who get tired and cranky and just want to shut out the world sometimes.

Our alternative is to squarely confront the truth: We're no different from anybody else. It comes down to our willingness to see and respond. The hero hype doesn't empower. It only serves to disillusion others and sometimes even deceive ourselves. Authentic heroes would never use the word "hero" to describe themselves. Instead, they would confess they are ordinary people who put their one ordinary foot in front of their other ordinary foot and walk the path and do the next right thing. This rarely feels heroic or courageous.

For me, toddler Grace embodied courage, which the *Oxford English Dictionary* defines as "the ability to do something that frightens one" and "strength in the face of pain or grief."

Grace was the most vulnerable among us and had been placed with strangers because she wasn't kept safe by those meant to protect her. Grace never volunteered to be placed in the terrifying position of falling asleep in the room of a person she'd never met before, but voilà—here she was, showing courage.

Sometimes, like Grace, we are in positions where we have

no choice in the matter. Other times, we are asked a question and must give an answer. If courage is a characteristic that only heroes possess, then we are all doomed. But if courageous "heroes" keep walking toward a situation we find difficult or overwhelming—then there is potential there for all of us.

Courage and convenience do not go hand in hand. Fear and untimeliness drown out possibilities before we even ponder the answers, crowding out the possibility of being invited to engage a worthy inconvenience.

Worthy inconvenience invites us to embrace the tension in our own lives—between the significant and the ordinary—and move toward others focused on relationship and not rescue.

Worthy inconvenience compels us to be transformed by love, knowing we have infinitely more to learn from others than we could dare hope to teach.

As I strive to see the Imago Dei—the image of God—in all people, I realize that sometimes it is God who comes to us disguised as a worthy inconvenience.

• • •

The knock at the door on Monday morning came right on time as planned. I'd had a lump in my throat about it ever since I got the call on Friday. It was time to say goodbye to Grace.

She had been with us for nine days. When she arrived at our house, she was wearing a dress a bit too snug, a soggy diaper, and sparkly tennis shoes. Now, Grace was dressed in an adorable outfit with pink polka dots with matching pink dress shoes. Her favorite pink flower clips adorned her curly black locks, and her hair smelled like apples. She looked like she was ready for a professional portrait, not being transported back to the government office to await a foster family who would say yes to her and then be driven to their home.

How do you tell a three-year-old girl that there's a shortage of certified foster families available to welcome her in the state's most populated metro area because they are all at capacity?

As much as I wanted to reassuringly whisper to Grace, "It's okay, sweet girl," as I buckled her in the car seat, I looked into her dark brown eyes and didn't.

Because *nothing* about this is okay.

Instead, I kissed her forehead and said, "Goodbye, sweet girl."

I tell you about Grace not to heap motivating guilt on you. Emotional arm-twisting may work for the short term, but it is unsustainable for the long haul. I'd never encourage someone to wade into the waters of foster care without careful consideration, but it's imperative that you know this: If you swim upstream from any issue that negatively creates ripple effects on families—addiction, incarceration, domestic violence, untreated mental illness—and you ask yourself, "Where do children *go* when their parents suffer with these things and they have no safety net of people who can adequately care for their children?" the answer is not a mystery! It's foster care.

I tell you about Grace to share the reality that while foster parenting is not for everyone, it *has* to be for more people than are currently engaged with it! And while foster care is undoubtedly complex and many improvements need to be made, there's clarity when we focus on the one whose very life is dependent on having safe parents/caregivers. Children like Grace are all around us, whether we personally see and know them or not. Grace and children like her don't need a hero—they need a healthy and safe *someone* who will reach out, embrace them, and accompany them on life's path.

• • •

Grace, in her pretty dress, sat in the child welfare office for ten hours—*ten hours!*—before a foster home was secured for her. She left our home in the morning and later that evening, a certified foster family picked her up and welcomed her into their lives.

Years later, I spotted Grace riding a mechanical bull at the fairgrounds, her hand triumphantly in the air. Life circumstances had bucked her off a time or two, but her preschool-age spunky resilience was undeniably present. She didn't recognize me, but I certainly recognized her, the girl we had the honor of sheltering for a short time.

When our local newspaper ran a series on foster care, Grace's story was featured. While I was grateful for the spotlight shined on one child, the reality is, Grace's story is very much a nonstory. It's a nonstory because stories like Grace's—shuffling between houses, compounding family traumas, waiting for hours in government offices to be seen and said yes to—are everyday occurrences in the world of foster care.

Every. Single. Day.

There's a Grace in every neighborhood.

The Wednesday after Grace left us, I stood at the kitchen sink doing the dishes. I had a houseful of energetic kids who were running around, inside and outside, despite the low December temperatures. I was calling out, "Please close the door!" every seventeen seconds.

As I took inventory of the beautiful crew of kids bouncing on the trampoline in the backyard, I saw my four children—my two daughters and my two sons. Elias, the fifth child, was swaying on the rope swing. Jennifer was with me, sitting on a stool pulled up to the kitchen counter.

While drying a saucepan, I thought about how out of the two women in the house right now, one had grown up in foster care and was deeply affected by the experience. I realized that out of the five children playing in my backyard at that moment, three had been in foster care. And in that moment, I felt a burden that the real story behind the newspaper articles and attention about Grace is this simple, yet unknown truth:

There's a Grace in every neighborhood.

Children in foster care are in our children's classes, standing next to us in line at the grocery store, and walking down our street. If we will only open our eyes to see them. They are there.

My thoughts were interrupted by a soft knock at the front door.

A friendly looking man with a little girl was standing on our porch, both of them bundled up in their coats and mittens. I'd never seen them before. "I'm sorry to bother you like this," the man said, "but this little one is new to the neighborhood and when she saw the tree house and heard children in your backyard, she begged me to bring her over. We live just across the alley."

I welcomed them inside our entryway and shut the door.

"When did you move here?"

"My family and I have lived in the neighborhood for a long time," he said, but his family was privileged to welcome this girl recently. They were brand-new foster parents.

I smiled at the youngster and asked her age.

"I'm eight."

Then I asked, "Honey, what's your name?"

"My name," she replied confidently, "is Grace."

16

THE LONG GAME

Reconnection

A FEW MONTHS AFTER RETURNING Elias to Jennifer in 2016, I was enjoying a rare late-night moment of sitting on the couch without multitasking when I got an urgent sixth sense/ mama bear/Holy Spirit immanence. Where in the *world* was that first grader with the winsome, tooth-missing smile who walked through my door thirteen years ago? Where in the world was Royal?

On every new calendar, I had faithfully circled his summer birthday. I had occasionally worn that chipped Mother's Day ring. I had carried him in my heart all these years, and Luke had searched on and off with no results, but now I intuitively sensed the moment was here. I needed to find Royal that *very* instant. I got on Facebook and searched by name and location and two seconds later—*BOOM!* A photo popped up—an image of a young man staring back at me with bloodshot eyes, a pick in his Afro, holding a cigarette and bottle of liquor in one hand, and flipping off the camera with the other.

It was Royal.

I tilted my head slightly, squinted a bit, and studied the familiar eyes. He now had sideburns and some scruffy facial hair. He was no longer the little boy missing two teeth, grinning at me over the handlebars of the scooter he'd learned to ride in our driveway, but it was Royal. I was sure of it. I slowly inhaled and then my fingers flew across the keyboard.

> Royal, you've been strongly on my mind tonight. When
> I compare that face and smile, even 13 years later, I
> totally believe it's you! My husband, Luke, and I had you
> and Dion with us when you were in first grade. We have
> pictures of you baking brownies, riding your first bike,
> taking a trip with us to CA. We remember you as an
> amazing kid with a good heart who had so much adult
> stuff on his plate to deal with. Through no fault of your
> own and not through our choice, you moved on to a pre-
> adoptive home that fell through, and then to a group
> home for boys, where we still visited with you before you
> were gone one day. I tried several times to get in touch
> with you, but I hit dead ends. I have no idea if you even
> remember us, but you have a special spot in our heart.
> Take good care, Royal! I wish you the best. ~ Jillana

I pressed Send and snapped my laptop closed, my heart and mind feeling a bit jumbled. *Would he remember us?* In the morning, I turned on my phone and saw I had several missed calls via Facebook Messenger and this written message.

> OMG!!! You're still MY MOM!!! I've been searching for you my whole life!!! This feels like a dream. I've never forgotten about my family. It was the best thing that ever happened to me. I feel like crying right now.

Hours later Luke and I huddled around a speakerphone talking with him. His voice was solidly a man's, with a hint of familiar inflection. "Mom, Dad, is it really you? I can't believe this." *Mom and Dad?* When he lived with us, he called us "Mr. Luke and Ms. Jillana." The change was both eyebrow-raising and a tad thrilling.

For the next twenty minutes, we got the bullet points of his last thirteen years, but there were a few things that didn't add up. He mentioned he had moved to the South. Why was he back in New York? Why was he delaying going to city hall to get an ID? I knew there was much more to the story, but this was a time to listen, not cross-examine.

As this first phone call was drawing to a close, Royal said, "Mom, you're the best mom I ever had. For real. Hands down. Dad, you were the only one to ever play football with me. The only man in my life. Ever. I love you to the moon and back, Dad. Love you, too, Mom. Talk soon?"

Yes, we agreed, and ended with both of us saying, "Love you too, Royal."

My blender of whirling prayers, wonderings, and concern for Royal Storm kept mixing.

• • •

Royal talked a tough game on social media, but he was very different when he interacted with us privately. It wasn't that one version of Royal was fake, and the other was real. They were both him. In person, he is thoughtful, intelligent, and kind. You'd never know this by his Facebook page with countless photos of alcohol, posts about smoking and selling weed, about women, and chasing money, accompanied with comments full of expletives. The dissonance between our conversations and the complicated code of the streets by which he lived was eye-opening to me.

Luke contacted his mom and stepdad in Buffalo, New York, and they were enthusiastic to connect with Royal, too, as they fondly remembered him. Soon afterward, Luke's mom and older brother took Royal out to eat. A week after that, Luke's older brother whisked Royal away to the suburbs to play football and eat dinner with the family on Labor Day weekend. As we always do during the holidays, we West-Coasters connected virtually with Luke's family in New York, so we could see everyone's faces. Royal was on the couch surrounded by Luke's family. My precocious six-year-old nephew, Winston, sat next to him and with a Vanna White–type hand-motion, confidently stated, "Aunt Jillana, I don't believe you've ever met our new friend, Royal!"

"Oh, I do know him! I knew Royal when he was your age!" Luke and I wanted to be intentional about cultivating a relationship with Royal without it being too much too soon, but what does pacing yourself look like when words like *Mom*, *Dad*, and *love you* were exchanged?

Royal was saying the same syllables and consonants to form the same words, but the difference in our experiential meaning was immeasurable. I have had one mom and dad my whole life. Family members who tell me they love me have always been there for me. Not so for Royal. Same words, different experiences.

Heaviness and trauma make words and their meanings fuzzy.

•   •   •

I always prefaced my phone conversations with "You know, Royal, I'm not trying to pry or intrude here, I'm just trying to understand."

He would endearingly reply in his nineteen-year-old gruff man voice, "Mom, I could talk with you all day. Ask away."

Royal had no memory of us ever picking him up at the group home, even though we did that monthly for a year. We had a photo of Luke holding year-old Sophia in one arm and seven-year-old Royal in the other. Despite that memory gap, Royal remembered the smallest details of living in our home.

"Remember Dad's cologne he would let me wear? Remember the kid Jimmy from next door and how you took us to Chuck E. Cheese? Remember the lunch box I took to school?"

"Honestly, I can't picture the lunch box, Royal."

Without missing a beat, he wisely said, "When your whole life is like a storm, Mom, in the calm I do remember that. I do remember the small details. And with you and Dad, that was the one time in my life there was calm."

Staring up at the ceiling at night, I couldn't help but be

gripped by a fierce hope and determination for Royal. His life was far from over. I was both keenly aware of and disconcerted by hurdles he'd need to jump over to make it anywhere different from where he was now standing.

One evening I asked Royal if he currently had anyone in his life whom he could emulate.

"What does that mean, Mom?" he asked. I told him, and he promptly told me he didn't. I asked him about his dreams for his life, and he told me he wanted to become an engineer. My mind churned with what it would take to get him to school, mentally making note of the community college within walking distance of where we live.

Royal's overview of his life after he left our home screamed loss, abandonment, betrayal. His life before he came to us screamed the same. I didn't want to pry but I told him if there was ever anything he wanted to share about his early life, I'd always listen.

"I remember being removed from my biological mom when I was three," he said. He shared hazy impressions and some pointed memories. "Yeah, I still remember," he mused, his voice fading. Then he said urgently, "I gotta go, Mom. I'll call you tomorrow."

Tomorrow was never tomorrow. Half the time his phone was disconnected, but when more than a week or two went by without hearing from him, I'd worry and reach out.

"Okay, I'll try to keep in touch. I just gotta get used to this, Mom. I never had anyone love me this much but you" was his instant reply.

• • •

Over the course of several months' worth of short, stilted conversations, he shared bits and pieces of his deeply uprooted life.

"Mom, I've gotta be straight with you about something. I just want you to be proud of me and all." With a slight crack in a steady voice, Royal recounted moving to the South, getting into fights, selling pills, getting expelled from school, and constantly running away, which led to juvenile hall. There, at age seventeen, he punched a juvenile detention officer. Royal was charged with a felony as an adult and transferred to the county jail. The jail released him without a safety net. Royal was given several years of probation, but with no family, no knowledge of where to get help, and no means of support, he fled, and as a result, a warrant was issued for his arrest. He slept in abandoned cars. He was shot in the leg by someone he encountered in the streets. At this point in the eye-widening overview, though I was hanging on to every word, I couldn't help but blurt out, "Who visited you at the hospital?"

"Mom, nobody. I didn't have nobody."

Then he secretly made his way to Buffalo. His siblings, whom he didn't grow up with, lived there, and they pitched in to get him a one-way ticket. With a calm and measured voice Royal then uttered the most vulnerable and haunting statement.

"Ya know, Mom, I think if I had stayed with you and Dad, I would've had a shot at a normal life."

I took a deep breath and thanked him for sharing the

truth. I pointed out that if he had been staying with us, it didn't necessarily mean he wouldn't be in the same predicament he was now. Royal immediately noted that even if that were true, the difference would be that we "would have *been there* for him," even if he got into trouble. I said that we now had a foundation on which to build.

"Royal, I don't want to lose you again."

"You won't, Mom," he assured me.

I could feel the turmoil across the three thousand miles that separated us.

"I would've had a shot at a normal life" kept me up that night, staring at the ceiling, long after everyone else had fallen asleep.

• • •

Royal never came across as needy, though I knew he couldn't have much. I decided to mail him a Target gift card to cover some basics.

He never got it. I tracked it with my receipt and saw that the day it arrived, it had been used to buy lots of beer and a pair of baby girl socks with a remaining balance of 96 cents. There was the chance Royal was lying and had someone buy beer for him, but I doubted it.

I cringed as I dialed to let him know what happened. A gesture intended to bless him would now become a source of pain. The siblings he was living with had presumably stolen from him. I implored him to keep his anger in check when I told him some disappointing news. He agreed. I softly and directly told him the gift card had been used.

He immediately went ballistic shouting, "Who stole what

my mom sent me? My mom sent something for ME! Who STOLE from me?" His tone was primal.

I heard a clamoring of multiple voices shouting and talking over each other.

"Here, talk with Mom," I heard a distraught Royal say.

A man with the same voice as Royal said, "Yo. Who this?"

"This is Jillana."

"Ms. Jillana! This is Dion." His tone was jovial. "I was adopted, and my name was changed to Tony, you know what I'm saying, but the adoption didn't work out. But it's me. Hey, how are you?"

"Tony, wow! I knew you as Dion. What name would you like me to call you?"

"Call me Tony."

Royal was ranting in the background as Tony casually talked with me.

"How are you and Mr. Luke doing?"

"Umm . . . we're well, thanks, Tony." The unfamiliar name rolled slowly off my tongue.

"I can't believe it's really you, Ms. Jillana! Where do you live now?"

"Portland, Oregon."

"That's so great. Wow! Royal is going crazy right now!"

"Tony, I don't mean to be rude, but I can tell that Royal is having a hard time at the moment. I'd love to talk with you more, but can you put him back on the phone, please?"

"You know what, Ms. Jillana?" His tone instantly changed from casual to hostile. "Royal was always your favorite. I'm done with this s—."

Click.

I instantly regretted my painful misstep. The sudden mood shift triggered haunting memories of nine-year-old Dion.

Royal texted me a short while later. "I love you, Mom. I kept my promise. I didn't hurt nobody over this. Can't believe my own family stole from me. I'll call you tomorrow, alright?"

A few minutes later, he posted on Facebook that he was high.

"I'm so litty!!! It's kinda hard for me to explain da way I'm feeling right now . . ."

● ● ●

I connected with Tony and profusely apologized. I said I didn't mean to disrespect him and that I wanted to start over. I told him that Luke and I knew he wasn't a bad kid, but a good kid who had experienced way too much at a young age. I told him his behaviors were the trauma speaking and not the essence of who he is.

He thanked me and said, "I sure do appreciate that, Ms. Jillana. I sure do."

The juxtaposition of the little boy who menacingly waved a steak knife in the air against his adult expressions of appreciation was staggering.

Then he reminisced, "Remember that time we had people over and we had chip and dip and we all watched football? Remember when you made me grilled cheese and soup?"

He recalled everyday, ordinary things from his sixty days with us. The only detail that he mentioned I could specifically recall was the Spider-Man poster hanging up in his room.

"Next time I'm gonna talk with Mr. Luke. I'm gonna tell him I remember him holding me down as I tried to break the window and telling me 'Dion, you are safe here. We love you,' as I struggled with him. Didn't change me running away, but I still remember that."

Six months later, Tony called me from the hospital. His girlfriend was having a baby, and I could hear her groaning in the background, so I rushed the conversation, wanting Tony to be completely attentive to her.

"Ms. Jillana, if we have a girl, we're naming her after you. Jillana will be her middle name."

When I said I was really surprised, he said simply, "I'd want her to grow up and be just like you. For real."

As I hung up, I was struck with how sixty days out of twenty-three years is absolutely nothing.

And yet, it wasn't.

• • •

A few months later, Royal called. It was midnight his time.

"Hey, Mom."

"Hi, sweetheart."

"I want out of Buffalo. I can't take this no more." His voice was soft and monotone.

"Royal, I can barely hear you. Where are you?"

"The train station."

"Why?"

"I had a fight with my girlfriend."

"Are you sleeping there?"

"Yes."

"Let me call Nana to come and get you."

"I don't deserve anything else than these streets."

"But you do!"

"I'm not going with Nana."

"Royal, we love you. You know Dad and I will fly out there and help you through this so you can live a different . . ."

Click.

". . . story."

• • •

The next day I received a voicemail that I still have saved on my phone.

"Hey, Mom. I just wanted to let you know, like, I'm safe and all. When you get this, will you call me back, please? Love you."

When I called him back, I shared that my dear friend in Buffalo, who also remembered Royal as a little boy, knew of some possible employment opportunities and an organization that might be able to help Royal with his legal situation. She picked him up, took him out for coffee, and texted me a photo of them together.

But then Royal called me the next day.

"Hey, Mom, Megan said she could arrange for me to meet with a lawyer who maybe could help me and look at my case and I don't want *nothing* to do with that. I have a life here, and I just want to move forward."

"Okay, Royal. Move forward without an ID? What does that look like?"

"I just need to think more on that, Mom." Long pause. "Does that hurt you, Mom?"

"It hurts me because I see potential in you, Royal, that

you don't see in yourself. I want you to have doors of opportunity opened to you. I want you to get this legal matter taken care of so you can get an ID. I want you to be able to support your family and live into your potential.

"But it's your life," I added.

"I'd just rather we didn't talk about this anymore," Royal replied.

And therein lay all the tension. Talking about the past was painful. Talking about his future was nonexistent.

On Christmas after opening up the outfits we sent him, he wrote, "Thank you for the clothes. My girlfriend and I are good. First girl who ever love me. She got my name tattooed on her chest, so I know it's real. I just wish things was different with my real family. Fighting all the time. None of us are together. Kinda sad on a day to be celebrating Jesus' birthday. I wish I was with you. Merry Christmas. Love you, Mom."

So much complexity packed into succinct little messages.

•　•　•

In the spring, nine months after our first contact with Royal, I flew to the East Coast for my brother's law school graduation. I couldn't be three hours away from Royal and Tony and not make the drive. At the time of my arrival, they were not on speaking terms with one another.

Buffalo had changed so much since we'd left a decade prior, but the East Side was still poverty-stricken with a palpable taste of despair. I pulled up to the house where Royal's girlfriend rented an apartment. It was situated between an overgrown abandoned lot and a boarded-up house covered with graffiti. I knocked on the screen door, halfway off its hinges. The screen door squeaked open, and there stood Royal.

After a long embrace, we headed to Applebee's. I could tell he was nervous. I was bursting with excitement, trying not to sound overeager.

"You know . . . I'd have recognized you anywhere, Mom," he said while we waited to be seated.

"Really? Well, I wouldn't have recognized you," I said back teasingly. The last time I'd seen him, a few of his permanent teeth were starting to come in. Now he was standing several inches taller than me.

We slid into a booth. A young waitress with mocha skin, just like Royal's, overheard him ask me, "What are you gonna eat, Mom?" as she plunked down our water glasses. She turned to Royal and said with a nod of approval, "I'm just like you. Black dad and a white mom. I'll be back to take your order in a minute."

Without any hesitation, Royal leaned forward and said with all sincerity, "Mom, I know I'm the son of your heart and everything, but she thinks I'm your *real* son, so let's just go with it."

•   •   •

Royal's quiet declaration of "Let's just go with it" at the restaurant became my internal mantra for the next few days. As I dropped him off at his house, he gave me a hug that felt natural. "See you tomorrow, Mom."

The next day I took him to Kohl's. He found one plaid button-down shirt he liked. Then he scanned the racks and whispered, "This here is white people, old man clothes, Mom. Can we go to Urban Trendz?"

At Urban Trendz, Royal held up a black hooded sweatshirt and asked me if he could get it. I was instantly reminded of what wearing a hoodie had meant for Trayvon Martin and countless others and voiced that out loud.

"Mom, you don't got to worry about me."

"But I do, Royal."

"I know," he replied. "It's crazy," he added with a sheepish smile.

On the third day, Royal asked if I could pick him up an hour later than we arranged because "I've gotta do something." I knew immediately what that something was.

We walked the gravel path circling the perimeter of the park on a blue-skyed, cloudless afternoon. It was the same park Luke and I had taken him to as a boy. I asked him about his dreams. He told me he didn't really have any.

I made explicit what we were offering in terms of walking alongside him to try and help clear the obstacles, so he'd have the ability to walk a smoother path in the future, maybe even pursue engineering like he'd talked about previously.

"I don't think I can do that, Mom," he replied. "My girlfriend has a kid who looks up to me. I don't want her kid to know I'm going back to jail."

My voice became wobbly. "I know you don't like talking about this, but I see you struggling to survive. And I'm just concerned . . ." With my chin quivering, I gulped back a tidal wave of emotions. "Royal, I'm concerned that you're going to die selling drugs on the East Side."

Tears fell down my cheeks. "Your story doesn't have to

be *this* story." His brown eyes were locked on mine, and he listened intently.

"Oh, Mom," he said and turned away, hands clasped behind his head for a brief moment. He studied my face for a moment. "I appreciate it—just with my girlfriend and everything . . ."

A fight broke out on a nearby basketball court that got our attention for a moment.

"I'll tell you what, Mom . . . I'm gonna let you know."

"Okay, sweetheart." I knew right then and there he wasn't ever circling back around with me on this.

I didn't arrive in Buffalo thinking I could somehow restore Royal's sense of purpose that trauma had stripped from him, but I needed to take the opportunity to tell him, face to face, that he had more options than were currently in front of him and that I was rooting for him.

• • •

"Any place you need to go?" I asked as I was driving Royal and his girlfriend home from lunch, a few hours before my flight. Royal asked if we could stop by the pet store.

Royal and his girlfriend oohed and aahed over the kittens and then moved on to the fish. I was several steps behind them. Sandwiched between cat toys and stacked cases of Friskies Tasty Treasures, I noticed gray kittens playing in the large, glass kennel. My eyes were drawn to the large poster underneath them. It had a giant photo of a tabby cat staring into the camera with a raised paw as if to plead, "Pick me."

The large, bold letters on the poster read:

IF YOU WANT TO TOUCH THE PAST,
TOUCH A ROCK. IF YOU WANT TO TOUCH
THE PRESENT, TOUCH A FLOWER. IF YOU
WANT TO TOUCH THE FUTURE, TOUCH A
LIFE. CHOOSE ADOPTION.

I stood staring at the advertisement for the Ten Lives Club
for cat rescue and adoption and was struck by how it's never
that simple. *There's no guarantee that in "touching a life," it's
all going to work out.*

As I waited for my flight home, I journaled impressions I
didn't want to forget. For example, after I took Tony and his
girlfriend out to eat, I handed him a framed photo of Luke
and me, sitting with him and Royal, a few days after he came
to live with us. He quietly studied it for a long time.

Finally he said, "I know I was labeled 'therapeutic' when
I was with you in foster care, and I know I was awful to you.
But I remember everything you and Luke did for me, and I
just want to say thank you."

I saw Royal all four days I was in town. We drove and
took pictures in front of his old school where I had dropped
him off every morning for first grade. We got out of the car
and posed for pictures in front of the home we had lived
in together, our heads tilted toward one another with the
driveway where he once rode his scooter in the background.

Back at his apartment as I prepared to give him one last
hug, Royal handed me a pencil drawing from a sketchbook
I'd sent him months earlier. He'd drawn two masks side by
side. One mask had narrowed eyes and sharp teeth with a

joker's sinister smile. The other mask had human teeth, a gaping mouth, and eyes shut tight as tears spilled down the cheeks. On it he wrote in cursive, "*Laugh now. Cry later.*"

I counted it an immense privilege to witness his vulnerable side that cries despite the mask he presents to the world in order to survive.

We have made it our pattern over the years to travel to New York to visit Luke's family every other summer, so it would be over a year before we would see them again. I was keenly aware that Royal and Tony could fall off the radar and I'd have no way to get in touch with them. They could be hurt or even killed. In the past six months, Royal was jumped and hurt but because he was in hiding, he didn't seek medical attention. Tony was also stabbed and hospitalized.

I showed up, knowing that my role was not to attempt to bandage the wounds of years of immeasurable losses. Such a notion would be ridiculous.

I simply showed up to be present to two young men whom I had the privilege of caring for as little boys. They didn't have a choice when they were placed with me in foster care. They do have a choice to engage with me now.

At the airport, preparing to fly home, I simultaneously felt the exhilarating joy of reconnection and a heavy heart. Upon landing in Portland, I saw a text from Royal: **I love you so much, Mom. Thanks for everything you do for me, including loving me.**

If life were a Hallmark movie, the lights would fade and cut to the credits right after that text. I picture him standing in my kitchen confidently helping himself to whatever was in the fridge. I imagine him sitting around our table. I think of teaching him how to drive, supportively standing alongside him in court to take care of legal matters, enrolling him in school, and seeing that he has a foundation on which to build.

But life is not a Hallmark movie, and the wounds of trauma create deep grooves that are hard to escape. I'd received multiple texts from Royal's girlfriend and then finally a phone call from Royal asking if I could pay their cable bill. I told Royal I wanted to see him thrive and not just survive, and the receiver clicked.

Royal, did you just hang up on me? If so, please call me back, I texted.

Look, Mom. If you can't pay it, that's fine, but I'd appreciate if you could just be direct, he shot back.

I didn't respond. Ironically, five minutes later he texted me, **Are you done talking with me?**

Royal, I wasn't done talking with you, but YOU hung up on ME. I love you. And I always will, sweetheart. If you value me being direct, in that spirit, I'll say this: I want to be seen first and foremost for who I am and secondly for what I can give to you.

My cell phone dinged.

Ok, MS. JILLANA, I don't care what you do for me anymore. It's not like I call you every day asking for money, but I don't need nothing else from you. Period. For real. So from now on you will not be hearing from me. Ever again. Don't text me or call me. I want nothing to do with you. It was nice knowing you.

As I looked at that instant text response with eyes widened, I wiped one tear that held far more than could ever be articulated. I wanted to cry and guffaw simultaneously.

My brain was flooded with *It was never real. He was using me all along. If he hangs up on me just because he thinks I won't pay something and then rashly cuts me off, it was always about what I could give to him and never about me.*

Before that skepticism could take root, a tender, unsarcastic, and almost out-of-body appreciation for his swift, life-survival skill of manipulation overtook me. *Oh, that's good! Very strategic, Royal.* I had just written him a note the week before, saying what a profound privilege it was to me to be called his "Mom." Like a pitch thrown down center plate, Royal hit it out of the park, referring to me for the first time as MS. JILLANA in all caps. This realization made me nod my head and slightly smile.

Sometimes it's easier to light the match and torch the relational bridge than to navigate the scorched planks of disappointment. Royal, like many kids impacted by countless losses, was an expert at this. Father Boyle writes: "You stand with the belligerent, the surly, and the badly behaved until bad behavior is recognized for the language it is: the vocabulary of the deeply wounded and of those whose burdens are more than they can bear."

I went ahead and sent Royal the little photo album I put together of our four days together. Along with it, I included a succinct note laying out that I desired for us to be reconciled, that my heart held so much love for him, *and* that I also had a standard of how I expected to be treated and was owed an apology.

It's brutal and I didn't do it often, but I occasionally checked his Facebook page to see if he was still alive. In his latest video, he'd asked someone to fight with him. He was red-eyed, holding a liquor bottle, with his fierce-looking "squad" in the background affirming him. He was laughing and pointing right at the camera with his finger shaped like a gun.

I could clearly see the angry mask overlaying the crying mask from the drawing he gave me.

"You were spared," a well-meaning person told me. And then added brazenly, "You were spared the *inevitable*. Too much trauma to ever change the outcome."

I wrestle that down.

An indelible path is carved for each of us, resulting from who we're born to, where we're raised, and what we're taught about ourselves by those around us. Life does not, however, automatically put us on a circumstantial conveyor belt leading to one predictable, statistical outcome. Royal was plodding along the statistical pipeline of foster care to juvenile hall to incarceration to homelessness that is gut-wrenchingly predictable for youth, especially youth of color impacted by foster care. Even in the midst of the heavily weighted unjust factors of life with their unquantifiable ripple effects, I believe there is a Creator whose plan for redemption, healing, and reconciliation is *relationship*.

Relationship is a game-changer.

It's the most humble, organic, radical way Divine Love changes the world.

While I hold the tension of all that shapes us and the Mount Everest that some people like Royal are forced to climb just to attempt to have what others of us are simply handed in life, I reject the idea that there's an automatic, inevitable storyline written for anyone.

Though it can be tempting to believe that love, nurture, discipline, good intentions, and faith by well-meaning people under the roof of a loving home is *always* enough to overcome, it is not. I know this well.

But I still can't help but wonder if Royal would be standing on that corner ready to fight, with total disregard for his life, if his bouncing had stopped in foster care at age six and not continued for the entirety of his growing-up years.

My heart expands big enough to hold the haunting tension of the forever unknown.

. . .

A few months later, Royal was still not in communication with me, but I snuck a peek on his Facebook page: "Just found out we gonna have a baby! Hope it's a boy so he can be a savage like me."

Royal. The boy who said he wanted to be an engineer, who's now selling drugs and fighting on the street corner, was about to become a father, having no father figure in his life except for one year with my husband. The boy whose school Christmas concert I sat in the front row and clapped for, who I baked with in my kitchen, who I buckled up next to on a roller coaster at Disneyland, who made me a mom for the first time—he was becoming a father.

Despite the profound longing for things to be different in his future, I felt compassion for the "stuck" narrative he was living and what happens when kids leave foster care without the steadfast, relational safety net of even *one* caring adult. I wanted to be that person, but I couldn't strong-arm my way into making him choose to be reconnected. As much as I felt intense heartache when thinking of and praying for Royal, I couldn't escape the fact that this kid brings me even more joy and delight.

Love has a way of doing that.

Through my year of reconnection with Royal as a young adult, I understood the biblical narrative of the Prodigal Son better than ever before. I will always desire to run to Royal and offer him a ring and a robe and invite him in to have a huge feast. Not out of guilt or manipulation but out of an exuberant love.

Whether I'm accepted or rejected, Royal will always be the son of my heart. I will always yearn for health and wholeness for him. With compassionate understanding and clear communication, I want him to know and to experience what we all long for in this life: an unwavering invitation to be folded in and connected, based on our inherent worthiness, and not on our performance.

• • •

Though wanting to respect the "Don't text me or call me" exhortation, I did send him one simple text five months later. **I miss you, Royal.** He called ten seconds later.

"Hey, Mom, it's been a minute, huh?"

I told him it had been. I could tell he was nervous.

"Sorry, Mom. Mom, I'm sorry."

It was said in such a rushed way that if Micah had said it to me, I would have likely made him start from scratch and add a little more depth and context.

But he is not my nine-year-old son who I've raised most of his life. He's a twenty-year-old young man from whom

I've spent a lifetime apart. I'm acutely aware that he's never circled around to utter those words before. Ever.

I told him in the first two sentences that I loved him, forgave him, and it was good to hear his voice.

"Thanks, Mom. Ummm . . . the bus is coming. I've gotta go."

His eagerness to be done with the call was obvious in the midst of his desire to be tethered. This short phone call further exposed the ever-present tug-of-war in his traumatized body and mind.

The son of my heart daily carries a hurricane of haunting memories. Family titles like "Mom" are convoluted for him. His reality twists with abject poverty, and he dulls the pain from a lifetime of abandonment.

My good-hearted Royal Storm.

17

MOM

Acceptance

ELENI, MY FIFTEEN-YEAR-OLD, is not one to fill any silence with words and out-loud musings or wonderings like her mother. One day, on the ride home from school, she overtly said, "Please do *not* ask me about my day, Mom. If anything interesting happened, I'll let you know."

After a few silent car rides, I felt like I wasn't taking advantage of our rare solo car time, so I said, "Roses and Thorns. How about if we both share one thing—anything—about our day? One positive and one negative." (Looking back, even I feel slightly annoyed at my own suggestion, but bless my eager-beaver-desiring-to-connect mother's heart.)

Eleni played along for a few days and then broke the news at a red light that she actually hated Roses and Thorns. "Could we just listen to music, Mom?"

Over my parenthood journey, I'm continually learning in a million ways that it's not love if you just check an invisible "good mom" box for yourself—whatever that may be—and the received felt impact falls flat. Eleni nonchalantly surprised me one day with a thoughtful gift: a customized "Mom's playlist" of music she knows I like and that she can tolerate, a win-win for the sometimes lively and sometimes silent drives.

• • •

As a child, I always knew I wanted to be a mom. I never had a specific vision, however, of what my future family would look like. All I can remember is deciding that when I was older, I wanted to be a mom *and* carry a briefcase. In my mind, being entrusted to carry around papers in a case with a combination lock was the ultimate act of importance. I've never once fulfilled my briefcase dreams, but I have always been fond of stylishly functional tote bags.

When I was young, I understood the title of mom to mean raising and loving children. With age, maturity, and experience, I've realized raising and loving our children is the general idea for all mothers, but we easily splice ourselves into categories, making assumptions about a culture of motherhood, based on one descriptor. There are no cookie-cutter shorthand assumptions, however, that can be made of any mom in any description, whether our mom descriptions are lifetime or seasonal.

Over my years as a mother, at one time or another, I've checked the boxes of:

- biological
- foster
- adoptive
- working
- stay-at-home
- homeschool
- special-needs
- volunteer

Admittedly, I only homeschooled Sophia for one year before Luke, Sophia, and I collectively decided that wasn't a good long-term choice. While I thought homeschool was forever in the rearview mirror, parenthood invites us to continually pivot. Five years later (as Charlie's self-esteem was plummeting due to the way in which he was engaged by teachers and peers at school), Luke and I looked at each other with a deep sigh and a knowing head nod: We would embrace the unexpected and start the homeschooling journey with Charlie with no clear exit ramp in sight.

Full disclosure: Though I do some volunteering, when it comes to sports and classroom sign-ups, I am the mom who brings paper goods and juice boxes, and I don't feel bad about it. Nothing to be impressed about here, folks!

But that's just the thing. While honoring the uniqueness of the experiences that shape us in our motherhood and the commonality of striving to love our children well, we can get lost in the labyrinth of superficial categories of parenthood, as if there's a one-size-fits-all path, or an automatic subculture of values assigned to each box. We then miss the opportunity to encourage and uplift one another because we're looking past one another into the assumed projection of what we think is true.

Every fall, I see magazine covers proclaiming, "Easy Costumes for Moms to Make." I have never ever sewn Halloween costumes for my children, and I never will because I don't know how and don't care enough to learn. When I learned to crochet in my early twenties (something I've now forgotten from lack of practice!), I made *one* blanket. I had lofty ideas back then to make stunning blankets for each of my children, but the reality of life changed my plan. So with each one of my babies, I've whispered, "Here, I made this for you" and wrapped them up in the *same* blanket for a season. Thankfully, none of them got attached to it. Someday I'll cut off pieces of that blanket and with a chuckle, give them each a piece of that handmade blanket I made for *all* of them!

Despite my good intentions, I've never kept updated family or child-specific photo albums. Instead, I have a clean, unused XL pizza box in my office closet designated for each of my kids, and when there's a photo or keepsake, I throw it in their pizza box which (perhaps one day) I'll sort through and arrange. I'd rather take out the trash and mow the lawn than cook dinner, which is why Luke and our teenagers take the lead in this role. I'm not a clever decorator who switches things around in my home the way others do effortlessly to "celebrate the changing seasons." Some people have a flair for putting together a Pinterest-worthy charcuterie board. My arrangement of crackers on a plate lacks pizzazz. I've been teasingly assigned to bring fruit salad for the past two decades to Luke's family functions because it's something that cannot be messed up. (Though I won't brag, I do want you to know I make a mean chocolate chip cookie!)

When I look at an incredibly narrow, stereotypical version I've created in my head of what "good moms" do, there are definitely areas where I fall short. But parenting is not about the specific amenities we offer our kids, but about the long game of consistent heart-posture and presence with which we offer ourselves to our children. Kids know when we're checking dutiful boxes of parenthood—Roses and Thorns—and when we're taking the time to engage and come alongside in a way they can receive. In all our motherly glory, we embrace our quirkiness and natural bents and pair them with a fierce desire for the currency of our attention to unquestionably lavish our children and others with the message:

You are loved and okay, fully accepted, inherently worthy, just as you are.

• • •

I clutched my plane ticket and held Luke's hand. One flight was over, and we had one more to go. The kids at home were supportive of our last-minute plans to be out of town on a day we were traditionally together. On this Mother's Day weekend in 2018, we were on the second leg of our trip to be with Royal.

Three months earlier, Royal's past had caught up with him and he was extradited to jail in a southern state where he had violated probation. I accepted his daily collect calls. He wrote heartfelt, open letters to Luke and me, and we faithfully wrote back to him. He'd had a few women play the role of mom in his life, but his first letter written to me on binder paper started out "To my favorite mother."

Luke and I were like-minded that in this moment we would do for Royal what we would do if it were any other child living under our roof. We asked him pointed questions about what he wanted in his future and got some direct answers. We were keenly aware a person may say or do anything to get out of their current predicament, but Royal communicated a clear desire to completely change his environment, to eventually move closer to be near us and work toward a better life. He believed that being surrounded by our family would give him a higher chance of those desires becoming reality.

We hired a private defense attorney and wrote a letter to the prosecuting attorney to give some life context surrounding Royal's charges. A friend of mine who had worked for Oregon's child welfare system for thirty years urged the prosecutors to let Royal reconnect with his family, the handhold he'd always deserved but never received. Lastly, Royal wrote a letter to his defense attorney about who he wanted to be in his life and the action steps he would take to become a law-abiding contributor to society, including his greatest desire: to be a present father. After outlining the shame and brokenness of feeling unloved and unwanted his whole life, he concluded, "Please help the judge understand I'm not an ordinary criminal."

In a head-turning decision with just four days' notice, I got a call that Royal was going to be released from incarceration on a suspended sentence. He needed to stay out of trouble for the next three years, and then he'd receive the possibility of having his felony record sealed. Without this hired attorney advocacy, he would have had to serve *years* behind bars and *years* on probation. This bypassed that.

I called my friend Megan, who has two decades of experience working with kids on the margins in Buffalo, and who'd taken Royal out for coffee to talk about legal matters. I told her Royal was getting a real-life miracle. This "miracle," my friend informed me, is what happens when white people who have an educated voice and money know how to navigate systems and use their power to advocate. I saw the truth in her hard-earned wisdom, and I have continued to educate myself more about the reality she named. The attorney we hired for Royal said that in her eleven years of practicing law, she'd never seen an outcome like this one. For countless other incarcerated young men of color with similar stories, there would be no advocacy and no head-turning decisions.

As we drove our rental car to the one motel in town, the clerk checking us in at the front desk asked us to please move it one parking space over so it would be directly underneath a security camera where he'd "watch it like a hawk all night." The intimidating reputation of this area was reinforced by the gentleman sitting next to me on the plane, who asked me where I was headed. When I told him, he raised his eyebrows and simply said, "Y'all don't stay out after dark."

The next morning, Luke and I were seated in the front row of the courtroom that looked like it was out of a 1970s time capsule. As Royal was led into the courtroom, shackled, the same big smile I recognized from when he was a little boy spread across his face. I had assured him on the phone the day before that we would be looking at him, the *person*, and not the orange jumpsuit. He went before the judge, and the bailiff escorted him back to jail to be processed out and released.

We came prepared with our cashier's check for the exact amount of his extradition fees. As we were waiting for everything to be uploaded into the computer so a phone call could be placed to the jail authorizing his release, Royal's defense attorney quietly offered us some behind-the-scenes conversation with the prosecuting attorneys that had happened the previous week. After reading our letters advocating for Royal and agreeing to pay his fines, the prosecutor asked the defense attorney, "Who are these people and why are they doing this? Don't they know what *these people* [referring to Royal] are like?" Apparently, that rightfully set off our attorney, who told us she responded, "Don't you know the story of the Prodigal Son? It's like that. It's not your job today to ask why, it's just your job to look at the facts of the case and this context and to make a decision." Apparently, a Bible lesson in the Bible Belt got some traction because less than a week later, Luke and I were standing in that courthouse.

We drove four blocks to the jail and parked our rental car on the side of the road near the back door of the jail. I looked around at the startling disparity between the sparkling, modern jail and the backdrop of an impoverished town with abandoned lots full of weeds, houses with peeling paint, and faded billboards. We were told it could take hours for him to be released. Luke and I, along with Royal's defense attorney, sat in our respective cars and eyed the jail's back door while we sweated in the unrelenting ninety-seven-degree heat. Royal had walked out of this exact door two years earlier, just barely a legal adult, to nobody waiting for him. That door would open up again electronically any minute, and it was our privilege to be waiting for him this time. With a loud buzz, the door opened and Royal walked toward us in street clothes, carrying a plastic garbage bag of belongings, just as he had when he walked in my front door at age six in foster care.

I jumped out of the car and sprinted to him. I threw my arms around him, and we rocked back and forth in an embrace, before I put hands on both sides of his cheeks and said, "I love you." Luke walked up behind me, arms outstretched to Royal. "Hi, Dad," Royal said.

It was the first time they'd spoken to one another in person since Royal was in second grade.

Royal had no ID so he couldn't get on a plane. His girlfriend was pregnant with their daughter, due the following week. *What was there to do?* We all jumped into our rental car and jumpstarted some mega family togetherness, driving through seven states for seventeen hours until arriving in New York. It was an undeniable whirlwind in the best of ways, one that we'd had no idea we'd be embarking on just a week before! The three of us did a long group hug as we said goodbye, and then Luke and I boarded a plane back to the West Coast. Royal and his family would move across the country to live near our family three months later.

• • •

Back at home, I ask my children what makes a "good mom." Micah, age twelve, rattles off that "a good mom is someone who takes care of you, feeds you, helps you, takes you places, has fun with you, and laughs a lot." It takes him fifteen seconds with no hesitation to share this. (Feeling brave, I also ask him, "What is something annoying I do as a mom?" and he acts as if he's just hit a buzzer on *Jeopardy!*, confidently replying, also without hesitation, "It's annoying when we're playing cards at the kitchen table, and you make us listen to instrumental nineties pop and then sometimes sing along!")

I ask Micah how he feels about knowing both of his moms—having us around the same dinner table at times or talking together in the living room, even though he's often just going in and out to play and doing other things. He says he likes how it makes him feel "special." Sometimes less is more, but this is a time when "more is more." After a decade with what has evolved into kinship, any notion of drawing a tight circle around me and Micah with room for only one mom has been erased. There's another loving presence in his life, rooting him on, desiring goodness for him. I'm grateful.

I had scribbled down Micah's response, and I look at it again—"Takes care of you, feeds you, helps you, takes you places, has fun with you, and laughs a lot." I see the many opportunities we have to not only pour into our own children, but also to contribute to the flourishing of other peoples' children. You don't need someone officially calling you Mom in order to have a nurturing presence. A friend of mine had recently picked up my middle-school-age daughter, who was having a hard time, and took her out for ice cream. It was good for her soul to be in the presence of a caring adult outside the walls of our home.

Sophia, sixteen, eating chips and salsa in the midst of her pandemic, sheltered-at-home school day, offers up that "moms know how to read people and situations, when to step in and when to let go."

I nod and am quiet. I think about a recent situation that involved peer bullying of one of my children and the long haul of sitting with them in their collective loneliness with an entirely virtual school year. I can't help but immediately notice in our dialogue that there's not the smallest bit mentioned about the stereotypical frivolities I've assigned in my head that align with being a "good mom." I prefer not to be a ragged mom, but a *real* one. There are worthy conversations to be had about balance, and in motherhood there's a decent amount of prioritizing, releasing, and letting go. I celebrate the many strengths and propensities in other women that don't come naturally to me in mothering. I love when my children get time to experience others' distinctive and caring styles of mothering, whether they're reserved or gregarious, a mom who knows pop culture and can sing along to the radio or one who's a bit behind the times, moms who let their kids take public transit around the city and those who prefer to drive their child themselves. For it is uniqueness that makes this world go round.

• • •

After the birth of his first child, Royal and his fiancée, her nine-year-old child, and their three-month-old baby rode seventy-one hours on Amtrak from Buffalo to Portland. Before their arrival, I searched for housing for them at dozens of apartment complexes. I was met with barriers at every turn until a manager at a family-owned complex, just a mile down the road from our home, gave them a chance. His rusty truck parked in the "Manager" parking spot sported a bumper sticker that read, "Believe in Miracles."

I picked them up at the train station, and they moved in. Over the next year, I continued to release the myth that living in close proximity and having family dinners, perhaps some heart-to-heart talks, and a pat on the back would overcome a lifetime of abandonment. We intentionally and interpersonally connected Royal with our friends in our network who had a personal relatability to his past, something that despite some pretty major mama bear empathy, I didn't have. There was no textbook on how to be present to a young man whom we parented for only one year of his life and now was a parent himself! If our journey with Jennifer had taught me anything, it was that with gentle, overt communication, healthy boundaries and grace, the next steps would reveal themselves. This was in no way going to be a straight, linear path walking into the sunset.

At the Thanksgiving table, Royal announced in a toast, "This is my first real Thanksgiving I ever had with my family, not counting the one when I was six years old and lived with you. Now I'm here with a family of my own, back with my true family, and that's what I'm most thankful for."

He stood in my kitchen many times over the better part of a year, and I caught him looking at the photos of his little and big self, plastered on my fridge and framed on the piano.

Royal got his first photo ID here in Portland and had his first work experience making what he calls "legal money." It's tempting to polish up the narrative for some fragrant flower outcomes, the making of a feel-good story. Keeping our hands on the relational vase to keep it from falling was hard; hard in many ways that made me put my head in my hands, close my eyes, and rub my temples at night. It was a front-row seat to examining our own well-intentioned offerings with a heavy dose of reality. It was bearing witness to countless ripple effects of what those coming out of incarceration with a box marked *felony* have to carry. It was witnessing, once again, how trauma and abject poverty form and shape one's worldview and the code of survival operating within that reality, so starkly different from my own. Most of all, it was an invitation to relationally be present and pay attention.

Royal's desire was to be tethered to us, a desire that alone holds so much beauty. Many were eager to see the buds of hope bloom into vibrant, results-oriented flowers before their very eyes. And while I can't deny that I wanted to celebrate any way in which he was moving toward health and stability, our primary focus was on the vase holding our relational connection. Royal's life will never look the way it would have if abandonment, neglect, trauma, and loss had never been part of his story. There will always be fissures and chips and perhaps entire pieces missing in that relational vase that may never be glued back together. Perhaps this vase won't be able to hold water. Perhaps it won't be able to hold what is being offered to him now, but we must, as Teilhard de Chardin puts it, "trust in the slow work of God."

• • •

I wear a silver bracelet that I bought at a fundraiser for one of my children's public middle schools. Its small hand-stamped lettering declares: *Attention is the greatest form of currency.*

As I turn it around and around on my wrist, I contemplate parenting in this age of great distraction. Our phones and watches are buzzing and pinging us relentlessly, diverting our gaze—and often the felt-experience of care—from the ones present in front of us. All of our distracted glances and "just let me respond to this one thing" add up exponentially.

To combat this, I wear an old-fashioned no-bells-and-whistles watch. I strive to throw my phone into the cupboard when the kids are home from school. Occasionally, I check in with my children about how I'm doing attention-wise. I give myself a solid B+ because a little affirmation never hurts. My children, however, offer me a pretty solid C, a few times better and sometimes worse. I try to reason them out of that grade, to paint how some parents are more distracted than I am, hoping they ponder my good points and perhaps recalculate my score a bit higher.

But at the end of the day, it doesn't matter where I put myself on the continuum of attention—it matters what they feel and how they *experience* my attention. Not in relation to others, but in relation to *me* and *them*. I want them to feel loved, heard, and understood for what may be said, and the undercurrent of what remains unsaid, in the flow of navigating life.

I remember once, when Sophia was five years old, the undercurrent of the unsaid finally bubbled to the surface. The day started off normally enough: We were all trying to get somewhere, and Sophia wasn't putting her shoes on.

"Sophia, get up and get your shoes on, please," I said as I hurried around the kitchen making last-minute lunches for us on the way out the door. I looked over to see Sophia hadn't moved.

"Soph, c'mon, go get your shoes on," I said a minute later with increasing urgency and a little irritation in my voice. As I put on Micah's shoes, I noticed Eleni's were on wrong on her chubby toddler feet, but at least she did what I asked. Sophia was slouched on the couch with her shoes next to her but made no effort to put them on. "Sophia Noelle, please get your shoes on *now*!" I said forcefully as I started putting on Micah's coat.

I wasn't yelling. I hadn't totally lost my patience, but Sophia looked terrified. Her little preschool mouth was twisted, and for a moment she was stunned before pointing and shouting, "DON'T talk to me like that! NEVER talk to me like that!" Her limbs stiffened. "Don't be a BAD mommy, because if you're a bad mommy, they'll take me away from you."

I had the diaper bag slung on my shoulder, keys in hand, and was standing by the front door when I was hit with the weight of what Sophia was carrying on her shoulders.

"Sweetheart, why would you say that?"

"Because that's what Karina [Micah's caseworker] does when mommies are not safe! And you're a mean mommy when you yell!"

Deep breath.

"Are you worried Karina might take you away from me, Sophia, when Mommy raises her voice?"

She nodded.

I walked over to her, let the heavy diaper bag clunk onto the floor, and slid next to her on the couch. "I'm so sorry I made you feel scared." With my head touching hers, I assured her she would not be taken from our house. I reassured her that Micah was taken from his mommy because she couldn't be safe and healthy enough to take care of him, but that she was learning how so she could one day take care of him again. "Even when I get frustrated and raise my voice, you're still safe with me. I love you. I'm sorry I scared you."

The rest of the day was fine, but the image of that little, twisted face haunted me. On the one hand, Sophia was confident enough to express honestly what bothered her and not to shrink down and sulk. *We must be doing something right in nurturing her,* I thought. I was glad she could assuredly call me out when she thought I was being inappropriate. She had absolutely no concept that there are mommies who, for a myriad of reasons, cannot kiss boo-boos, pack lunches, and set up playdates. And why would she?

But it was also a good wake-up call for me to pay attention and be intentional about explaining our family's special circumstances. I want my children to learn from me the power of a frequent and genuine apology—the ability to name a mistake or to acknowledge something that didn't feel quite right, a response said or received that was wonky or fell flat, or an overt trampling on someone's feelings.

• • •

After nearly a year living near us in Portland, Royal's fiancée was pregnant again, and they made the difficult decision to return to Buffalo. Royal expressed he'd wished he'd had more time living in the same neighborhood as us. We talked openly about our claim on one another, redefining family and imperfectly walking out that idea, whether near or far.

When it was time to go, I received special permission to escort them to the train. They had all their worldly possessions piled high on a stroller and in dozens of reusable shopping bags.

"Mom, where are our seats?" Royal asked, and I stepped onto the train, holding their baby, to show them. A moment later, I heard "All aboard," and saw the passenger car door close!

"I'm not on this train!" I waved and called out assertively to the conductor as the train began to slowly chug . . . chug . . . chug.

"What are you doing here? Only ticketed passengers are allowed on board. I can't put the ladder back down, so it looks like you're headed to Seattle!" When I asked if there was *any* way I could get off, he said (though he wasn't supposed to) he could open up the door if I was willing to jump.

I handed Royal his baby, kissed him on the cheek, and at the conductor's signal "Now!" I jumped. (Mind you, I was jumping onto the pavement, and it was only about six feet down, but I'm telling you, I landed it like it was no big deal and something I do all the time.) As the train picked up speed, I walked through the desolate train yard with a sly smile, my baseball cap covering up my messy hair. *Maybe if my non-profit work needs a little adrenaline boost, working on the side as a mid-forty-year-old stunt double would be a suitable possibility for me.* That fantasy came to an abrupt halt as I realized I was locked inside the train yard and did not have the skills nor desire to scale the twelve-foot chain-link fence. I knocked on the door marked Staff around the back of the station and waited for what seemed like an eternity for someone to open up and escort me back through the train terminal. Still, jumping off a moving train felt like a fitting ending to this particular season.

· · ·

Before the end of the year, Royal was back again—alone this time, to live under our roof—in a desperate attempt to get a job and save up for a place for his family. He and his family hoped to move to Portland again. I cherished the simplicity of knocking on his bedroom door and saying, "Goodnight, love you!" I was content watching him liberally take piles of chocolate chip cookies off the kitchen counter. And my heart aligned with his in frustration as I drove him to yet another job interview where his record went before him like a parading trumpeter.

He was here for Christmas, just as he had been when he was a little boy. At the Christmas Eve candlelight church service, we were all given a small white candle to hold. Royal, always one to sit on the very end of the pew for smoke breaks, tipped his lighted candle to the wick in mine. I watched it flicker as we sang about a thrill of hope and how the weary world rejoices.

When the carol ended, I prematurely blew out my candle. Royal smiled and teasingly shook his head as he relit my candle. Who in the world could have ever predicted that he'd be here and *choose* to be sitting next to me. He lent me light as I held my candle, wearing the same jagged-gem mother's ring on my finger.

Later, I tried to snap a selfie of Royal and me around my

kitchen table, and for the life of me (like the tech-savvy, cool, fortysomething I am), turned on a video instead. "Welp, anything you have to say?" I asked him.

"You're the definition."

"Of what?"

"Of being a mom. You're the definition to me of what it means to be a mom."

Father Boyle shares that we hope (against all human inclination) to not model the "one false move" eye-in-the-sky kind of God to others, but rather the "no matter whatness" of God. This *no matter whatness* erases shame and fills us with tender mercy. It allows us to truly see the person in front of us. My ever-evolving mothering with all my children, through the uniqueness of their histories, the indelible imprint of trauma, and their innate wirings, humbles me. Spun together with the currency of attention, the power of apologies, and unconditional acceptance, being a mom stretches and beckons me to continually learn from and alongside my children. It invites me to not sweat the small stuff, but to link arms, bear witness to the struggles, and celebrate the strengths of those around me.

As parents, we have a tendency to repeat things to our children—both mundane and significant—throughout their days and throughout their lives. The reminders are for them, yes, but it's also reassuring to us to hear these things voiced aloud so that perhaps this time, they can internalize the message at a deeper level. Sharing with my children in word and deed "You are loved and okay, fully accepted, inherently worthy, just as you are" draws me in and nudges me closer to the no matter whatness of God.

VIBRANT FAMILY IN A THICK GRAY REALITY

ON THE WALL OF OUR DINING ROOM hangs a large, dark wooden sign, a meaningful gift from a friend many years ago. In white, hand-painted letters it proclaims:

Do Justice. Love Mercy. Walk Humbly.
Micah 6:8

Both under the roof of our home and outside of it, in ways both big and small, Luke and I imperfectly strive to walk out that verse in our lives. Our chaotic and divided world keeps on turning. There are questions Luke and I have purposely wrestled with over the years, centered around our partnership, our parenting, and our next right thing. Though answers to these questions have varied over the years, "do justice, love mercy, walk humbly" have always served as directional arrows.

It's been five years since Royal and I reconnected. In the three years since his incarceration, Royal has beaten the statistical odds. He's stayed out of trouble and as a result, is currently in the process of having his felony record sealed. While the path to getting a job is now smoother for him, he still faces many obstacles. He knows—and I have overtly told him—that I will love him just the same whether he takes full advantage of this opportunity or squanders it. As much as I have high hopes for his life, I cannot turn hopes into reality and walk the path *for* him. At the end of the day, it's *his* path to walk, though it will always be my privilege to walk alongside and encourage him.

There's a recent photo of Royal sitting in the hammock tied to the tree in our front yard, his arms folded across his chest, grinning. It sits framed atop the same piano in the same place where, in early 2009, I instinctively grabbed the 8 × 10 photograph of baby Micah; the one I threw into my purse at the last minute before driving to the courthouse. As I walked into that juvenile courthouse for the first time, introduced myself to a disheveled woman, and held out a framed photo of her baby, how could I have ever known that "I'm rooting for you"—genuine words that tumbled out of my mouth, surprising even me—would be mutually transformative?

Jennifer's kinship has profoundly influenced my life.

In December of 2021, Jennifer celebrated six years clean and sober, the longest uninterrupted span of days since she was a preteen. Jennifer called it the "proudest accomplishment" of her life. I'm continually learning from her as she actively engages her sobriety. Before walking alongside Jennifer, I would have been tempted to say, "Shoot for the moon! Name your shot! If it's your intention to be clean and sober, why not just proclaim here and now that you'll be clean and sober *forever*?"

As I've had a front-row seat to see her walk, stumble, and then get back up again multiple times over our more than thirteen years of doing life together, Jennifer has mirrored a priceless life lesson back to me: It's all about making a choice for the moments that make up *today*, and then waking up the next day and making the same tenacious choice again. This mindset is valuable to anyone who ever struggles, which is to say, all of us. *Today*: It keeps us centered, inviting us to pay attention to what's before us, and carrying us forward to our next right thing.

Jennifer's father passed away while she was still in her active addiction, and in the last five years of her sobriety she's lost the other two biological family members she's held most dear—her mother and her grandmother. Jennifer and I are not just family in theory or as a cutesy, inclusive thing to be said about an outer circle of people. We are family to her, and there aren't many others. She is squarely family to us. Currently, we are walking alongside one another with a comfortable gait. There is mutuality. There is trust. We are here for the long haul to accompany one another wherever it leads.

Jennifer and I are raising full biological brothers in two different households across the same city from one another. It's like a real-time close-up of a nature versus nurture experiment. We compare notes, share strategies, and talk about how to best uplift our boys. "You're a good mom, J," I tell her often.

A few years ago, for Elias's birthday and several years into Jennifer's sobriety, Elias asked Jennifer if Micah could please go with them to the movies, the three of them together. Jennifer texted me, asking if it might be possible for her to pick up Micah and bring him right back after the movie. I deferred to Micah. He wanted to go, and so Jennifer came to my door, hugged me, and asked Micah, "Ready to go, bud?" The last time he'd been alone with her was when he was two months old. Later that night, I asked Micah how he felt as I sat on the edge of his bed to listen. "I had fun, Mom." He was genuinely content to both go and come back.

Recently, Jennifer got a tattoo on the top of her hand between her thumb and pointer finger. She texted a picture of it to me: a scrolly initial *M* with a crown. When I showed it to Micah, he smiled unabashedly. The next time we saw Jennifer, I invited them to stand together for a photo. She proudly draped her arm around Micah, now standing slightly taller than her, showcasing the *M*. Had I seen that photo before living this journey, or had someone told me that Jennifer would be going out to the movies with Micah post-adoption—so unlike anything I had considered or envisioned or seen lived out by example before me—I would have sprinted the other direction out of fear. I would have felt threatened by all I didn't yet understand about how love can multiply and not divide. And I would have missed out. Missed out on a cherished, influential person in my life. Micah—both my son and her son—also would have missed out on the ease with which he knows both of his moms, the comfort of having us around one another, knowing we love him, and we love one another. The whole picture is one of grace.

• • •

Our one-hour drive to the state capital of Salem is full of natural conversation. Jennifer and I talk about the kids and whatever else life has put in front of us. We pull up to a building, take the elevator to the fourth floor, and walk into a large classroom. We are invited to come here monthly. Years before, the judge who had terminated Jennifer's rights asked us to share at a convention for hundreds of attorneys and child welfare staff about our "unlikely partnership," an example of what's possible when two imperfect moms walk toward one another for the sake of loving the same child.

Getting off the elevator, Jennifer and I turn to the left and walk into a classroom together. We find an audience of fifty new state child welfare staff, all with eager expressions, watching us. They have large cards in front of them identifying them by name, role, and which child welfare office in Oregon they'll be headed to upon completion of their training. This is their last training class. Beyond the innumerable state policies, procedures, and protocols they've learned, today's focus is to hear the human element from parents who have worked in and around the "system."

A water pitcher, cups, and a microphone are placed in front of us. I am seated between Jennifer and another woman who appears to be in her midfifties. As the trainer introduces us and gives us the floor, I turn to the woman on my left and ask her if she'd prefer to share her story first or second. She says she'll begin and clears her throat. With poise, she introduces herself.

She shares that she now has a master's degree and a leadership role in an organization that helps child-welfare-involved women regain custody of their children. Though you'd never guess it, three decades ago, in a relationship wrought with domestic violence, she deserted her kids to run after a high. Addiction led her to being behind bars for years. When she was released, her youngest child was a toddler in foster care, and adoption had already been set in motion by the court. She suspects his adoptive mom read her file, saw the effects of what her child had endured, and was fearfully protective.

Reaching for a tissue, she shares straightforwardly she can understand why. She speaks of being lost in a bureaucratic labyrinth, the social workers who didn't seem to care, and the one person who believed in her. Despite jumping over countless towering hurdles in her life to sit where she sits today, she pines to know her child, who is now an adult. She longs to know his story and perhaps even to be invited to share hers with him. She wonders about her son every day; his life is a daily question mark, a haunting mystery. She wishes his adoptive parents had been open to meeting with her, even once. Having a child taken into foster care never to be seen or heard from by her again has been an irrevocable, indelible loss, she believes, for both of them. For more than two decades she hasn't changed her cell number or her landline, in hopes that her son may still reach out to her someday. She sits back in her chair and looks down at the floor.

A gray reality thick with the life-altering immensity of foster care hangs in the room.

Jennifer and I look at each other. The story of the woman seated next to us could have easily been *our* story.

I give her an encouraging nod and Jennifer begins to speak.

"Hi. I'm Jennifer and I always start out with saying that I'm an addict. I grew up in foster care and have had all four of my children involved at some point in the foster care system. Today I'll be sharing as the biological parent and Jillana as the foster and adoptive parent."

She turns it over to me, and I continue, "We fully recognize that relationships take two, and certainly not all biological/foster/adoptive relationships can or are meant to look like ours. Also, if you had polled us at many points along our story, we *never* would have thought we'd be before you today. As you'll soon hear, we have experienced every emotion under the sun with or toward one another over the years, and we're not going to sugarcoat the hard parts, but as we share our story—popcorn style—we do so with the hope that maybe one day, our story will not be *quite* so unusual."

As Jennifer takes it from there and continues with her raw sharing that draws others to her, I look out to the faces in the audience hanging on to every word she's saying.

Jennifer and I have had no blueprint for the relational bridge we've built in the fog over the last thirteen years. Walking the path of the unexpected, we have taken the dare to love against the grain. At times, the planks on this relational bridge toward one another have been rickety at best, but in this moment, for today, we are standing squarely together on a sturdy one.

In the midst of the sacredness of the everyday, the world overflows with countless things that *are*, yet should not be. Surrounded by brokenness, I am extended a continual invitation to walk the suspension bridge between reality and hope. Right there in the blurry middle, there are some things I've learned about this life and still many things I do not yet know. I am confident, however, of this: *Proximity* to others is what holds the marrow of life. The gift of proximity has exposed me to Divine Love showing up in the world in limitless ways. Sometimes that Love has come like the beating of a drum, and at other times like a whisper. It has widened my definition of family and has given me the wild and precious life that is mine.

MEET MY FAMILY

LUKE, ROYAL (AGE 6) & JILLANA IN 2003

ROYAL (AGE 24) & JILLANA

JENNIFER &
JILLANA

MICAH, LUKE, JILLANA, CHARLIE, SOPHIA & ELENI

ACKNOWLEDGMENTS

Expressing gratitude is important to me, and there are so many people to thank.

Tara Brown, you and I got to know each other sitting around the table for our monthly dinner club, which met for two years. (Full disclosure: I was the only non-foodie in the group, but I do love eating and talking over a good meal!) You were kind enough to express interest in my writing, and I handed you a very rough manuscript. You saw potential in it and connected me with Kathy Helmers of Creative Trust, who became my literary agent. The fact that both of you, Tara and Kathy, believed that my story was worth telling put wind in my sails.

To the whole team at Tyndale, I feel like I won the lottery because everyone I have engaged with has been a member of the Dream Team! Thank you, Sarah Atkinson and Jillian Schlossberg, for first meeting with me. Thank you, Jillian, for having a vision for this book, for being endlessly patient with all my questions, and for exuding grace and encouragement from beginning to end. Bonne Steffen and Annette Hayward, your keen eyes as you read every single word of the manuscript and asked clarifying questions made *A Love-Stretched Life* so much stronger. I can't thank you enough for your teamwork! Lindsey Bergsma, Christina Garrison, Andrea Martin, Kristen Schumacher, and Cassidy Gage, thank you for your creativity and collaboration in getting my book out into the world.

Heartfelt gratitude goes out to Andrea Zimmerman, Missi Thurman, Anne Bumbalough, and Louise Biela for graciously reading the entire manuscript amidst full lives and offering invaluable insight. Thank you, Brooke Jarvis, Kat Bonham, and Aubrey Page, for your keen feedback on specific chapters. Thank you to the friends in our affectionately named "Garage Crew" for letting me hijack some of our hangouts to whip out large Post-it notes, stick them on the garage fridge, and take notes while we talked about friendship and titles for this book. To everyone who took the time to read and offer your endorsement of the book, as well as those who used their influence to share *A Love-Stretched Life* with others, I'm humbled.

To the families that comprise Family Feast, you are my people. I'm beyond grateful for the rhythm of life we've established. The names of all those I hold dear who have been supportive of me are too many to list, but I'd be remiss not to mention those who offered specific encouragement to me as I wrote this book: Allie, Emily, Andrea, Bethany, Anne, Audrey, Missi, Laura, Jenny, Barbara, Megan, Becky, Emilee, Shanelle, Glenda, Amy, Kelly, and Summer. Thank you to Norene, Miriam, Cathy, Marilyn, and Renee, who fall into the category of both trusted friends and mentors.

Luke's mom, Louise, was the earliest cheerleader to pore over the manuscript. My loving parents, Jeff and Judy, poured out their support by offering me a room at their house to write in, free from distraction. Thanks, Mom, for poking your head in the door every once in a while and offering snacks. You provided me a cozy bed so I could wake up early and write for a few hours before heading home.

To those at The Contingent with whom I work: Thank you for consistently demonstrating the "Third Way," for taking big swings at complex social issues with an eye toward redemption and inviting others to be a part of a larger story outside of themselves.

While I have learned from and been influenced by many at the organization, a special shout-out to Ben Sand, Anthony Jordan, Brooke Gray, Shelly Winterberg, Marcus Gillette, Vennisa Gomez-Gerberg, and everyone who works, volunteers, and believes in the mission of Every Child. I'm a better leader due to the privilege of learning and serving alongside you.

Thank you to my home church, Imago Dei Community, without whom Welcome Boxes may never have become a reality tipping into this wild ride of a community mobilization movement. A special thank-you to Pastors Rick McKinley, Seth King, Ruben Alvarado, Josh Butler, and the foster/adoptive support group at Imago Dei led by Mike and Renee Pinkerton. You have continued to humbly model what showing up looks like in a myriad of ways!

Jennifer, I think the world of you. Thank you for teaching me through your example and trusting me to share our collective story. Doing life together has been one of the best surprises this life has granted me. Elias, Auntie loves you.

Royal, you are the son of my heart, and I will always want good things for you. I'm forever in your corner.

To my family under my roof: Sophia and Eleni, growing up in the city and in our home, you have been continually invited to see people and situations with color and texture. You have a lived understanding of trauma and invisible brain-based disabilities. You "get" things I had no inkling of at your age. Your honesty, vibrancy, resiliency, humor, and ability to dance in the midst of our messy, colorful family gives me hope for the world. Micah, you're brave and kind and you have a tender heart. Thanks for trusting me to share some of the details of the lives of both of your families and how we are interwoven, with you at the center. Charlie, you may be my life's greatest teacher. You help me see things I never would have noticed before, and your laugh fills me with indescribable joy. Sophia, Eleni, Micah, and Charlie, may you always know you are deeply loved, no matter what!

Luke, you have been there for me every single step of this

writing process, from beginning to end—binding pages, parsing sentences, giving your loving and sometimes too-honest feedback. This wouldn't be what it is without your loyal support. When we said yes to one another in 2000, we had no idea what adventures this life would hold, but there's nobody I'd rather be creating this love-stretched life with than you.

NOTES

page 20   ***"Blessed are the pure in heart":*** Matthew 5:8.

page 25   ***"'Hope' is the thing with feathers":*** Emily Dickinson, *A Letter to the World* (n.p.: MacMillan, 1968), 43.

page 49   ***learn to be "safe and healthy" parents:*** Without intentionally using the adjectives "safe and healthy," the narrative can quickly dive into "good" or "bad" labels, which aren't always fair when you acknowledge the complexities child-welfare-involved parents face.

page 53   ***an inner-city after-school program:*** Peace of the City is an incredible organization I've supported for nearly eighteen years. See peaceofthecity.org.

page 54   ***"To love at all is to be vulnerable":*** C. S. Lewis, *The Four Loves* (New York: Harcourt Brace, 1960), 121.

page 60   ***an AA or NA meeting:*** Abbreviations for Alcoholics Anonymous and Narcotics Anonymous.

page 60   ***"You give and take away":*** "Blessed Be Your Name," music and lyrics by Matt and Beth Redman, © 2002 Thankyou Music/Adm. by worshiptogether.com songs.

page 76   ***"The path of prayer and love and the path of suffering":*** Richard Rohr, *Everything Belongs: The Gift of Contemplative Prayer* (Chestnut Ridge, New York: Crossroad Publishing, 2003), 14–15.

page 81   ***For the Israelites, the stones of remembrance:*** See Joshua 4:1-7.

page 110   ***resolutely or dutifully firm and unwavering:*** Oxford Lexico dictionary online, s.v. "steadfast," accessed October 1, 2021, https://www.lexico.com/en/definition/steadfast.

page 117   ***having FASD (Fetal Alcohol Spectrum Disorder):*** *Fetal Alcohol Spectrum Disorders (FASDs)*, Centers for Disease Control and Prevention, last updated May 21, 2021, https://www.cdc.gov/ncbddd/fasd/facts.html.

page 117   ***most common preventable cause of intellectual and developmental*** *disabilities: Fetal Alcohol Spectrum Disorder*, The Arc, accessed October 1, 2021, https://thearc.org/wp-content/uploads/forchapters/FASD.pdf.

page 117 ***more prevalent than autism:*** Kerry Lyons, "1 in 100 Babies: The Fetal Alcohol Spectrum Disorder Pathway," *Nursing Standard* 31, no. 13 (November 23, 2016): 18–20, https://doi.org/10.7748/ns.31.13.18.s22.

page 117 ***more prevalent in foster care than in the general population:*** "FASD: What the Foster Care System Should Know," National Organization on Fetal Alcohol Syndrome, accessed December 8, 2021, http://www.nofas.org/wp-content/uploads/2012/05/fostercare.pdf.

page 121 ***Over 60 percent of individuals with FASD:*** Ann P. Streissguth et al., "Understanding the Occurrence of Secondary Disabilities in Clients with Fetal Alcohol Syndrome (FAS) and Fetal Alcohol Effects (FAE)," Centers for Disease Control and Prevention, August 1996, http://lib.adai .uw.edu/pubs/bk2698.pdf.

page 129 ***we would never tell someone who is blind:*** Diane Malbin, *Trying Differently Rather than Harder: Fetal Alcohol Spectrum Disorders* (self-pub., 2017), Kindle.

page 132 ***"the body keeps the score":*** Bessel van der Kolk, *The Body Keeps the Score: Brain, Mind, and Body in the Healing of Trauma* (New York: Penguin Publishing Group, 2015).

page 134 ***"A piece of pottery that has been shattered":*** Sarah Thebarge, *Well: Healing Our Beautiful, Broken World from a Hospital in West Africa* (New York: Faith Words, 2017), 254.

page 149 ***"I've learned that people will forget":*** Maya Angelou, *Rainbow in the Cloud: The Wisdom and Spirit of Maya Angelou* (Thorndike, ME: Center Point, 2015), 58.

page 151 ***mentoring program called Faithful Friends:*** This mentoring program offers support and stability to children. Find out more at https:// faithfulfriendspdx.org.

page 153 ***Help, Thanks, Wow:*** Anne Lamott, *Help, Thanks, Wow: The Three Essential Prayers* (New York: Riverhead Books, 2012).

page 161 ***"We'll call them Welcome Boxes":*** Find more ideas on how to prepare Welcome Boxes at https://everychildpdx.org/welcome-boxes/.

page 162 ***international movement called Advent Conspiracy:*** You can find more information at https://Adventconspiracy.org.

page 165 ***do a "makeover" of the visitation rooms:*** Nancy Anderson, "Volunteers Spruce Up East County Child Welfare Office to Make It Warmer for Children," *Oregonian*, November 16, 2012 (updated January 10, 2019), https://www.oregonlive.com/gresham/2012/11/volunteers_spruce_up _east_coun.html.

page 167 ***He wrote a feature article with the headline "A Revolution . . .":*** Steve Duin, "A Revolution in Portland's Foster Care," *Oregonian*, January 9, 2013 (updated January 10, 2019), https://www.oregonlive.com/news/oregonian /steve_duin/2013/01/steve_duin_a_revolution_in_por.html.

page 167   *under the umbrella of their non-profit:* This organization was later named The Contingent. Per their website, "The Contingent is a venture nonprofit that addresses many of the largest injustices and vulnerabilities facing Oregonians today." Learn more at https://thecontingent.org.

page 169   *another article, "Redefining the Shadow . . .":* Steve Duin, "Redefining the Shadow of the Church and Aiding Foster Children," *Oregonian,* May 20, 2013 (updated January 10, 2019), https://www .oregonlive.com/news/oregonian/steve_duin/2013/05/steve_duin _redefining_the_shad.html.

page 169   *"The families we see are beset by domestic violence":* Steve Duin, "Redefining the Shadow."

page 171   *Every Child is now the branded name:* See https://everychildoregon .org/about-us/how-it-started/.

page 171   *It has drawn interest from several other states:* Steve Duin, "Feds Celebrate Oregon's Every Child," *Oregonian,* February 23, 2020, https:// www.oregonlive.com/opinion/2020/02/feds-celebrate-oregons-every-child -steve-duin-column.html.

page 171   *share about our work on a local TV station:* See KGW Straight Talk: "Oregon's Foster Care Crisis," Part 1, June 8, 2019, video, 17:00, https://www.youtube.com/watch?v=eu_gylvoHSY and Part 2, June 8, 2019, video, 7:54, https://www.youtube.com/watch?v=q6P2Pz1D8v4.

page 171   *the non-profit With Love:* Find out more at withloveoregon.org.

page 173   *"I am only one, but still I am one":* Quoted in Edwin Osgood Grover, ed., *The Book of Good Cheer: A Little Bundle of Cheery Thoughts* (Chicago: P. F. Volland and Company, 1909), 28.

page 175   *recognize that "Where there is love, God breaks in":* Luke Goble, "A Theology of Foster Care," unpublished paper 2013. This was circulated to several Portland area churches.

page 196   *"At the end of the day, we can endure":* Laura Almeida, "Quotes from Frida Kahlo," Denver Art Museum website, posted December 28, 2020, https://www.denverartmuseum.org/en/blog/quotes-frida-kahlo.

page 204   *"The expectation that we can be immersed in suffering":* Rachel Naomi Remen, *Kitchen Table Wisdom: Stories that Heal* (New York: Penguin,1996), 52.

page 206   *the importance of various types of rest:* Dr. Saundra Dalton-Smith, "The Real Reason Why We Are Tired and What to Do about It," TEDx Talk Atlanta, March 2019, https://www.youtube.com/watch?v=ZGNN4EPJzGk.

page 208   *"Joy is the most infallible sign":* Attributed to Pierre Teilhard de Chardin.

page 215   *"Once you are Real, you can't become unreal again":* Margery Williams, *The Velveteen Rabbit, or How Toys Become Real* (New York: HarperCollins, 1975), 16.

page 228   *"The ancient Desert Fathers, when they were disconsolate":* Greg
Boyle, *Tattoos on the Heart: The Power of Boundless Compassion* (New York:
Free Press, 2010), 159.

page 232   *"This is the most profound spiritual truth I know":* Anne Lamott,
Traveling Mercies: Some Thoughts on Faith (New York: Doubleday Anchor,
2000), 264.

page 239   *"the ability to do something that frightens one":* Oxford English
Dictionary, s.v. "courage," accessed October 7, 2021, https://www.lexico
.com/en/definition/courage.

page 244   *"My name," she replied confidently, "is Grace":* To read the newspaper
accounts of Grace's saga, see Steve Duin, "Claiming Grace, One Child at a
Time," *Oregonian,* November 27, 2014, updated January 10, 2019, https://
www.oregonlive.com/news/oregonian/steve_duin/2014/11/steve_duin
_saving_one_grace_at.html. See also Steve Duin, "'Grace' Finds Her Foster
Home," *Oregonian,* December 3, 2014, updated January 10, 1029, https:/
/www.oregonlive.com/news/oregonian/steve_duin/2014/12/steve_duin
_blog_grace_finds_he.html.

page 264   *"You stand with the belligerent, the surly, and the badly behaved":*
Boyle, *Tattoos on the Heart,* 179.

page 281   *"trust in the slow work of God":* Pierre Teilhard de Chardin, quoted
in Boyle, *Tattoos on the Heart,* 113.

page 287   *the "no matter whatness" of God:* Boyle, *Tattoos on the Heart,* 52.

ABOUT THE AUTHOR

JILLANA GOBLE has been a foster mom, biological mom, and adoptive mom—in that order—since 2003. She is a connector and collaborator who has walked an unlikely path in creating unprecedented relationships—with the children who have walked through her front door, their biological families, and the state's child welfare agency. She is the founder of an initiative that has been the catalyst for Every Child Oregon, a robust movement that has paved the way for unprecedented partnership between the community and Oregon's Child Welfare Program.

Jillana holds a master's degree in teaching English as a second language. She is a sought-after speaker on various topics relating to foster care, community partnership, adoption, special needs, and walking the suspension bridge between reality and hope. She continues to mentor and walk alongside many parents navigating this journey. Jillana and the biological mother of a child she fostered (and later adopted) regularly co-speak to state caseworkers, sharing their unlikely journey of collaboration over the past decade. She is regularly invited to share in the training classes prospective foster and adoptive parents take to become certified. Jillana also co-presents training for caseworkers about how to best engage with foster parents. She enjoys speaking, sharing, and continuing her learning at retreats and workshops.

Jillana and her husband, Luke, have been married since 2000 and live in Portland, Oregon, with their family. Five remarkable kids, ranging in age from preteen to young adult, call her Mom.

When not engaging with her family, Jillana enjoys drinking coffee—half-filled with cream—with friends at neighborhood coffee shops. Her favorite things include leaning in to engage others' real-deal stories, taking walks, and reading in the tub way too late at night.

DISCOVER WHAT FOSTER PARENTING REALLY LOOKS LIKE.

Filled with practical suggestions and insight for prospective foster parents, *No Sugar-Coating* is exactly what you need to better understand how to welcome vulnerable children through your front door.

Learn more at Jillana-goble.com.